MADNESS VISIBLE

MADNESS VISIBLE

A MEMOIR OF WAR

Janine di Giovanni

BLOOMSBURY

First published in Great Britain 2004

Copyright © by Janine di Giovanni 2003

The moral right of the author has been asserted

Bloomsbury Publishing Plc, 38 Soho Square, London W1D 3HB

A CIP catalogue record is available from the British Library
ISBN 0 7475 6056 0

Typeset by
Printed by Selwood Printing Ltd., West Sussex

For my big sister, Judy

"While shaving, I had a conversation with myself about the incompatability of being a reporter and hanging on to a tender soul at the same time."

ROBERT CAPA, LONDON, 1941

"History is an argument without end."

PIETER GEYL

Contents

Acknowledgments

In early June 1999, shortly after the "liberation" of Pristina, I sat in a field in Kosovo with a family of Gypsies watching the retreat of the Serbs. It was a few days after the NATO war had officially ended, and the Gypsies—some of whose ancestors had been in the Balkans since the fourteenth century—were running away from the Kosovar Albanians.

The Albanians were returning to Kosovo with vengeful spirits after their much-televised exodus two months earlier. They were ready to kill and loot and burn, and to attack anyone they believed had aided the Serbs. The Gypsies were terrified. They protested their innocence. They said they had done nothing other than try to stay alive during wartime.

They said they were neither pro-Serb nor pro-Albanian. Still, like the Serbs, they were running, and the Albanians were repeating another violent Balkan cycle by hunting them down and expelling them. They were doing to other people exactly what had been done to them only a few weeks before: using fear as a weapon to gain territory and power.

For years, I had watched angry retreating soldiers, columns of desperate refugees, shells exploding on civilian targets, and battles beginning and ending in the country that was once called Yugoslavia. It was, seemingly, a war without end, a war between former neighbors. I saw cease-fires which ended in mortar attacks; diplomatic negotiations breaking down or causing wide divisions; cities under siege; morgues crammed full of bodies, one on top of the next; bones jutting out of the flesh of children with no medicine to treat them; and my friends—poets, teachers, doctors—burning their books instead of firewood and driven to madness and despair.

Where I was sitting, in that field in Kosovo six months before the new millennium, the war was considered over, and so were the series of backyard wars that had gutted the Balkans. But from where I was sitting, I could see that the war was definitely not over. The Serbs may have been driving their tanks north and the international community may have been moving toward control of Kosovo, but there was too much anger, too much unfinished business. The Serbs had just lost their fourth war in eight years. Slobodan Milosevic was two years away from being sealed inside a U.N. detention center in The Hague. Franjo Tudjman, the first president of independent Croatia, was still alive. Retribution had not been paid to families of victims in Srebrenica, Foca, Gorazde, Knin, Vukovar. What was once Bosnia was divided in two and its remains were ruled by foreigners, the Office of the High Representative, in Sarajevo. Gangster cultures prevailed. No one talked about Brotherhood and Unity, the old Tito-era mantra that for years had kept ethnic tension in check. Reconciliation seemed a long way off.

Brecht said war is like love, it always finds a way. But I believed, and I still do, that the wars in Yugoslavia might have been stopped years earlier. While the memory of World War II atrocities sharpened ethnic divisions between Serbs, Muslims, and Croats (and early on, Slovenes) in post-Tito Yugoslavia, the destruction of the country was not inevitable. A *New York Times* article from 1992 describes well the demographic mix that characterized Bosnia and Herzegovina on the eve of the war, and touches on its eruption.

> *Bosnia and Herzegovina was the most ethnically mixed of the six republics that made up Yugoslavia after World War II. Muslims, Slavs whose forebears converted to Islam during the centuries in which Bosnia was ruled by the Ottoman Turks, were the most numerous group in Bosnia and Herzegovina, with 44 percent of the population of 4.5 million, as measured in the 1991 census.*
>
> *Serbs, an Orthodox Christian Slavic group that predominates in the neighboring Serbian republic, were 31 percent of the Bosnian total. Croats, who like the others are Slavs and speak Serbo-Croat but are Roman Catholics, are 17 percent of the population.*

The remainder identified themselves to the census takers as Yugoslavs, embracing a non-ethnic nationalism that today is all but crushed.

Those groups were interspersed throughout Bosnia, with many towns and villages having no majority ethnic group, and many Muslims, Serbs and Croats living next door to each other. Mixed marriages among all three ethnic groups were commonplace.

Slovania and Croatia declared independence in 1991, but the Bosnian leadership was leery of following suit, having watched neighboring Croatia plunge almost immediately into vicious fighting with the Serb-dominated Yugoslav armed forces. But the Sarajevo leadership scheduled a referendum on independence for Feb. 29 of this year. The Muslims and Croats voted yes, while the Serbs boycotted and insisted on dividing the country into three ethnic cantons.

The Bosnian government refused to accept the cantonment of the country, and war erupted early in April, after the European Community officially granted recognition. The Yugoslav Army and the Serbian irregulars quickly overwhelmed the lightly armed defenders.

The plan, it is evident now, was to seize enough territory to forge links between the Serbs in Bosnia, the Serbs in Serbia and the Serbs in neighboring Croatia. As many as half of Bosnia's two million Muslims live in the areas picked to be corridors between the various Serbian regions. The Muslims were to be exiled forever in the policy the Serbs call ethnic cleansing.

In the last decade of the twentieth century, the will of the international community—having promised that the Holocaust would never be repeated—should have prevailed. Diplomacy could have been more effective. The guarantee of human rights for ethnic minorities—such as the protection of Serbs in Croatia while Germany stubbornly insisted on premature recognition of Croatia in 1999 without weighing the consequences—should have been carefully considered. Action should have been taken long before March 24, 1999, when NATO began air strikes against Serbia.

It is estimated that 2,000 people died in Kosovo in the wave of ethnic violence that preceded those air strikes. But one hundred times that number of people died in the Bosnian war before the Bosnian Serb military infrastructure was crushed by bombs, beginning in August 1995. Did that mean, cynically, that the life of one Kosovar was worth hundreds of Bosnians? Or did it mean that much-needed help did not really arrive until NATO's reputation was at stake? It was geopolitics, not compassion or the desire to achieve peace in what once was Yugoslavia, which launched the 1999 air strikes.

I often think about what might have happened if the political will to stop the war early on was more forceful, if Milosevic and Tudjman and their generals and paramilitary and foot soldiers had been halted in their paths in the early 1990s. If that had happened, the fields around Srebrenica would not now be haunted by the 7,000 dead Muslims who were murdered by Serb forces while French generals, Dutch soldiers, and Japanese special envoys to the United Nations did nothing to protect them. The children who were gouged with shrapnel while playing football or sleigh riding would still be alive. In the Lion's Cemetery in Sarajevo, row upon row of tombstones containing the dead who were born in the late 1960s and early 1970s would not be full. And an entire generation would not be tainted with bitterness, remorse, and despair.

The wars what once was Yugoslavia killed more than 250,000 people between 1991 and 1995 alone, and displaced 3.5 million out of a prewar population of 23 million. What would have happened to all of them if someone had not lit the fuse? Or rather, if someone extinguished it while it was still a spark? If the map of their country had not been deformed, chopped to bits, and then sewn back together again?

This book is a journey around the region over a ten-year period. Hundreds of people speak through it, and I have tried to present their stories, and their lives, in their own words. I am grateful to many, some of whose names have been changed.

All my friends in the former Yugoslavia: Dragan Kljajic; Zlata Filipovic; Klea, Zoran, and Deni Jokic; Mario Susko; Aleksandar Brkic; Jelena Komad; Said Spasic; Dessa Trevisan; the Sandic family; Dane Gvero; Ivana Antic; Irena Sutic; Adil, Fikreta, Dzenana, and Adela Dragonovic; Zjelko Kapanja; Albasa Kurbegovic; Sasa Djurkovic; Roy Gutman; Dr. Ejup Ganic; Alija Izetbegovic; Denis Begic; Advia Sehomerdjic; Raifa Mehic; Munira Subacic; the Movement of Mothers of Srebrenica and Zepa; Melika Malesevic, Irfan Ajanovic, and the Association of Former Prison Camp Inmates of Bosnia and Herzegovnia; Braca Grubacic; Anthony Borden and the Institute for War and Peace Reporting; Mirella and Ismeta; Ahmed Buric; Suzana Andjelic; Orhan and Alma Pasalic; General Jovan Divjak; Benjamin Vojnikovic; Mirza Hajric; Leonora Luttoli; the Tarifi family; Enis Ahmedi; Gordana Mikulic; Marko Vesovic; Drasko Vojnovic; Suleiman Redzic; Ibrahim Busatlija; Zoran Kusovac and Sonja Pastuovic; Vesna Cengic; Alexandra Steiglmayer; Abdulah Sidran.

Marco Predieri and Casa Giovannina, Positano, Italy

Meredith and John Shelton, Impasse Guermine, Paris

Lieutenant Colonel Stephen Kirlpatrick and the Princess of Wales's Royal Regiment, Kosovo

Major Dave Wilson and the Royal Marines 415th Commando Group, Kosovo

Major General David Richards

John Owen and the former Freedom Forum, London

Amnesty International

Kris Janowski and UNHCR

Jim Landale at ICTY, The Hague

Kathryne Bomberger at the International Committee for Missing Persons, Sarajevo

Joanne Mariner and Human Rights Watch

Mark Laity, NATO

The Crimes of War Project

To the memory of Juan Carlos Gumucio, Kurt Schork, and Miguel Gil Moreno De Mora.

This book would never have been written without Graydon Carter, editor of *Vanity Fair*, who published the article, also called "Madness Visible," from which it sprang. Henry Porter and Bruce Handy, my editors at *Vanity Fair*, were instrumental in fashioning its final form.

Nor could I have completed the book without the unstinting support of my colleagues at *The Times*: the editors under whom I have served, Peter Stoddhard and Robert Thomson; my foreign editor, Bronwen Maddox, and managing foreign editor, Martin Fletcher; Gill Morgan, editor of *The Times Saturday Magazine;* and others who supported and encouraged me: Ben Preston, Sandra Parsons, and Graham Paterson.

Kyle Crichton of the *New York Times Magazine* ran my story about being bombed with the KLA and sent me to various other places where no one else would go. Fiona Mirch and John Thynne of the BBC enabled me to travel through post-Dayton Bosnia.

For their patience and assistance: Laura Kang of *Vanity Fair;* Richard Beeston; David Watts; Gill Ross; Jenny Heyes; Alex Blair; Dan Wallis; and Matt Gibbs of *The Times* of London.

My agents in Britain and the United States, David Godwin, Kim Witherspoon, and David Forrer, were enthusiasts for this project from the beginning. My wonderful editors, Ash Green of Alfred A. Knopf and Alexandra Pringle of Bloomsbury, understood a reporter's stress and deadlines and never hassled me for my manuscript. They let me take my time. I also wish to thank their assistants, Luba Ostashevsky and Chiki Sarkar.

I could not have stayed sane without the love, loyalty, and support of my tribe: Stel, Roy, Sweetie, Allegra, Ariane, Connie, Bettina, Marina, Lucy, and Chas, and, of course, Christopher. Alex Majoli and Thomas Dworzak of Magnum Photos kept me company during those days and nights in cold trenches and other miserable places. And love to my family—most notably my beautiful mother, Cat, who often had to learn about my life through the headlines of a newspaper.

Finally, my husband, Bruno Girodon, whom I met in the lobby of the Holiday Inn in Sarajevo in 1993 and met again in Algeria in 1998. He waited for me in Kukes, Albania, while I was caught in an aerial bombardment in Kosovo in 1999, and enlisted the aid of French Special Forces when he thought I was dead. He calmly gave crucial advice when I called from Grozny as it was falling: "The best reporter is the one who gets out alive to tell the story." *Bien-aimé.*

Janine di Giovanni
London
February 2003

MADNESS VISIBLE

Chapter One

Exactly how much time passes from the moment a
man is wounded until he starts to feel pain?
Sometimes it's a second.
Sometimes it's an hour.
Sometimes it's more than an eternity.

Artyom Borovik, *The Hidden War*

Albanians Killed as Kosovo Village Is Blown Apart; At Least 60 Civilians Die

More than 60 Albanians were killed and scores more
badly wounded late Thursday night when bombs
blew apart a village in southwest Kosovo, near
Prizren, Yugoslav officials and journalists at the scene
said Friday.
The attack in Korisa, was said by Yugoslav Government officials to have been carried out by NATO
warplanes. . . . NATO officials in Brussels said they
were investigating the report and were reluctant to
comment before their work was complete. . . .

New York Times, May 15, 1999

KLA Forward Base Camp
Near Kosare, Kosovo
May 12, 1999

Much later, I remembered the stillness, the quiet of chaos.

The wet, late spring.

The way time slowed down until each second seemed elastic. The sixty seconds that it took four men to lift the youngest soldier, dead, boots still on, and lay him carefully on the back of a truck bound for the morgue. How everything surrounding that minute— the tears of the soldiers lifting him, the way a hand was cupped over a match to light a cigarette, the Kalashnikov thrown angrily on the ground—stretched to hours.

In the background, the low rumble of noise. It seemed so far away, over the mountain even, but it was right there. Some soldier crying: "My two brothers died. . . . I don't want to die."

Or the way the sky changed. The early-morning breaking light during the first wave of bombing, deepest blue with the faintest brushing of the stars. Then lighter azure, then premature streaks of pink. The sun finally rising over the harsh mountains. Then finally light enough so that I could see the sleeping soldiers next to me, dotting their way down the trench. In the darkness, I mistook them for tree stumps.

Or the way that the wounded looked when the others carried them into the trench. The way they did not scream or beg, just submitted. The childlike surprise on their faces. One minute sleeping quietly, the next, the leg they can still feel, no longer there.

One of them was a half-dressed teenager. Face, neck, chest covered in blood, brighter than the blood dried on his gray sock. The sock was still on his left foot, but his right foot was gone, as was his right calf, his right knee. The last bomb blast caught him, surprised, down near the riverbed twenty minutes before, and he must have been feeling the pain by then. But he silently lay on a stained stretcher and waited as though he were waiting for a bus.

First step of first aid: Expose the wound. So they cut away his T-shirt to see where he'd been hit, and he was there in the wan sunlight, topless, shivering. Next to him, another boy, skin slashed with hot shrapnel, chest peppered with wounds that were dotted like measles. The medic, a twenty-three-year-old architect who lived in Switzerland, moved from body to body, wrapping field dressings with elastic bandage, injecting morphine, and washing away blood and dirt and mud.

The boy without the leg looked forgotten in the chaos of the morning bombing. It was too loud in the ditch for anyone to hear him whimpering. He lay alone, throbbing with pain and watched those scenes of anger inside that ditch: of soldiers running from their positions, some running away to the forest. A commander shouted for them to come back. They continued to run.

Ali, the Moroccan commander, shouted, "The Serbs are two thousand yards away." He told everyone to prepare for a ground assault. "Every soldier, grab your arms and ammo, and go, get to the front." The soldiers stared at him blankly. Some moved. Others just stared.

The medic, moving between bodies, said, "Help me." He stood over a teenager with acne and an exposed bone in his leg, a cut over his left eye. The Swiss medic held the flesh together and moved the needle as if he were mending a button on a shirt. The needle did not pierce the flesh easily. The medic cursed. He pushed the needle through the flesh again, harder this time, and the boy underneath him winced.

Nearby in the ditch was someone else: a body with a mangled leg, deep in shock. We pulled down his trousers and the medic threw the bloody fatigues in the ditch. The boy looked at him, startled, confused. He's not embarrassed that he's lying there without trousers; he's dreaming he's back in Pristina in a bar, because he keeps reaching into the top pocket of his T-shirt and pulling out a crumpled packet of L&M cigarettes. He put one in his mouth, offered another to me.

I wiped blood, took the cigarette out of his mouth. But he kept offering the pack. The medic jabbed him with something and looked up over the trench to see a seventeen-year-old girl soldier called Jacky. She had a blond ponytail and a small Koran on a leather strap around her neck. Everyone claimed she was sleeping with the commander, but she said, in a small, tough voice, that she was there to fight. She ran with a box of ammunition and a friend with short spiked hair and a Walkman tuned to hip-hop. She left the music on even during the shelling.

The medic was a veteran of the Kosovo Liberation Army (KLA) for several months. He was cynical, suspicious of NATO's intervention, of the sudden interest of the West. "I believe in the KLA," he said. "I believe we will get what is best for our country." He had steely round glasses. As he looked up at the sky, there was another flash of light and it caught his lenses. "But I don't believe in NATO."

He rolled the boy with the cigarette onto his side, checked his breathing by sliding his finger under his nose, and moved down the trench. He told me to watch him.

The boy slept, soft hair falling across his forehead, his wounds. The cigarette pack was left in the mud.

It has been nearly two months since the NATO bombing campaign inside Kosovo began, a response to a wave of Serbian military and paramilitary attacks on Kosovar Albanian civilians. Those attacks included assassinations, mass killing, burning villages. Then the refugees began pouring into neighboring Albania, Macedonia, and Montenegro. They passed on donkey-pulled carts, in vehicles, or on foot, slipping on the ice, in the mud, in the snow, carrying their lives in shopping bags.

In one week alone, between March 31 and April 2, 1999, the United Nations High Commissioner for Refugees (UNHCR) noted that 230,000 people had fled, Europe's biggest refugee exodus since the war in Bosnia. At one point, Jamie Shea, NATO's spokesman, announced that 4,000 ethnic Albanians were leaving every hour. "We have to recognize we are on the brink of a major humanitarian disaster in Kosovo," Shea said from his perch in Brussels, "the likes of which have not been seen in Europe since the closing stages of World War II."

Someone took a photograph during those days: a mass of refugees forced to leave Pristina by train in Macedonia, huddled together like cattle, thousands stuffed inside ancient railway cars. Some were forced to walk alongside the tracks. A blind man tapped his cane along the railway telegraph wires for guidance.

Forward bases, front lines like those at Kosare, sprung up. The Ushtira Clirimtare e Kosoves, the UCK, or KLA, was swelling with soldiers who wanted to push back the Serbs, liberate their country, and rescue the refugees who were stranded in the hills. The soldiers I was with in Kosare were trying to push through to the town of Junik. They had taken the position from Serbs a few days before, and now we were getting hit, unsure of who was bombing us.

"We don't know who's killing us," Ali said, "NATO or the Serbs."

I was sleeping in Ali's tent, along with other soldiers, most of whom were in their early twenties. Ali was older and experienced. He made it clear that he did not like my being there. A devout Muslim, he prayed five times a day and had come from North Africa to fight for his Balkan Muslim brothers.

The bombing, he said darkly, was a punishment. "It's because of last night," he said. The night before was someone's birthday. Everyone sat around a fire, drinking, smoking, singing. "Allah is angry. Women. alcohol."

Because he had been a captain in the Moroccan Special Forces, and because most of the younger soldiers were silent with fear, he began to take control. He moved down the trench carrying a stack of old helmets, which he threw like footballs to the soldiers. Mine landed in the mud: it had no strap. He then separated us, fifty meters between each person. "Because when more bombs fall, I don't want to lose all of you."

I stayed where I was with the injured boy. I watched Ali moving away, heard him calling, his voice growing fainter: "Be prepared for everything," he said. "Be prepared for anything."

The boy slept. His face was hot, his body did not move. He continued breathing. But outside, another boy, dark, Arabic, with a beard, pulls down his trousers. He squats. He's covered in blood and is in too much pain to be embarrassed. He's got shrapnel wounds all over his leg, his arm. He lifts one hand. "Water," he says, in English.

I passed him the bottle. He drank from it, collapsed on the ground. The sky changed. Morning had come. The pink light softened the rocks on the mountains, the jagged cliffs. The grayness faded, then brightened to blue.

"Oh my God," someone said, "it's a perfect day for bombing."

At some point later, I looked at my watch. I thought it was late afternoon. But it was only nine o'clock in the morning.

Café Drenica
Durres, Albania
May 3, 1999

How did they get here, to this field in Kosovo?

Sometimes, I sat with them outside the tents and listened to their stories. Why are you here? What made you come? Everyone had a different story, but most of them, in the early days, before they got to the front line, all seemed so young. When you looked hard at the recruits, and saw fresh haircuts and spotted skin, you realized they lied about their age. When you saw them hold a gun, imitating someone they'd seen in the movies, you realized they had no experience. When you saw them at night, saying prayers or leaning across their sleeping bags to borrow a match or a Swiss Army knife, or sitting outside the tent alone, talking about their girlfriends or their mothers, you knew: this was the first time.

When you saw the drawer full of their passports from America, Sweden, England, and read their dates of birth—1975, 1981, 1978—you realized then they were kids who read something about war in the newspaper and, triggered by patriotism or adrenaline, bought a plane ticket. They paid their own way, found gear from Frank's Army & Navy store in the Bronx, packed fatigues, red bandannas like Rambo, maps and water canteens. Then a cheap flight to Rome, train to Bari, boat to Durres in Albania. Then two days on a minibus, north to the war.

But first they stay a few days in southern Albania. Getting acclimated, sitting in a café drinking coffee, watching the other recruits. In Durres, there were bandits, thieves, and Albanian Mafiosi, all jostling for position. During Roman times, it was called Dyrrachium, one of the great cities on the eastern Adriatic. Now there are prefabricated white houses slouching toward the sea, belonging to wealthier Albanians, and piles of trash—plastic bottles, tins, toilet paper—by the Roman ruins. There's tenth-century Byzantine church, neglected, because there is more important business going on here; down the road is Vlora, the port city where high-speed boats loaded with illegal aliens set off for the Italian coast each night.

Further inland, there's Fier. Fier is spooky and dark. As we drive through the dusty wide streets, the locals, sitting in roadside cafés, pause from their coffee and stare without smiling. In the center of town is a former chicken farm with wire fencing. Behind it live Kosovar Albanian refugees who escaped the Serbs. The aid agencies have forgotten they're there. At night, Mercedes with tinted windows roll up and men in black leather jackets try to entice the prettiest girls to come out from behind the fence and talk to them. They tell them they will give them jobs as waitresses in Italy, jobs as au pairs.

"But they get there and there are no jobs as waitresses," Anna told me. She wore tight jeans and a pink T-shirt, was a student of German literature before the war. She spoke for a few moments and then started to cry. The blue mascara she had applied that morning in front of the single mirror all the women shared ran down her face. Her words came out faster. She was desperate, she said.

Because of these men who came from Vlora and Durres, aided by locals, looking for refugee girls, she said, she was afraid to go anywhere without her father. He stood behind her, dark and quiet, and said he could no longer protect his daughter from the gangs, and would we take Anna out of Fier? He said that the day before, they had gone to the village to make a telephone call. When he left Anna alone to use the bathroom, he returned to find her surrounded by men.

"Because we're refugees," she said, "we have no rights."

Anna told me she was afraid to go to sleep at night. She said that when she closed her eyes, she could not forget there was a Mercedes parked at the gate, and inside the car were men who had guns and more power than she did. Some of the women in the camp had already gone willingly, but there were stories that others were taken.

I believed Anna, and I found an Albanian policeman who confirmed the story, as did a French intelligence officer, who said that the Greek consulate in Tirana provided the girls with visas. If they did not go to Greece or to Italy—where one in three prostitutes come from Albania—they went to Saudi Arabia or the Gulf States. It is believed that since Albanian independence in 1992, 10,000 local women have been taken to Italy and 20,000 to Greece.[1]

In Durres, there is a murky sense of illicit transit. Near the biscuit-colored beach are cafés where people wait for boats. Some of them are young women, some are families, some are biting their nails, others are wearing bright-colored track suits and holding baskets of fruit. They say they are going to Italy but don't want to say with whom, or how.

In another café, young KLA recruits sit clustered together, a pack of Marlboro Lights in the center of the table along with a lighter and an overflowing ashtray. A waiter serves small cups of coffee with no eye contact. There is a hostile attitude toward foreigners here, a legacy of the Communist dictator Enver Hoxha, along with the concrete bunkers that rise up out of the earth every few hundred meters. On the one hand, they love anything Western. On the other, they fear it.

"We grew up waiting for an invasion of any kind, intellectually, militarily," said one young Albanian. By May 1999, their town *was* being invaded by a largely foreign militia who had come to launch an assault in Kosovo, where the majority is ethnic Albanian. The recruits were young and could barely speak Albanian.

They gathered at the KLA recruiting center in the Café Drenica. The outside was guarded by soldiers with Kalashnikovs, and the red and black flag with the double-headed eagle flew overhead. A veranda wrapped around the back of the building, looking out toward the sea. Boxes of ammo were stacked.

One year ago, there were a few hundred KLA soldiers, more guerrillas than fighters. They had sprung from clans and come together in their villages in an attempt to rid themselves of the Serbian policemen and a Belgrade government that, they believed, repressed them by forbidding them to speak their own language and elect their own leaders.

The conflict in Kosovo, like all the conflicts in the former Yugoslavia, was rooted in history and vengeance. For the Serbs, Kosovo is not a wasted, impoverished province, but a mythic place. During the battle of Kosovo Polje in 1389, Prince Lazar was defeated by the Turks. In Serb legend, he was offered the choice of an earthly kingdom or a heavenly one, and chose the latter, justifying the Serbs' image of themselves as the chosen people. The Serb minority that lived there were traditionally loyal both to Belgrade and to their homes in Kosovo.

The separation between the ethnic Albanians and the Serbs in Kosovo had occurred long before the NATO bombs. Following the first proindependence demonstrations by ethnic Albanians in 1968,

Tito redrew the Yugoslav constitution in 1974, giving Kosovo an autonomous province within Serbia and additional political rights. By 1989, however, Slobodan Milosevic had revoked autonomy. This was a political move, for he was using Serb nationalism as a tool. His words to a crowd of Serbs in April 1987—"No one shall ever beat you!"—set in motion a cycle of nationalism and ethnic hatred, first in Slovenia and Croatia, then Bosnia, later Kosovo. It played to the Serbs' resentments, recent and ancient. It became their rallying call.

For the Albanians, it marked a catastrophe. By 1990, Yugoslavia had sent in troops to impose control and dissolve Kosovo's government. In 1991, separatists proclaimed Kosovo a republic, recognized only by its neighbor Albania. The following year, Ibrahim Rugova, advocating a peaceful path to independence, was elected president of the separatist republic.

Rugova and his party, the Democratic League of Kosovo (LDK) built up their own parallel state in quiet defiance of Serb institutions. Albanian doctors had been fired from Serb hospitals, so they established their own. They had their own schools, clubs, social services; they collected taxes. Kosovo moved toward a form of apartheid.

The KLA was born out of frustration with Rugova's peaceful policies. Its supporters were young radicals, former prisoners, policemen, and soldiers. The Dayton Peace Accord that ended the Bosnian war had not addressed Kosovo. In 1996, a number of pyramid schemes in Albania collapsed, and in the meltdown and civil disorder that followed, gun depots were raided. Arms poured across the border into Kosovo. In addition, money was raised abroad by the Albanian diaspora for KLA weapons and training.

That same year, the newly born KLA claimed responsibility for bombing Serbian police targets—classic guerrilla warfare. In July and August 1998, it had seized 40 percent of Kosovo before being routed in a Serb offensive. The Serbs gained momentum following an attack on August 27 in Senik, near Pristina. Serb troops, discovering human remains believed to be Serb villagers murdered by KLA fighters, retaliated with artillery and tanks, terrorizing 4,000 inhabitants. Of the Senik aftermath, Fernando del Mundo, a spokesman for the UNHCR, called the aftermath of the battle "a scene out of Dante's Inferno." Sixteen civilians were killed; fifty wounded.

The attacks began to shift focus. As the Serbian Ministry of

Internal Affairs (MUP) police launched more assaults on civilians, a pattern emerged, reminiscent of the early days in Bosnia, when the term "ethnic cleansing" first came into use, meaning expulsion of Muslims from towns that were deemed Serbian.

As events progressed, the U.S. State Department, in a later report on ethnic cleansing, went further when it said, "What began in late February 1998 as a Serb government campaign against the separatist Kosovo Liberation Army has evolved into a comprehensive, premeditated and systematic program to ethnically cleanse the Serbian province of Kosovo of its roughly 1.7 million ethnic Albanian residents."

Throughout the autumn, fighting continued as diplomacy failed. A guerrilla pattern emerged: the KLA would launch attacks, the Serbs would retaliate. In January 1999, in Racak, a fleeing column of 45 people—including 3 women, a twelve-year-old boy, and a sixty-year-old man—were shot and hacked to death by Serbian interior ministry police and paramilitary. The incident incited the international community—which had basically stood by and let Bosnia be butchered—to outrage that Belgrade would not observe the October 1998 cease-fire.

"When I think of those days, right before the NATO war," my friend Suzanna from Pristina, told me once, "I remember this strange feeling that we were on the edge. Something was going to happen. But no one got ready."

In February at the Rambouillet peace conference, both parties arrived with no thought of real negotiation. The Serbs had no intention of giving up land that held mythic significance. The Albanians, the ethnic majority, wanted autonomy. The outcome was predictable. Milosevic declared, "We will not give up Kosovo, even if we are bombed."

Eventually, the major powers reached an agreement on wide autonomy for Kosovo and demanded an immediate cease-fire. The Kosovo Albanians conditionally accepted a draft accord subject to a two-week delay. The Serbs initially agreed to autonomy, but attached conditions. Meanwhile, Belgrade refused to allow NATO peacekeepers in Kosovo, or to permit a referendum on Kosovo's future after three years of interim government.

The failure of diplomacy opened the way for NATO air strikes, and a gloom descended over the Balkans. It was clear the next steps would be drastic. On March 20, the OSCE mission pulled out and Richard Holbrooke, the U.S. special envoy, left the Presidential Palace in Belgrade on March 23, having failed to convince Milosevic to back down.

On March 24, NATO launched massive air raids against the Serbs. It was coalition warfare, with nineteen separate governments contributing under the direction of General Wesley Clark, the American Supreme Allied Commander in Europe. Watching from the ground was like watching a patchwork quilt of nations haggling for power and political motives. It gave both factions—the Serbs and the KLA—more chance, more space, and more impetus to fight.

Immediately after the bombing started, Serb forces began a rampage against Albanian civilians, murdering scores, using entire communities as human shields, and forcing thousands from their homes. They looted, stole, raped, threw bodies into trucks and dumped them in rivers. They forced villagers to dig their own mass graves.

The refugees we saw on the mountains passes in Montenegro or Albania carried stories as well as shopping bags with woolen socks and tins of food. The tales were of people being pulled out of their houses and shot, screaming in the night. Images of houses on fire, children running down roads, refugee women giving birth in the woods.

One of the first mass killings—for which Slobodan Milosevic would later be indicted—took place the day after the bombing began, March 25, 1999, in the villages of Velika Krusa and Mala Krusa. More than 100 Kosovar Albanian men and boys were killed by Serbian police after they were rounded up and put inside an uninhabited house. The room was sprayed with bullets.

During the first five days of the bombing, a systematic push drove hundreds of thousands of Albanians out of Kosovo. By the end of March, it was estimated that 500,000 people—nearly a quarter of the population—had fled.[2] On March 31, an estimated 100,000 were driven out of Pristina alone by security forces.

In response, the Albanian diaspora, which numbers close to a million, began recruiting soldiers around the world. By late April, the KLA claimed to have as many as 8,000 training camps inside Albania proper and thousands of recruits arrived. By the end of May, the estimated number of fighters was 17,000. They were described to me variously as freedom fighters, guerrillas, terrorists, thugs, and rebel partisans.

Or, as Bilal Sherifi, a KLA official told me one afternoon in his Tirana office, "The KLA is a collection of various groups of Albanian patriots." Within that group, in May 1991, two primary factions struggled for power. One was headed by Bujar Bukoshi, a German-based physician, allied to Ibrahim Rugova, the former political leader of the Kosovar Albanians. Hashim Thaci, who was the Kosovo representative to the ill-fated Rambouillet negotiations, which precipitated the war, led the other side. Thaci would later emerge as a powerful force and go on to become a leading political figure in postwar Kosovo.

The hierarchy and the fundraising of the KLA were kept secret, with operations based throughout Europe and North America. Zurich was one center for KLA organizational activities, New York another. Much later, after the bombing had stopped and the Serbs had retreated from Kosovo, vowing to return, the KLA would come out of the shadows and begin to court the West. It would not forget its original intentions for its land: much later, in what seemed like another lifetime after the war in Pristina, Jakup Krasniqi, the KLA political spokesman, stressed to me that it had fought for an *independent* Kosovo, not an autonomous one. The KLA people would back the U.N., he said, *for now*, but they would not give up their vision.

At the moment, however, the KLA was still fighting to regain its land. To do this, it needed men. The first entry to its world was the Café Drenica, past the guard with the black bandanna and the AK-47 with its safety catch off.

Inside, the café was dank. It smelled of too many men living and working closely together. Bored soldiers sat drinking coffee. Others were loading boxes of ammunition. Posters were taped up on the wall: of Adem Jashari, the rebel fighter now elevated to the status of national hero since he was murdered, along with most of his family, at Prekaz in March 1998 by the Serbs. In the picture, Jashari held a Kalashnikov and an ammunition belt, and wore a long dirty beard. Underneath, in big letters: HOMELAND IS CALLING.

Suzanna and I headed for the back stairs to the office of a recruiting officer called Taf Tafa, the Albanian corruption of the English "Tough Tougher." He pulled out a laminated German driver's license. "It's my real name," he said, opening a locked drawer, moving an ancient World War II revolver, and pulling out a sack of recruit passports from Germany, Sweden, Switzerland, Norway, American, Canada, and Britain. "It's like the European Union. A real international army."

Once the recruits dropped their passports and signed up in Durres, they traveled north by minibus to secret locations in northern Albania. Since Albania was not technically involved in the war, Taf Tafa explained, the Albanian camps did not officially exist. The recruits then moved, once trained, into Kosovo. Their priority was to get to safety the estimated 500,000 to 700,000 Kosovar Albanians trapped in the countryside and to reclaim land.

By late April, the guerrillas had managed to establish at least ten enclaves in southwestern Kosovo, just over the Albanian border, and had opened a narrow corridor from northern Albanian, near Tropoja. The original plan was to punch through a bigger corridor with the aid of American Apache attack helicopters, to free more refugees and get supplies to the KLA troops. The Apaches, however, never left the Tirana airstrip except for training exercises.

While the KLA did not have enough weapons, uniforms, or trained soldiers, it did have manpower. The number of volunteers— said to be 8,000 in training—seemed high. The problem, Visar Reka, a KLA official in Tirana, later told me, was that once they were trained, often too quickly, they didn't have enough guns. "We're scavenging," he said, and admitted they were no match for Serb artillery and airpower.

Later, during attacks, it became clear how poorly trained the KLA soldiers were. A commander turned to me, seeing his men get sliced up by shrapnel, and shouted, "We need help. We're not ashamed to admit it." Another soldier, much younger, just said, "When are those damned Apaches going to get off the ground?"

Tirana, Albania
Early May 1999

From Taf Tafa, Suzanna got a nom de guerre on a piece of dirty paper, and we moved to Tirana, trying to find a way to the camps. A few days later, I got a phone call and was summoned to a meeting in the park across the street from the Rogner Hotel. I walked alone, passing children eating pink gelato and older men playing cards. I sat in the café for one hour with an untouched lemonade in front of me. No one came.

The next day, the same thing happened, and the third. On the fourth night, a commander was sitting at my table. Behind him were two beefy bodyguards, well armed. The commander himself looked vaguely familiar—large, blond, full beard. He stood politely and shook my hand and said he was a commander in Sarajevo during the war. He had driven straight to Bosnia from Pristina when the fighting broke out. We had common friends, and we talked about Zuc, a front-line position. He said that a famous commander in Sarajevo we both knew had died of cancer. "And his dog died of heartbreak," he added.

The commander ordered a beer. He said there were no training camps inside Albania. He said that his forces were holding out but had few guns. He said he was working alongside the Americans. He said Albania had nothing to do with the war. "Officially," he added, dropping his voice. He spoke a bit more, and before we parted, he said a minivan would pick us up at dawn along with a group of recruits, not to bring too much, and not to tell anyone where we were going.

The van left from a Tirana marketplace a few hours past dawn. There were two guards sent by the commander—one a former Yugoslav National Army (JNA) officer called Kadvi, the other a recruit. He was young, rawboned, and wore a polyester red track suit. His name was Male. He had spent the past seven years living in London, working as a bouncer in a club off Bond Street, and had come back to Kosovo to fight.

"Do you know anything about fighting?" I said when we settled in for the drive.

Male cracked his knuckles. He had a funny, lopsided grin. He said he had broken up fights at the club and he knew how to use a gun. "Everyone from Kosovo knows how to use a gun."

But Male was young. He fell asleep on my shoulder, mouth slightly open. Inside the elastic waist of his trousers, pointing down, was an ancient German-made silver pistol that he claimed belonged to Enver Hoxha. His father had given it to him.

We drove out of Tirana, past cramped houses, worn Soviet-style blocks of flats, into green countryside. The road swayed, turned, coiled, went deeper and deeper north. The driver announced that the road was impossible and that some aid workers were killed on it a few weeks before. "My tires aren't great," he said cheerfully.

The day passed, the color changing outside the window. Kadvi and Suzanna smoked. It grew dark.

"He won't tell us where we are going," Suzanna said. She wore a knitted skullcap and looked tired. Since she had left Pristina nearly six weeks before, she had worn the same clothes every day. She was getting thinner. "I don't like food," she said. Her skin looked gray.

Male woke up briefly.

Kadvi fidgeted. He was crushed in the last seat of the minivan, next to cardboard boxes full of supplies. He pulled out a tattered wallet and showed photographs of his children: girls with pigtails and ribbons; girls sitting at a party with other children. He had spent many years in prison under the Serbs but would not talk about it. He wouldn't tell us his rank, the name of his commander, or where he was going. "I have a delivery," he said. When we got to Kukes, flooded with refugees and recruits, he jumped out of the van and disappeared.

The swarming recruits had paid their own way and were not anywhere near the front line. In the restaurant of the run-down Hotel Gjallica, I met Vasel Lulgjuvgjaj, a thirty-three-year-old maintenance engineer from Greenwich Village who had brought his own guns and tent, and was now waiting, growing more frustrated. He had been in northern Albania for one month and had not been paid or sent to the front.

"I spent eight hundred dollars, for what?" he said, holding out a plate of cevapcici, small sausages that he stared at with disgust. Everything about Albania was intolerable, he said: the weather, the food, the Albanians, and the fact that he was a long way from the fighting.

Vasel looked like a caricature of a soldier. He had faded fatigues, a blue bandanna wrapped around his head, three crosses on leather straps around his neck, given by cousins and aunts in the Bronx. An ethnic Albanian, he was born in Macedonia and had been living in America since childhood. He had come to save his people.

"I've got gas and electricity at home, I've got money and a job, but my conscience wouldn't let me stay home and watch TV," he said. "My brothers and sisters were being slaughtered by Serb cowards."

At dawn the next day, Vasel stayed behind and we climbed back in the van: Male still in his red track suit; Alex Majoli, a photographer from Magnum; Suzanna; me; a couple of others from Kukes. We left in the light drizzle and drove further north, rounding curves, overlooking crystal lakes and hills. It grew colder. I slept, woke at an abandoned school now used as a base for soldiers. The driver unloaded us like boxes of produce. He turned and drove off.

A teenage soldier led us to his commander, who threw his hands in the air. "I have no rides for you north of here!" he said. "You might be here for weeks! We've got no fuel!"

We bought some candy bars from a rickety roadside kiosk for a late lunch. Suzanna and I washed with water from a rusty pipe. Alex came shouting. A truck had arrived, the driver was going north. He was delivering ammunition to the front. He was happy, he said, to drive us to Kosare.

Papaj
Northern Albania
May 6, 1999

We reached a camp on a hillside at nightfall. All the commanders were eating dinner, and the sentry stood nervously telling us to leave and come back in the morning.

We walked to a farmhouse down the hill, through a field. Somewhere was the sound of water flowing. At the door, the farmer took us in. They stared in wonder at our shoes, our hair, our faces, so unused to strangers. They gave us their sofa and their blankets. The mother pulled quilts and pillows from a cupboard and poured cups of tea. "You are from outside," she said shyly.

She had dark hair and a face that was soft and rounded but etched with hardness. Everything at the farm was done by hand. She served us bean stew and thick bread, and yogurt made from soured milk. Later, she took a candle and led Suzanna and me to a hut in the garden.

"Here," she said gently. She pointed to a water pump and held it down as we washed our faces with icy water and a small sliver of green soap that she had produced. There was the distant sound of muffled shooting. The mother threw up her hands. She handed us a clean towel and led us back to the darkened house, her plastic clogs sticking to the mud. The war was so close to her, but she seemed utterly unaffected by it.

In the morning, her young daughter-in-law showed us pictures of her wedding. She touched the photograph herself in a white, meringuelike lace dress and said, with sadness, that she married into a clan and left her own family, and now this was her family.

"The night before you marry is the saddest day," she said, "because you leave your family behind." They lived too far away for her to see them often, but she had a baby now, a solemn child with fuzzy, pale hair. She made coffee and pulled out the sour yogurt. Then we dressed and walked uphill in the cold mist, led by the youngest son, who wore a KLA uniform.

Inside the camp were young men still uncomfortable with guns. Standing in front of one group, looking at them with great dismay, was a British trainer from Hereford. Jon was a former gunner in the Royal Air Force. He spoke fluent Croatian, learned during his time with the Croatian Army, and said he had come to train the recruits.

Jon led us to the canteen, fed us again, and arranged for us to stay in his quarters. He was only twenty-eight, but as a mercenary had served in Vukovar and Krajina. He loved the Balkans, he said, and he almost died in the Balkans. In Knin, leading a house-to-house clearing operation, he got shot in the chest by a Serb with a rifle. A 7.62-mm bullet penetrated his flak jacket and lodged itself a fraction of an inch from his heart.

He spent four months in a coma in Zagreb, four more months in rehabilitation. The Croatian Army recruited him after his recovery, and he later sat up in bed to write a training manual for the army. He got engaged to a Croat and decided to stay in Zagreb. But the relationship fell apart and he drifted back to England, where he got a job working for Autoglass, a company that replaces windows.

"One day I'm replacing windows," he said. "The next I'm blowing them out with Kalashnikovs."

He hated civilian life. He grew bored with the daily rhythm of life without war, and the dreariness of Britain, the gray skies and the endless cups of tea. Monotony set in. When the war in Kosovo broke out, he watched the images flash on his TV screen and went out and bought a plane ticket with his MasterCard.

In Tirana, he found some commanders he knew, Albanians who had fought in Croatia. Most of them spoke Serbo-Croatian, even if they didn't like to admit it. They gave him the rank of major and told him he would train a Special Forces unit called Delta Force, or BVD unit.

The BVD, he claimed, were the elite. "They'll lead the way, like the American Rangers or the British Royal Marines," he said, but the soldiers in Papaj, skinny, dejected, miserable in the rain and the cold, looked years away from that kind of experience.

"Wait until I'm finished," Jon said, perhaps overconfidently. He had sent fifty-one men to the front already, and all of them were still alive. The ones here spent their time jogging up a 750-yard hill loaded with 11 pounds of sand, or running ten miles in mud. Sometimes, he had them do 250 push-ups, or firemen lifts up stairs. In the afternoon, they had weapons training with Kalashnikovs, AK-47s, rocket-propelled grenades, and other explosives. Later, they learned mine detonation. The Serbs had laid a nine-mile stretch of minefield between Kosovo and Albania, and anyone going near the front line had to recognize mines.

Fifty percent of his soldiers dropped out each week or were kicked out. The ones who were training did not look like they would get past the first round. They had young, spongy faces and wore uniforms donated by Germany. Underneath their camouflage, they wore pink, red, and blue T-shirts that read "Love Parade 1997," provided by sponsors of an annual techno celebration in Berlin largely composed of gays and transvestites. There were some who could not wait to get their hands on a gun and live ammo, but most of them had no idea what they were doing there. In their other lives, they were students, artists, musicians, computer programmers. They did not volunteer to serve, they were forced, either morally or by their families, to fight with the KLA.

The camp had been part of a farm before the war started, and the soldiers were living in the stone buildings, sleeping in bunks or on the floor. In the morning, the roosters and cows walked by unnoticed amid the gunshots from the training exercise. Jon watched them, his optimism fading. Some, like Batman, his assistant, were clearly not going to make it home alive.

"He'll be dead in an hour on a front line," Jon said one morning, drinking weak tea from a plastic mug. "How can I send someone like that up the hill?"

Batman was a miserable character. He had crossed eyes, rarely smiled. He came from a small village in Kosovo, had a wife and children who had not yet escaped into Albania. He bore his lowly duties and Jon's complaints with stoicism. At night, he sat outside his barracks, staring toward the East. "I don't want to be here," he said simply.

Most of the other soldiers did not want to be there, either, because Camp Papaj was limbo. It was still fifteen miles from the front, close enough to sense war but not close enough to be in the middle of it, or to feel that you were actually fighting. The nights were lonely and cold. The mornings were drenched in a heavy mountain mist. A few times a day, a farmers' truck with an open back drove into the camp, and the British commander would point out a few of his best soldiers, who would quietly gather their kits and head up the hill toward Kosare.

Before we left with a group, moving up the hill to the front, Jon said that he was proud of all of them when they left, but he felt bad sending some of them off. He knew, maybe, that some were going to their deaths. You could always tell, he said, who was going to make it and who was not, by some strange look in their eyes.

KLA Forward Base Camp
Near Kosare

May 12–14, 1999

The thing about a front line is that once you get there, having begged and cajoled and crept at last inside, once the fighting starts, you can't run away. You are stuck inside, like the soldiers, who look as scared as you do, as fearful and afraid and unable to stop their hands from shaking.

Breakfast, before the bombing started, was stale bread, tea in pink plastic cups, outside the commander's headquarters. A radio blaring BBC World Service balanced on a makeshift wooden table, reporting that Serbian troops were pulling out of Kosovo.

"Milosevic is backing down," one of the soldiers said, chewing hard on the bread.

Before the KLA had turned it into a front line, the camp had been a farm, with small houses scattered across rolling hills. Flowers were slowly pushing up through the plowed earth. Each morning, an elderly woman still took her cow out to pasture. There were some horses down closer to the river, and the fruit trees were getting ready to drop their fruit.

The soldiers in Kosare were experienced, more experienced than those in Papaj. There were Kosovars, from Pristina, who spoke good English, had traveled, lived abroad. There were also foreigners: from America, France, North Africa, the Middle East, Bosnia. In my tent, everyone spoke English. The day I arrived, Ali, the Moroccan commander, told me an Italian named Francesco had died the week before and asked if I knew how to get in touch with his family.

I asked for his last name. Ali shook his head. "Don't know. He never said."

"Passport?"

Ali didn't have it, didn't know where it was. It could have been back in that drawer in Durres, or in Kukes. Francesco had no identification when he died; now he was in the morgue in Bajram Curi.

"I want his family to know he's dead," Ali said. It was a chilling thought. Francesco was lying in a morgue in a northern Albanian city; no one he loved even knew he was there.

Kosare was a front line that had recently been captured from the Serbs, and there was a precarious sense to it. Outwardly, there was a semblance of normality. The soldiers ate, washed with stream water, cleaned their weapons, rolled cigarettes as they sat in the sun. But there was a pervasive sense of fear and waiting, punctuated by the sight of a constant stream of bodies brought on stretchers from the first front, over the river and the hill. The small triage hospital was full of the wounded.

Sometimes, there were reprieves, when bodies were not carried in and bombs did not fall. Then the camp looked almost idyllic in the bright sunshine, when the animals continued walking across the green hills and the sound of the water coming down from the mountain was the only thing breaking the silence.

But it was an illusion. Within minutes, when you relaxed and lay in the sun, or got a cup of tea from the makeshift kitchen, or opened a book or began to talk to someone about life beyond war, something would happen.

That day at breakfast, making jokes about Milosevic, listening to the radio, none of us saw the plane.

When the blast came, it crackled loudly and shook the earth beneath us. It was louder than a mortar. Later, we learned it was a rocket, 300 yards away. My cup dropped from my hand, the lukewarm tea running down my trousers, but I didn't even feel it, didn't feel the red burn I would later find. The soldier next to me fell to the ground. As he dropped, he said, "It's a bomb."

I dropped too, under the table, useless protection, but I moved with the same sense I had when I was small and would climb under my bed. Then I remembered that I had heard a bomb early that morning, around 5 a.m., but it was distant and far away, and seemed to me, from my fuzzy haze of sleep, familiar: like the hundreds of mornings I had woken up in my bed at the Holiday Inn in Sarajevo. I turned and, with a terrible complicity, went back to sleep.

It was the same with the snipers. Most of the people I knew who had been shot by Serbian snipers in Sarajevo told me that at first they did not leave their houses, or they ran across intersections in groups. But after a while, they got tired of staying inside and they believed nothing would happen to them. There was one boy who got shot in the spine. It was such a beautiful day, he said, how could he not go outside, even if they were shooting?

But this was not a shell or a sniper. It came from a plane. A commander ran out of the Command Post. He screamed at us to move, that the plane was circling and coming back.

I rolled out from under the table. The radio was still playing, knocked to the ground. The soldier I was eating breakfast with was gone. Some others were running up a steep hill, guns in front of them. I ran after them.

Who is it? Who is bombing us?

One of the soldiers turned. "I don't know. Nobody knows."

We went down a bramble path, stumbling over bushes, and along a narrow ridge that took us past the Triage where the nurse, Nasi, was already outside. We ran past the chicken coop and past some dilapidated shacks used as outhouses. Then another blast came, and we dropped to the ground, lying flat on our stomachs. I looked at the soldier next to me, his face under his helmet. He seemed young, scared. I felt a strange rumble in the earth. "Get up," the soldier said to me softly.

We got up again and ran. Someone was coming behind us, panting. An older soldier with a big belly. "Keep moving, keep moving." He overtook us and moved ahead. "Don't stay here, you'll be killed. They're dropping them by the river." His voice sounded like it came from the bottom of a lake. He ran down the path and was gone. The two soldiers ahead of me suddenly stopped.

"Where should we go?" I said.

One fell silent. The other said, "I don't know."

Another shudder of a rocket, and the two others were gone, off the trail. I did not see where they were, because my head was buried in the dry grass. When I looked up, away from the smell of the earth and of early summer, I was alone.

I ran to my tent. It seemed the point furthest away from the river, where the last bomb had fallen. Once inside the plastic dome, I dragged my sleeping bag into the sunlight, thinking that if they bomb the tent, at least I'll have something to sleep in. Around me, outside, there were soldiers charging forward with guns, soldiers with antiaircraft guns, a soldier trying to get a signal on a satellite phone, supplied by NATO, presumably to tell them they had the wrong coordinates and had hit the wrong target.

I looked for Alex, for Suzanna. Suzanna was sitting on the grass, a strange look in her eyes.

"NATO is bombing us," she said plainly.

"Who told you that?"

"The soldiers."

Around her were the wounded who had been taken from the river, where the bombs had fallen, to the trench. There were bodies and stained stretchers spread across the green grass, some sitting with their skin ripped by shrapnel, others unconscious. Out of the corner of my eye, running across a field, I saw Male. He was holding the gun that belonged to Hoxha, the one that he was so proud of, but he was holding it straight in front of him, as though he did not know how to use it. He still wore the red track suit, dirtier now than when we rode the van north a week ago.

His friend saw him and motioned him to move toward us. "Male, get down! Get down!" he screamed. Suzanna stood up. "Male!" she called. Another soldier shouted, "Male! What do you think this is, a picnic?" Male made it to the trench and threw himself in. He was breathing hard. His eyes were wide, panicked.

Ali told me to get in the trench and help with the wounded. He said he thought the first wave of bombing was NATO, the second wave was a Serb plane that got shot down by NATO or by some of the soldiers at the river.

"I don't understand," I said.

He said, "I don't care who did it. It doesn't matter now. There's body pieces everywhere. Hands, feet, lying near the riverbed. Don't go wandering off."

Suzanna sat in the trench. She did not seem frightened, but dreamy, almost stoned. Her long hair was pulled back into a messy chignon, like a thick rope. She was helping a soldier pull off his socks. His foot was full of blood.

"I'm okay," she said, turning to me, eyes darkened.

"Are you?" I said.

Suzanna was never okay, not really. She was sitting in a Pristina café with her best friend when a group of Serb paramilitary razed the place with bullets. She woke up lying in blood and glass, and, searching around for her handbag, found the dying body of her friend. Sometimes, she says, she still dreams about it, and she wonders why it was her fate to live and her friend's fate to die. "I wonder if there will ever come a time when I don't dream about it," she said.

I climbed into the trench with her. She asked for a cigarette.

"Did you hear there were pieces of bodies down near the river?" She drew on her cigarette.

"Yes," I answered. "They shot down a plane. Ali said there are hands and feet and pieces of bodies scattered around."

Suzanna fell silent. She smoked some more.

"Can we go look for the hand?" she asked.

I turned, startled, to look at her, but she was dead-serious, her face as flat and expressionless as a stone.

The next hours slid down a rabbit hole—no sense of time, of minutes, of hours, of seconds, like being on a drug that stripped you of any sense of reality. What I thought had been an hour of bombardment was really three or four minutes. Minutes lying in a trench were actually hours. My watch had no relation to the reality of what was happening inside the camp. The world outside, where people were eating and drinking and reading newspapers or sitting in front of their computers, did not exist.

All that did exist were the small things, things that previously had been effortless and now had to be done in a mechanical fashion. The time it actually took to walk in the dark from the tent where I slept to the command post was twelve minutes, but it felt like twelve hours. The time it took me to fall asleep, next to a sleeping soldier, so close I could hear his breathing, was forty minutes, but it felt like days. The time it took to wake up at the first crackle of a bomb somewhere outside and scurry out of the tent took forty seconds at most. But untangling my boots from my sleeping bag, shaking off the last remnants of sleep, grabbing my flashlight and sliding out the door down a hill all made it feel like it was much longer.

No one knew what was happening. It was an assault, but where were the Serbs, how many were there and how close? Who had dropped the bombs? In the Command Post, they might have known, but they weren't saying. News filtered down: there would be another push, it would be tonight, it would be either by ground or by air.

In the tents, the soldiers were as confused as we were. They were being sent in shifts up over the hill to the first front line. The training they had gotten in Papaj or another camp suddenly did not seem like enough to prepare them for this. They were scared by Ali saying

we were being punished by Allah for drinking and smoking and staying up late the night before. "It's only fair," Ali said with a weird glint
in his eye, "to expect retribution."

There was a Swede from Malmö sharing our tent, a former U.N.
soldier who had served in central Bosnia. After the war, he went back
to Sweden but realized one morning he felt more alive in war than in
civilian life. After Ali left, it was the Swede who organized the tent,
who described the missiles that had fallen, the ones that might fall,
and how infrared devices could detect bodies sleeping in tents. He
talked about bullets, wounds, bullets entering guts, exit wounds,
amputations, shrapnel injuries, sucking chest wounds. He called me
Journalist.

During the first day of bombing, the Swede had excused himself
from the trench where we were all cowering—which in fact was a
latrine—and carefully climbed out to rinse his arm of the mess that
had stained his uniform. He held it under a small stream that came
from the mountains above. "For a moment, I am going to forget
about the war," he said, rolling up his sleeve and scrubbing the arm.
He smiled when it was clean, rolled down his sleeve, climbed back in
the trench.

The younger soldiers listened to the Swede the same way they
listened to Ali, because they knew about positions: the difference
between incoming and outgoing, clearing houses, urban combat. He
talked about Bosnia, about Srebrenica. Perhaps it was not all true,
but everyone in the tent listened: Dardan, who was twenty-five and
whose father was a well-known journalist in Pristina, and who was
studying broadcasting in Canada; his best friend from grammar
school, Arden, who lived in New York and worked at a restaurant in
Midtown Manhattan. Dardan had lived in London, like Male. He
worked as a bartender and was so good at mixing cocktails that
Loaded magazine voted him the fifth-best bartender in Britain.

They had fresh faces, Dardan and Arden. They had never fired
guns before, but were now holding Chinese Kalashnikovs in their
arms. They wore Ralph Lauren ski hats under their helmets, and
they were genuine and honest about being afraid and missing their
women and not wanting to die. They had been pulled abruptly out of
bars and restaurants and not given enough time to get acclimated to
the roughness, the harshness, the unfamiliarity of the place. They

wanted to save Kosovo because they thought it was the right thing to do—but they did not want to die for it.

Dardan left Pristina in 1992. "My whole generation did," he said. "We didn't want to get drafted by Serbs and fight against the Bosnians."

He talked about London. About buying vegetables on Portobello Road, about bars in Chelsea, about Soho on weekends. Our voices were drowned out by machine-gun fire somewhere over the hill, an invasion of reality. Dardan dropped his eyes. He was due to go over that hill in the next shift of soldiers.

He got married two years ago, to a Kosovar girl. He said, half-joking, "I don't want to die. All I want to do is sit in Starbucks in London and drink a good coffee."

At night, we put out the fire and the Swede told us what to do. There was going to be bombing that night, he said, and they would focus on the tents because they could see them. "At the first crack of the bomb," he said, "wake up and run, in orderly fashion, out of the tent into the nearby ditch. Spread out fifty meters apart. No flash-lights, no matches, no talking—most of all, no panicking. Just go, and quickly. Sleep in your boots."

"What if I don't wake up?" asked Arden.

"Then you're dead," said the Swede casually before climbing, boots first, into his bag. He fell asleep within minutes: I watched him, heard his first snores.

In the corner, an older man, a Bosnian, a former commander from Travnik, sketched out a map of the base camp, a defense plan against the assault. He spoke quietly to one of the soldiers and motioned with his pencil, marking the page.

When I met him that day, I knew, as with the Albanian commander in Tirana, that I had seen him before. There was something written on his face, some sorrow, beyond the battered skin and the deep-set eyes. There was a kindness to him, a gentleness. He spoke so softly it was difficult to hear him. I remembered, in a sudden, sharp image, that I had seen him in central Bosnia in the autumn of 1992, at a destroyed hotel in Travnik taken over by the Bosnian Army.

There was a footbridge that led to the hotel, near the blue mosaic mosque. There was a smell to that town then: Bosnia in the late autumn, before the snows, the odor of gymnasiums and schools packed with refugees following the fall of Jajce. There was a hospital, and a bus station near a hotel taken over by more soldiers, where we slept, barricading the door.

I remembered walking down and down the stairs to the basement of the hospital, where the intensive-care patients were kept, and how that smelled of blood and urine. There was low, primal moaning, like that of an animal, and I followed it to the bed of a twelve-year-old called Salko, whose torso was ripped open from chest to pubic bone. He was writhing in agony. Shrapnel was lodged in his intestine. He was a Muslim, trying to escape from Turbe, his burning village, when the Bosnian Serb Army lobbed a shell into a fleeing column of people.

Salko was separated from his father in the confusion. His mother was killed. He was alone in the hospital for nine days, and the exhausted doctor had only enough painkillers to give him an injection once a day. The doctor told me stomach wounds were the most agonizing because they healed slowly. "You cannot imagine the pain he is feeling," he said.

I remember how hard it was to sit with him, to not be able to help other than giving the painkillers I had to the doctor, who was sure Salko would not live over the next few days. I came every day, checking for his father, bringing orange juice that he could not drink. But he watched me, with his long, sad, gray face, his mouth gaping with pain, his head bathed in sweat. He did not cry, but he called for his mother.

The doctor said he had to be medivacked out, which seemed unlikely. "He's probably going to die," he said.

"What do you expect?" said a passing nurse. Not unkindly, just honest. "He barely has a stomach left."

In Travnik, at the hotel, I waited for days to get permission to go to Maglaj, a city north of Zenica under siege by Serbs, a place that had not gotten humanitarian aid for months and was totally forgotten. A few hours later, driving into Maglaj, a mortar dropped neatly on the car in front of us, slicing it open like an egg, and the people inside were killed. We waited in a ditch for the shelling to cease, and I was frightened because it was the first time I had been that close to exploding shells.

In Maglaj, people were living like rats underground for months, and without the benefit of knowing that anyone cared about them at all. Sarajevo's plight was already well known; but no one could even spell Maglaj, and the frustration and the terror were driving the few living inhabitants to the brink of madness.

I finally understood war for the first time in Maglaj. I saw a beautiful woman at the entrance to the town lying without any clothes on in the middle of the sniper's path. Everyone walked—or rather ran, because it was in full view of the Serb snipers—over her body and she would laugh and laugh as though there were some secret she knew that no one else did. The people would scream at her to get up, try to drag her, finally beg her to move. But she stayed, smiling, lying there, spread out, waiting for the snipers to take her away from this place forever.

There was a woman dentist living underground with no drugs left, pulling infected teeth from soldiers and trying to hold on to her last spoonful of coffee and her last pack of cigarettes. Bosnians used to joke that they could take anything but being without coffee or cigarettes, and she was hoarding her last remnants in a tin that she kept behind a pile of books. I did not want to leave her, because I knew she would feel abandoned. I searched in my bag for something to give her and found a bottle of Tylenol. She took the plastic bottle between her fingers, held it like a diamond, and wept, hard tears that shook her body, at some small act of kindness from a stranger.

When I looked in the face of the Bosnian commander, who was no longer a commander, just a simple soldier in the KLA trying to fight for Muslims in the Balkans, I saw this: Maglaj, Sarajevo, Travnik, a flood of refugees, a cycle of grief, death, destruction. Now he was in Kosovo, another amputated limb of the former Yugoslavia, watching more blood, more violence. I saw unbearable sadness, sadness that was so strong I could not look at him for long, the way you cannot stare into the sun.

Later, he told Suzanna that his life ended in 1995, the year the Dayton Peace Accord was signed, effectively concluding the war in Bosnia. The war was over, but he had lost all his family in a Sarajevo mortar attack. "Which is why I am here," he said simply.

The Bosnian commander continued to sketch his plan, and Dardan and Arden and the Swede had fallen asleep, and Suzanna was resting quietly inside her sleeping bag, playing with a strand of her hair. Alex, next to me, was breathing quietly. But I could not sleep.

Ali left the tent and I went with him.

"What's going to happen?" I asked.

He shrugged.

The darkness was so dense and so real and the stars so incredibly bright, and the silence of the camp so deep, except for sometimes the bellow of a cow. Ali knelt down in the mud, and began to pray.

I tried to sleep. I fell into a strange trance, sleeping without dreaming. Sleeping in a strange half-state, always aware that we would be woken up by someone above us flying in a dark sky dropping a bomb wherever his infrared directed. In the darkness, my senses were acute, like a dog's. I could detect everything: the sound of the soldiers, snoring, of small movements, of fear. Which of us will be living tomorrow and which will be dead?

When it came, the crack, I was not really sleeping. The crack in the sky, the whinny, the thundering noise, and the Swede awake in seconds, shimmying out of his bag, grabbing his gun. "Wake up, Journalist!" he yelled, nudging my leg. To the others, he shouted: "Ten seconds and exit! You have ten seconds!" Then he was gone, leaving the tent flap fluttering.

Everyone moved except Suzanna, who sat on her bag, bleary, with infinite slowness lacing her shoes, completely unaffected by the bombing. I flicked my flashlight briefly and someone hissed, "No lights! The plane is coming back."

"Suzanna," I whispered, "Suzanna, hurry."

She took her time, tying her shoes. "I'm coming," she said sweetly. But she was not rushing.

Alex was already outside the tent. He called out quietly, "There's a ditch here." We slid down into the coldness of the night air, into the trench. It was a ditch used by soldiers as a latrine, but it was below ground level and was safe.

Suzanna and I moved further up, slowly, inching our way in the mud, placing one foot in front of the other, and trying to see in the night. We found a tree, and lay down. Ali pushed Dardan and his friends into sentry positions.

Suzanna huddled against me, and I felt something warm on my shoulder. It was a sleeping bag that the Bosnian commander had retrieved and laid over us. He told us, in Bosnian, that he was there, and not to worry.

"Try to sleep," he said. He lit a cigarette, cupping the orange ember.

We slept, but woke to see the lightening of the sky, sometime between 4 and 5 a.m. It turned from black to blue to a fainter, milky, color, and as the first strains of pink came up behind the mountains, I saw an old woman who lived on this land before the KLA turned it into a forward camp. She was taking out her sheep. She was leading them, in the midst of a bombardment, into a pasture as though it were the most natural thing in the world.

She calmed me, the old woman. I drifted and woke to a shell landing close by, and this time I sat up and shook the blanket off my legs and looked around and saw the battle in harsh daylight.

There were soldiers, exhausted from the past forty-eight hours; there were Kalashnikovs spread across the grass like toys; there were soldiers loading heavier artillery into carts to bring it further up the hill, toward the first front line; there were wounded soldiers with fear in their faces and bloody bandages sitting in ditches; there was shit in the ditch too. I shook myself from sleep and forced myself to concentrate. Next to me, Suzanna's yellow hair was spread in the mud. Alex was asleep farther on. "Wake up," I said, shaking her. She turned over.

The Swede, Ali, and the Bosnian were gone. "They were called to the front," said another soldier who had been in my tent. "Everyone with experience had to go to the front." He looked gloomy and told me what he knew. The Serbs had taken the village next to us; there were reports of scores of dead. A rumor swept the trench that the Serbs were trying to break our first line of defense, that we should prepare for an infantry attack.

Dardan was still there. He stood above me, on sentry duty, with his helmet on and his old Kalashnikov slung over his shoulder like a soldier from World War II, smoking a cigarette out of the corner of his mouth. He was staring at the sky in amazement, bright blue flecked with pink and orange—a perfect Turner landscape. For a moment, he forgot the war. He was talking to himself, mumbling, but excited as a child.

"Look. Look at that light, look at that beautiful light!"

Then he saw me, saw that I was awake, and he turned to me with joy. "Look at that sky! We're still alive! Isn't it wonderful? We're still alive!"

I fell asleep again, and when I woke up, he was no longer in guard position at the edge of the trench. Someone said he had gone to the front.

By daylight, we counted some of the bodies. "Seventeen dead," Suzanna said, her voice steady and even, like an accountant announcing a tax bill. "And that's not counting the ones by the river." We had been forbidden to wander toward the river, or the first front-line trenches, or the place where the Serb plane had been shot down.

"I'll take you," said one soldier, a local, who knew the fields. In the chaos, no one noticed us moving toward the riverbed, where the forest grew deeper. There was the Serbian plane, a smashed taillight and pieces of metal, parts of the door with Cyrillic letters. There was puddle of blood near some rocks, and tattered clothing. There were remnants of the NATO rocket that had shot the plane down.

By a bend in the river was the tent where the first bomb had landed, killing four soldiers inside, including a sixteen-year-old boy. I had watched the soldiers load their bodies onto a military jeep the day before. When they loaded the bodies, the uncle of one of the younger boys was crying, weeping, and kicking the ground because he had told the boy to go to the tent because he thought it would be safer. On the jeep, the bodies were not yet stiff, and their eyes were closed, like sleeping children; but they were blackened from the fire.

When those soldiers chose that spot to sleep, it must have seemed safe. When the bomb came, one must have been outside on watch, because there was a pile of cigarette stumps he had smoked, bored, waiting. Half of a soldier's life is boredom. The other half is the unexpected. For him, the unexpected was the bloody tarp, the sleeping bags with congealed blood, one gray sock with stains of red, a book with ripped and burnt pages.

Suzanna could not move. She was staring at the ground, fascinated. "Try to imagine what it felt like," she said quietly, her eyes never moving from the spot. "Try to imagine what they felt."

We moved on, closer to the front. The sun was higher as we climbed, past fences to keep cattle inside, past small white farmhouses, now abandoned. It appeared at first to be an alpine village, but when you looked closer, something was wrong, the signs of the bombing were everywhere: deep holes bored into the earth, great pieces of rock that seemed to be in the wrong place. There was a cow with its hind legs blown off, covered with flies. Then further on, lying on the side of the hill, a beautiful white horse, poetic in its stillness, startled by bombs and apparently dead of a heart attack. There was a farmhouse, idyllic, with a garden in the front and someone's washing outside, hanging on the clothesline, left when they ran.

At the commander's post in Kosare, we ate: beans, bread, tea. The commander said the Serbs were sending over bombs with poison gas, like World War I, and the soldiers on the first front had to use gas masks. The ones who did not complained of terrible stomach cramps.

"I don't have any masks for you," he said. "But you can go if you want." He sent us with two antisniper soldiers as guards. One of them was Suzanna's cousin from Pristina, and after he kissed and hugged her, he gently fitted his ancient gas mask, like something from the Somme, over her face.

We waded across a river, avoiding scattered car parts and the military jeep half-buried in the water, hit by a mortar. Every day, someone made this trip to bring the soldiers food and supplies, often carrying them on his back.

"We send someone who runs very fast," Suzanna's cousin joked. "The Serbs can see everything from here."

At the top of the hill Serb snipers were within close range. The cousin said, "Run when I say run. One at a time, single file." He timed the shooting on his fingers, and when my turn came, I ran, across a field made hot by the spring sunshine, dotted with blue and yellow wildflowers and high, yellow grass.

We reached a white house, and the shooting began, closer, over our heads. The cousin threw himself down. "Fucking Serbs. They see us."

When the shooting started, I maneuvered myself over Suzanna. I wished she had not come. I wished I had told her to stay behind, to wait for us by the tents. I lay on top of her while she burrowed herself into the dirt, trying to shield her from the bullets that pinged over our heads and landed near the grass. She did not seem frightened. She was calm and her breathing was even. "I'm all right," she said. "I'm all right." She began to hum again, quietly.

For fifteen minutes, we lay there. Then the antisniper cousin looked at his watch and began crawling on his belly through the dirt, moving forward up the hill toward a barn, motioning with hand signals not to talk; to move left; right; to go forward. We crawled like worms, reaching an abandoned stable.

Inside were soldiers, but these were not recruits. They were front-line soldiers who had been there for days together. Now they were eating—beans in plastic cups, chunks of bread—and resting. Some had spread hay in a corner and were sprawled out, their guns next to them. There was no sweetness or youth in their faces.

They were too tired to talk. They wanted cigarettes, chocolate, matches, anything we had in our bags. After a few minutes, they told us to go because they were launching mortars. Run down down the hill before the Serbs start firing back, they said. In English, one said, "Get the fuck out of here."

We ran up higher, up the hill, to another unit, and these guys were high on a small victory; they were laughing and shouting and high-fiving each other like kids in a basketball game, hugging each other's skinny shoulders. They had freckles and T-shirts and sneakers, and they said they took out two Serbian tanks and dropped a mortar that killed 60 men. But they also told us to leave. Go, go, they said, pointing toward a forest. Something's going to come in soon.

We wound through the trail, climbing higher, a trail laid with pine needles, the leaves making a canopy over our heads, winding closer and closer to the edge of the mountain, the tops of the Serb positions.

Suzanna's cousin said, "Look! Up near that eagle's nest is a ridge, and on that ridge is this damn sniper, the one I can't get day after day." He vaulted over a log. "He's my nemesis." Along one side was a sheer drop of the mountain. But near that drop was a trench with camouflaged soldiers with branches over their heads. You could step on them and not notice they were there.

One of them suddenly popped out of his riding place, and Suzanna, who was facing the hill, turned around, as if in slow motion. The soldier climbed half out of his trench, covered in a blanket of branches, and stayed squatting. He wore a helmet, fatigues; camouflage paint on his cheeks and nose; and a baffled expression. A gas mask hung around his neck.

He watched Suzanna, and then his face changed too: something like a smile broke the deadness of his mask.

Suzanna stared at him. He called her name. As if in a dream, she walked over and looked down. Her expression softened and they spoke quietly in Albanian. Gently, she touched him lightly on the hand. Then the shooting started, louder, closer.

Suzanna's cousin said, "Okay, now this time is real, let's get out of here."

Suzanna looked dazed, as though someone had hit her. "That was my first boyfriend, from Pristina," she said. "I haven't seen him in three years. I wanted to give him a hug. He was waiting for me to give him a hug. But I couldn't do it. There were too many other soldiers around and there was no one to hug them. It wouldn't have been fair, would it?"

She put on her gas mask. For the next few weeks, she played with the mask, putting it on, off, or looking at it with a strange, loving smile. Once, she told me, she dreamed of so many things, of moving out of Kosovo, of becoming famous. She was pretty, with her soft yellow hair like corn silk and her wide brown eyes. She sang to herself like a small child, and walked with a strange, lilting gait which was not altogether unattractive. But something happened to her that night in the café in Pristina, something was taken from her. She no longer talked about the future or becoming famous, or about boys. Instead, she said things like, "I don't want anyone to touch me," or "Do you think I will go mad?"

Walking back, we passed the Triage where Nasi, the only trained nurse, was working. The Triage was a barn where the farm animals were kept, but she had lined up a few cots and lit a few candles to see in the darkness without electricity, and there were some boxes of medications that were out of date, from Switzerland and Germany.

Nasi's name means "wild rose" in Albanian, and she was nice-looking, with soft hair and fair skin, but with huge black rings under her eyes. She was thirty-eight years old but looked younger. She spoke some English, and we sat outside on a bench and smoked and talked.

Halfway through her cigarette, Nasi began to cry. "I can't take it anymore," she said. "I'm drained, emotionally and physically." She wanted to go home, she had not slept in days or weeks, and she could not close her eyes without images of boys with their legs blown off coming to her.

"I can't help them, I can't stop the pain," she said, wiping her nose on her sleeve. "I can't lie to them anymore, that they will live or that their leg will come back. I can't lie." She lost 17 boys in the past day, she said. Seventeen. She remembered every single one of their names. Their eye colors. Their injuries.

"The commander won't let me go home," she said. "He needs me, I'm the only nurse. But I feel like I can break if I stay here."

She saw a ring on my finger, a silver ring, and she touched it. I took it off and handed it to her.

"Go anyway, don't listen to the commander," I said.

"I can't," she whispered. "It's my country. My city may no longer exist, but my country, I have to do everything I can."

She put the ring on her finger and blew her nose. I slipped 50 Deutsche marks (DEM) into her pocket. "There's a truck going to Bajram Curi later," I told her. "You should take it, get out of here for a few days."

Nasi wanted to do something for me. So she loaned me her room for an hour, in one of the farmhouses, to boil water and wash. There was still fighting in the hills, but I didn't care. I wanted to wash, wanted to be alone, away from the scenes of blood and the sound of shooting. Her stone farmhouse set on the edge of the jagged green hill seemed safe, even if it was not.

I climbed the hill to reach it and found the water pump and the fire. As I waited for the water to boil, three snipers sat chewing on a piece of bread and watched me. One was sitting in a tree. He motioned to me, as if to say, Don't worry, we're here. You are safe.

I took the water inside and sat in Nasi's room surrounded by her bags of out-of-date antibiotics and rolls of bandages. What a strange world. The few articles of clothing she had were filthy, covered with grime. On a bench, I began the laborious process of washing the past days off of me—the blood and the latrine and the mud and the sick. I tried to think of other things, tried to take myself somewhere else, where the war did not exist, but I could not. Earlier, walking to Nasi's house, I passed Ali, who looked somber.

"The Serbs are in the last stages of losing Kosovo and they are desperate," he said, shouting over machine-gun fire. "They want to leave their mark on Kosovo now."

"How close is that machine-gun fire?" I yelled. "How close?"

"Three hundred yards," he shouted back. He had no fear. It was all fatalistic stuff, as he explained to me before: we had no choice in our fates. "They're trying to penetrate our base."

There was sunshine that day, and if you did not look out over the ridge and see the tents and the rows of artillery lined up and the soldiers sprawled on the grass in position, you would see that valley as it lay for five hundred years, a hamlet straddling northern Albania and southern Kosovo. A place that until now was utterly unremarkable.

Nasi left before she cracked in a million pieces. A few days later, I got a ride in the back of a truck, with Alex and Suzanna, bumping our way back to Kukes, which looked like a grand metropolitan city after Kosare. There was food to eat and packs of cigarettes to buy from kiosks, and electricity for a few hours a day.

There, I met a French intelligence officer who tried to piece together what had happened inside our camp, who grilled me about what kind of guns were being used there. He knew everything going on there during those four days, down to the last hour and the number of casualties. NATO sources later told me that what had happened in Kosare over those few days was that the former Serbian position had changed hands and NATO had not yet learned of the shift.

I never saw or heard from Dardan or Ali or the Swede again, but some time later, I saw Nasi in Tirana and she was wearing the silver ring.

A year later, in London, when the war was over, I got a letter from Pec.

"I'm finally home," she wrote. "I will never forget you or those days in Kosare." She said that she often thought of me, that she was trying to live beyond the war, but everywhere were things that reminded her. She still had bad dreams, about the people she saved and the ones she could not. In the corner of the envelope, folded and no bigger than a postage stamp, was the DEM 50 note.

Chapter Two

When a state becomes a party to the Geneva Convention, it undertakes to recognize that women shall be especially protected against any attack on their honor, in particular against rape, enforced prostitution or any form of indecent assault.

Geneva Convention IV, Article 27

Pristina, Kosovo
June 8, 1999

Afterward, Suzanna remembered every detail of their faces, their clothes, their smell. She remembered they were old, older than her father. Their dirty hair, their rancid skin. The strength in their arms when they shoved her, herding her off the bus.

She was separated from her mother and her sister and she thought the best thing would be to find her father. Someone had given her money and she got a bus from Kukes, heading for Tirana. She climbed into the bus and sat quietly, her hands folded in her lap, wearing the same pajamas she had worn when her mother came with her sister and took her out of the hospital in Pristina.

"Come on, we have to go now," her mother said as Suzanna dragged her feet out of the bed and placed them unsteadily on the floor.

It seemed unreal, the scene unfolding in front of her that day in the hospital. The wards crowded with people, wounded and confused, and outside, the grayness of Pristina broken by fire and shooting.

She wanted to go home and get her things. She was only twenty-one; she liked her clothes, her Versace minidress, her books, her photographs. "Wherever we're going," she said, "I need my pretty things." Her mother shook her head. Instead, they went to a basement and hid for three days. Suzanna wondered where her father was, where her friends were. Her neck still ached where the shrapnel had sliced it open, low, near her collarbone. A doctor had stitched up the worst of it into small butterflies with black thread. He told her if she wanted, after the war, she could probably get plastic surgery. "You're still beautiful," he told her. "Don't worry."

A few days before, her life had been entirely different. She was sitting in a café after curfew with her best friend and her professor from the university, drinking coffee and talking about the theater. It was the first day of the NATO bombing, the first day the bombs started cracking, the sky started slicing in two. She tried to continue to do what she had always done, which was go to the café, drink coffee, see people she knew, appear normal.

Later, she would say, she had had a bad feeling all along.

That day, she sat with her back to the door. They were talking about modern theater, about performing. That was the last thing she really remembered: the foam of the cappuccino, looking down into her cup, the words of her friend, the slowness of the minute hand. Maybe the world had not gone mad. Maybe they were not really at war.

She did not see the gunmen come in, but she heard the bullets spray the café. She felt the room shake and saw her friend fall to the ground, and the professor get hurled across the room and heard the glass shattering around her, tables crashing, chairs falling. Her last conscious thought was to put her head in her hands.

Someone moved her and she woke up. She remembered she was on the floor, surrounded by glass and debris. The café as she knew it was gone, blown up. She began crawling through the glass and there was the body of her friend.

Her friend would not wake up. Her body was still and her mouth was open. Suzanna began to cry, then she tried singing. She started to rock her. Don't leave me alone in this world, she whispered to her friend, because she had loved her. Later, Suzanna would think that her friend had died only because she wanted to drink a cup of coffee.

Someone pulled Suzanna's arm and lifted her up, out of the café. She fought them, tried to make it back to where she thought she had left her bag with her documents, her papers. She couldn't find her handbag.

When she woke up in the hospital, someone told her she had been reported dead on Pristina Radio.

The doctors examined her and operated. She wasn't too badly wounded: there were cuts from glass and debris all over her body. She would have scars, but she was alive. She lay in the hospital bed wondering what madness had descended on Kosovo in the past twenty-four hours. She lay down and willed herself to sleep. Then her mother came, grabbing her from the bed, telling her they had to leave.

They found a nurse who signed her release form, and she put a coat over her pajamas and they hid in a basement for three days while her mother found a way for all of them to get out of the country. By bus and car, finally a truck, stuffed in with other people running away.

The day she left, she looked back at Pristina, and as they drove out, in the direction of the Albanian border, she thought, still in shock, I'm a refugee now.

They crossed the border and were headed for Kukes when they had to stop, delayed by the backup of thousands of people crossing over. She was crammed on the back of a truck with the others. Her mother and sister were sleeping. As the hours passed, she grew bored, leaning against the metal frame of the truck. She didn't have anything to read.

She was half-asleep when a young journalist approached her truck and said, "Does anyone here speak English?" She had studied English at school and spoke it along with Serbian, Albanian, and German. The journalist was young and looked friendly, like someone she would have wanted to drink a coffee with in the old days, so she decided to help him.

"I speak English," she said quietly, more to herself than to the journalist, and jumped off the back of the truck. The reporter needed help interviewing other refugees, asking them their names and ages and what had happened to them. When she was done, she looked up and her truck was gone and she was in her pajamas and her mother and sister had headed somewhere else, up the road, still sleeping, not even realizing that she was left behind. She ran up and down the road, trying to find their truck, but it had disappeared.

She stayed a few weeks in Kukes, working for journalists, found some clothes to put on, ate dinner in a place called the Chicken Shack. But she moved as if in a daze, still not believing what had happened in that Pristina café. She wanted to find her family, and someone said her father was in Tirana, so she got a bus ticket one afternoon and went.

She was alone on the bus, dreaming and looking out the window, when the men climbed on board with guns. They said they were from the Albanian police. They asked if there were any Kosovar women, refugees, on board. At first, she didn't say anything, but it was hard for her to hide, to shrink into her seat: a small, blond, slightly disheveled young woman with no papers and no luggage. "I'm from Kosovo," she said.

One of them took her away and said they would help her get new identification papers. She remembered how badly they smelled, in the car, on the way to what she thought was the police station.

There was no police station. Instead, they took her to an alley and raped her, all of them, touching her roughly, pushing themselves into her brutally. She had never had sex before, so it was difficult. But they were determined, and they did not care how much it hurt, so they bit her and hit her too. She cried and told them she could be their daughter. They were old and they smelled, she remembered. They pinned her to the wall and she cried and cried but they did not listen.

Afterward, they left her alone in the alley. She gathered her clothes together and walked back toward the bus stop. She does not remember how she made it to Tirana, but she did. On the way there, she decided she would not tell anyone, that it was part of this continuing bad dream that had begun in the café back in Pristina. She was not from a provincial village, but from a professional family and wealthy family. But to be raped in Kosovo was still so drastic that women didn't call it rape, they call it "being touched."

Suzanna moved the next few days as though she was inside a cloud, letting each day pass and watching the wounds on her neck and arm slowly healing from scabs to angry purple-blue scars. Sometimes she wore a scarf around her neck, but other times she wanted to see those scars. Even though it seemed like a dream, she did not want to forget that dream.

The rape was different. She spoke about it one night, late, in Tirana when she was talking about how bad her head felt at night, as though there was cotton wool inside of it, how strange she felt and how she thought she might be going crazy. That day, and for weeks before, Suzanna had been with refugee women who had also been raped, but they called it being touched because they could not bring themselves to say the word. And every day, she sat and talked to them and learned about their stories, for weeks and weeks she translated and interpreted their stories and comforted them when they cried. And she never once told her story.

Dragacin, near Suva Reka
Kosovo
April 1999

Around the same time Suzanna was pulled into the alley in Albania, five women in the Tahiri family were touched by Serbian soldiers. No one in this family said the word "rape." It was too harsh, too hard, too damning. No one in the family knew about the Geneva Convention or The Hague or crimes against humanity, or what happened in Foca, in Bosnia, where women were held for months and forcibly impregnated by Bosnian Serb troops as a weapon of war, a device to attempt to dissimilate society.

It has nothing to do with them—war or The Hague or Foca—with their world, which before all of this catastrophe happened, was so small and contained it could fit into the palm of their hands.

Much later, when they all had fled their homes and were gathered in a refugee camp near Kukes, one of their older cousins spoke for all of them. She had not been touched. Perhaps it was because Sherife Tahiri spoke Serbian, so when the Serbs arrived around 9 a.m. in the first week of April and circled the village, she was the one who was sent out to talk to them.

Sherife is a tall, raw-boned woman. That day, she was afraid, but she did not want the Serbs to know that as she walked in front of the crowd, trying to hold her head up, hoping to find the commander. She did not know if they were military or paramilitary. Some of them wore masks. The ones who did not leered at her, and she did not linger, or look in their eyes for very long.

She remembered it was a cold morning; there was mud on the ground from the spring rains. The village seemed ghostly, empty. There were around eleven men still left in Dragacin, but just the old ones, who could not defend the women; the others had fled to hide or to join the fighters. Later, she learned why her village was punished so harshly.

"It's a stronghold for the UCK, the terrorists," said one of the younger Serb soldiers. "And the rest of you knew it and kept them safe."

That morning, the Serbs talked to her and asked her where the fighters were. But she didn't know, she said, she really did not know, the men had all left days, weeks before, into the forests. The Serbs grew angry and separated the old men from the women. The other women, her cousins, her friends, had come out of their houses by then, and were huddled together with their children, wearing scarves and boots and their winter jackets. The children stared, some cried, but Sherife remembered those moments were strangely quiet.

The soldiers marched them to a house in the center of the village, one of the biggest, which belonged to a wealthy farmer. Some of the women were crying; they did not know what was going to happen, whether they would be killed or not. For three days, they stayed inside the house, without getting food or water. Every time they wanted to use a toilet, they asked the soldiers if they could go outside. The soldier would laugh at them but tell them to go, pointing with their guns in the direction of the woods.

Sherife was only forty-four years old, but she had the face of a

woman at least twenty years older. Her brown skin was etched with
lines from years of working on a farm in the full sunlight, bringing
up child after child, serving her husband. It never occurred to her
that life could be easier. It was the way of her mother and her grandmother, and everyone in the long line stretching before her. Everyone she knew lived the way she did.

Dragacin is so small that it is not on most maps. Life there was
small too. Before the war, life was simple; there wasn't money, but
everyone knew what to expect: winter followed autumn, summer followed spring. Planting, harvesting, selling at the market, bringing
the cows to pasture. In the late summer, the time of the shooting
stars, you could lie on your back in a field and watch the constella-
tions flicker, and then an explosion of light, and a star falls, landing in
another world.

In Dragacin, you lived your life day after day in the same way,
and you expected nothing. Because nothing ever happened.

There were Serbs, neighbors, but no one bothered anyone else,
not in the beginning. Later, much later, there were suddenly more
Serb policemen in the village, heavy, potbellied men from Belgrade,
and when you saw them, you gathered your washing and moved a
little faster. When things got harder, when the repression came,
when it became more and more difficult, your younger brother and
husband disappeared at night to meet with other men—meetings
they did not talk about. You heard the letters UCK. But you never
asked.

You didn't think of yourself as a Muslim or as anything different
from anyone else. Most families in Dragacin were Muslim and celebrated Eid, the end of forty days of fasting for Ramadan; but they
weren't especially religious. When you were small, you didn't learn
about religion. When you were very small and went to school, you
walked with friends and stopped by the side of the road to copy each
other's homework. In the summer, you swam in the nearby river,
which got warmer in June.

When a father was asked how many children he had, he would
reply by giving the number of his sons. It was clear from early on that
a woman did not count, not really.

When a young girl reached puberty, she began to think of marriage. It happened when she was about sixteen, and always on a Sun-

day morning. You got a new dress, the other girls helped do your hair in an elaborate style. The night before was spent with the other village women, commiserating about the life that lay ahead of you, which you already knew would be hard. Your mother told you that; her mother told her that.

There was a special song that the village women sang that night before the ceremony; it meant goodbye forever to your own family, to your small freedom, to walking barefoot in the grass with your friends on summer mornings. When a rural Kosovar woman married, she belonged to her husband and his family. Her mother-in-law was expected to use her like a slave. Then, when her husband touched her for the first time, he was the last man to touch her. No one else came near her, not for the rest of her days.

If that was your life, you learned things. You washed your clothes from a pipe of running water that came from the mountains above the village. You rose at dawn to bake the round, high bread and to soak and cook the beans into a thick stew, which everyone ate for lunch. When you got pregnant, the other women came and delivered your baby. Your husband touched you again, and perhaps a year later there was another baby. And another. Most women in the village had between five and ten, which infuriated the Serbs, because they saw it as a plan for Greater Albania.

But you didn't see it like that: you are a mountain person with mountain ways; you don't understand politics or the notions of war.

Occasionally, if there was time, you gathered for coffee with the other women. Your friends helped you; there was a common solidarity among all of you because your life was not easy. You talked to each other. Sometime in your life, your husband might go away for several years at a time to earn money in Switzerland, Sweden, or Germany. He sent home Deutsche marks and wrote letters, but you didn't see him, and maybe you didn't speak to him. You got news of him from other women whose husbands had also left. If you were alone, you helped each other.

But strangely, after you were all raped, you did not help each other. You did not talk to each other. No one spoke about what happened. Some of the women who were not touched taunted and teased you. You passed days and weeks and months in a strange place, a refugee camp with ten or twelve in a tent and one bathroom set up in a field for a hundred people. There was no room for your own grief.

Then you did go home, eventually, but something happened to your village during the war: the fabric and culture bound together by generation after generation has frayed bit by bit, like a half-knit sweater that begins to unravel.

You waited and you waited and you tried to repair the damage in some small ways. Your husband didn't know, but he suspected. You didn't talk about it, not ever. Not to anyone.

After a while, the silence inside your head becomes unbearable.

"You understand," said Sherife after all this happened to the women of Dragacin, "for us rape is the worst thing that can happen."

In Dragacin, the war began like this: NATO bombing of the Serbs, then retribution against the Muslims, which happened quickly. The Serbs swept through the village like so many angry bees, they were looking everywhere for the men, whom they called terrorists. You stood outside and watched, with fear deep in your stomach. Then the burning began: house after house after house. You went and found your mother weeping and gathering her things to take away.

The soldiers came for you. You were put in the house with no food or water and you waited. You didn't know what they would do to you. There was crying all around: other women, wailing, but you did not cry. You waited.

They took the youngest and the prettiest, like Zoya, who was twenty-three and had long dark hair and a two-year-old son. Her husband worked in Switzerland and sent home money. Her house was burnt down around April 5, she can't quite remember: for two weeks, she stayed with a group of other women in a house until the day the Serbs came to "take" her.[1]

Zoya slept with only one man in her life. She said, "I do not know a lot of the world." But she knew what they were coming for, and she cried as they led her away, roughly, and brought her to a house in the middle of the village. All the women knew about that house. After a few days, it became notorious.

The soldiers were in their late twenties and early thirties. Inside the house, they told her to take off her clothes. This, for Zoya, was the most humiliating part: no one, except her husband and the woman who helped deliver her son, had seen her naked. She slowly peeled off her knitted vest, rolled down her dress, her undergarments, hanging her head in shame.

The soldiers who watched seemed to understand how painful this was for her, and they used that as a weapon. They made her walk through the rooms naked; they made her spend most of the day naked; they told her to boil coffee and she had to serve it to them, naked. She had to clean the house for them like that, crying quietly as she did it.

One of the kinder ones sometimes gave her his shirt. The others were not so gentle. They make her stand in front of them, her arms crossed across her breasts, trying to hide herself, and they fired questions at her in Serbian, which she remembered a little from school. Their voices seemed to come from all over the room, from the walls, from the ceilings. They shouted at her and pushed her, grabbed her arm when it appeared she was not listening. One roughly turned her face toward him when she looked down, taking her chin in his hand, and squeezing. His eyes, she remembered, were light-colored, but there was such hatred, such rage in them.

How old are you?
Where is your husband?
Is he with the UCK?
Who is leader of the UCK?

She was confused by the language and by the questions, and she stood silent, terrified, unable to speak. When they realized they could get no more from her, they gave up. Then they sat back, laughing, drinking, and eating chestnuts, as though they were at a sporting event, as though humiliating her was a game.

They asked her for Deutsche marks. "We know you have them," they said. Zoya said she didn't have any money. She did, of course, have the money her husband sent her, but it was hidden; it was all she had in the world and she was not prepared to give it up to them. Then they began to push her. She tried not to, but she started to cry.

"Okay," said one, who seemed to be the chief. "Let's go." He was wearing a uniform with lots of insignias, but Zoya couldn't read them; they were in Cyrillic. She tried not to look into his eyes as they pushed her into another room. One took out a bottle and they began to rub body lotion onto her. She was crying. She asked them to stop. They laughed. There were three of them, and they laughed together while she sat there, crying, her body covered in a thin film of pink lotion.

She told them she was a mother and asked them if they had children. "We all do," one said. "But it's not your concern."

"It made no difference," Zoya said later. "That I was a mother, that they had children. They started it, they finished it."

She remembered that she was wearing underwear, that they had allowed her to put it on before, when she made coffee. What happened next is too painful for her to describe, to even remember clearly. She only says that she "passed out" and woke up sometime later, in bed with two soldiers. Her underwear was no longer on, and someone had washed her between her legs.

Zoya stayed three days with those soldiers before they got tired of her. She began to feel like an empty doll, empty of emotions, of feelings. She moved through the rooms as though she were no longer a person, a human, or even an animal. She made the coffee, she cleaned, she fixed lunch. They touched her. She never used the word "rape." She never actually said they had intercourse, but later, when she was in the refugee camp, her greatest fear was that she would be pregnant.

"I will kill myself," she said, "if I am pregnant."

After a while, they let her go, after she gave them her money—Swiss francs her husband sent her—everything she had saved. They let her go, then they took her younger cousin in her place.

Sherife, with her fluent Serbian and her respectable age, tried to find out what happened to the women of Dragacin. The Serbs did not touch her, she said, because she was older, because she spoke their language. She also lied. She told them her parents were Serbian, that she had married an Albanian farmer and gone to live with his clan.

She shrugged. "It's a lie, I had to do it," she said. "They lie to us all the time, so why not?"

But five of her cousins, five of the Tahiri girls, were touched. Sherife saw them coming back from the house "wearing only their shirts." Later, they told her that the Serbs "were touching us all over our bodies and did that thing to us." She didn't know the exact number of men that took them; she thought there might have been six who took the girls away at gunpoint, another three who stayed in the house the entire time.

After the war, some of the men did find out what happened. They took it badly. They felt it was a reflection on them, their inability to protect their women, and that their clan has been tainted. The Tahiri clan numbered one hundred, and of those hundred, five had been raped. Another local man, whose daughter and daughter-in-law were raped, told a friend that he would rather be dead than have to bear this shame.

A story went around the village of a beautiful blonde, a voluptuous twenty-year old girl, the loveliest in Dragacin. She was with her husband when the soldiers grabbed her. One held her by the arm and said, "You're our woman," dragging her off while her husband stood by, at gunpoint, helplessly.

They took her away, and when they brought her back one hour later, she was beyond distraught. She tried to stick her fingers into electrical sockets to kill herself. She wept so hard she could not breathe. Despite this, she denied the rape, telling the men—her husband, her brothers, her uncles—that nothing had happened. If she admitted it, her life, and to an extent theirs, would be ruined.

Another woman in the refugee camp in Kukes said that after one of the Serb men raped her, they kept telling her, "You Albanian women are strong. You can have lots of babies. You're so strong that you can have sex with the entire Serb Army."[1]

While they were holding her down and hurting her, she said, they kept repeating, over and over, how strong she was.

Zoya said she had no power left in her soul, but in the refugee camp, later, she tried very hard. Every day she got up and attempted to wash, to put on some clean clothes and act as though life was just going on as normal. She did it for her son. She stood in the food line waiting, along with the 10,000 other refugees there, for her bread, her portion of sugar and oil and high-carbohydrate biscuits. She slept under a scratchy wool blanket with 12 other people in her tent, and during the day she took the boy for walks and tried to teach him new words. She met with the other women. No one talked about what happened, because there was nothing more that could be done.

Most of the time, she did very little. When I met her, one cold spring day, she sat in the midst of the camp, ruffling the tiny boy's hair. She was wearing a cranberry-colored sweater, and it picked up the delicate color in her cheeks, her light freckles. She was beautiful, but worn.

She tried and tried to move beyond those days, she said. It just got harder as time passed.

"I will never forget what happened to me," she said, trying to hold the small boy firm in her arms, "until the day I die."[2]

Suzanna had been listening to the stories of women raped for weeks, saying nothing, not telling anyone of her own trauma. But when Zoya told her story, Suzanna had laughed, a strange, bitter laugh. "You would laugh too," she said, by way of explanation. "It is the only thing you can do."

She began to write again in her diary, about what had happened to her. Even though she had never actually had sex, aside from the rape, she wrote one night, "I think I might be an erotic woman." But the thought of having sex with anyone was something she could not imagine. She did not want people to touch her, to put their arms around her, to touch her skin.

Most of all, she missed her friend who had died in the café. She said her friend was the image of Cleopatra, and when she looked at a man, he was lost. That's how beautiful she was. The only thing she took, when she entered Albania, aside from her pajamas, were her friend's cat-woman sunglasses, which she wore constantly. "I miss her so much," she said.

Her dreams were always violent, and sometimes she heard voices. Most of the time, she wandered, slightly lost, as though she had no idea where her legs and her eyes were taking her. Sometimes, she tried to convince herself that since so much grief had come to her, she would somehow be protected. Fate would not allow it, some act of evil, to happen again.

After the war, she drifted to one European country and then another. She found it difficult to connect, to make friends, impossible to work. She thought she heard voices; she wandered dreamily down the street often talking to herself. With her family, she was combative and at times had to be restrained. A doctor who examined her said she had a complete break with reality, that the trauma, the stress, the memory of war was so painful that she had entered another place where it was easier to survive. But sometimes, when she did think of it, she found it hard to feel safe.

It was difficult to slot herself back into life. To believe that evil things would not happen to her again.

Chapter Three

Why did the Yugoslavs choose to perish? It must be reiterated that it was their choice, made out of full knowledge. On none of them did their fates steal unawares.

Rebecca West, *Black Lamb and Grey Falcon*

Rozaje, Montenegro, on the Kosovo Border
April 5, 1999

Mehije had the deadest eyes. She sat on a pile of old blankets in the corner of a converted factory and silently watched me cross the room. Except for her eyes, her face was still. When I knelt next to her, she stared, oblivious to the whimpering of the two-year-old at her feet—her daughter Duka.

It was cold enough in the factory for breath to come out in small clouds, but Mehije wore only a sweater, muddy carpet slippers, and thin cotton socks that once were pink. Her dark hair was braided loosely in a plait that ran down her back.

She did not return my tentative smile. Instead, she handed me a package of loose rags tied with a pale blue ribbon.

I held the package, weighing it between two hands. Mehije motioned for me to open it. When I did, untying the knots in the ribbon, moving the soft cotton away, I saw the bundle of rags was alive, a tiny baby with a gaping bird's mouth. It made no sound at all, could not see me with its cloudy, newborn milky eyes. It was Mehije's seventh child, a boy, born four days before in the woods while she was fleeing Serbs.

Mehije silently took in my shock. Then she began to talk about her flight from Kosovo. She was an ethnic Albanian from a village called Mojstir, near Istok. To calculate her age, she had to think of seasons, years, marriage, births before coming up with thirty-eight years. She was married to a farmer called Abdullah, with five daughters and two sons.

When she left Mojstir, her village was burning. Along with 800,000 other people who fled Kosovo, she was leaving behind a gutted place, and she was not sure when or if she would ever return.

Holding the baby, she described life since March 1998, when the war began to escalate. A simple life. One that she never questioned: chickens, cows, the older children in school, Abdullah earning a meager living. But in the past few years, even she, who was not political, remembered changes. There were more Serb policemen. There was an antagonism toward the Albanians; it became harder for them to find work.[1]

From the moment Mehije became pregnant with Leotrim, she had a bad feeling—nagging, ominous. This baby, she thought, will not be born into a happy world. Her sister-in-law Sedjeije, who is nearby in the factory, living on her own blanket, described it like this, "We felt something different, strange in the air."

Mehije, from her perch on the cold floor, does not understand what is happening to her world: she does not know about the NATO maneuvers, the 4,000 people per hour pouring out of Kosovo. What she does realize is that her village, if she ever gets back, will not be the same. The only thing she knew how to do, she said, was to be a mother, bake bread, milk the cows. "I just want to go back," she said firmly. "Even if things are burned. I want to be on my land, near my home."

To think back over the past ten days was difficult for Mehije. She tried to remember the day she shut the door to her house and began her journey into the woods. She remembered that the fifth day of the NATO bombing was a Sunday, because it was Eid, an important Muslim holiday, when traditionally the six children were scrubbed and dressed in their best clothes and sent out to see relatives. In a normal world, Mehije would spend all day making roast lamb, or burek, a pastry stuffed with meat or cheese, for her family.

She was preparing the food that day in her kitchen, or starting to, when everything happened. Abdullah was outside repairing a fence. Mehije had her back turned when the door flew open and her Serb neighbors burst in.

Mehije had known these neighbors all her life. They were villagers together, worrying about the same things: the weather, their children, the livestock. But now they were different people, as though someone had gone inside their heads and changed their character. They carried guns into her kitchen, they shoved them in her face and ordered her, her husband, and her children out of the house.

She tried to calm them. She thought she might try to cajole them to give the family time, to let them stay until the baby was born, but looking up, she saw the anger and the determination on their faces. Nine months pregnant, she sank to a chair and asked if she could pack a bag.

"Take nothing," her neighbor replied in a calm but determined voice. "Just go. Go quickly."

Mehije, dazed, wandered outside. She had to find the children and dress them quickly. "We're going on a trip, not far away," she said to each one, to quiet them. In each one of their pockets, she placed pieces of bread. Then, with Abdullah urging her to hurry, she began to run, down the street, away from her house, toward the forest.

"I had the birth pains when I was running," she said. "But I ran anyway."

There was no car. Outside, there was chaos in the street with all the villagers fleeing, moving in the direction of the forest. Abdullah met a neighbor with a tractor who made a place for Mehije and the children. The men walked. They came to a forest where they spent the night, bedding down with leaves and branches for blankets and mattresses, trying to build a temporary hut with branches. Mehije, resting on the ground, could recognize faces in the dark. Around 200 Albanians, all from her village, were making fires and looking around in the snow for small animals for food, or for water.

But families had become separated. There was the sound of wailing children. People kept asking her, stumbling in the dark, "Have you seen my father? Have you seen my sister?" Most of them did not have their identity papers, a crucial part of existence in the former Yugoslavia. Either they had left them behind in the rush to get out of their houses or they were "liberated" by Serbs when they left, as insurance that they would never return to Mojstir again. Later, when she crossed the border, Mehije heard Serb soldiers were charging fees to refugees who were leaving Kosovo by car.[2]

As it grew later, and the camp grew quieter, someone told Mehije the village was on fire and that everything was already destroyed. What was not destroyed—the television sets, radios, stereos, clothing—were put on the back of trucks and driven away.

"To where?" she cried. "Where did they take our things?"

"To Belgrade," someone replied, shrugging. "Where else?"

Mehije gathered her children closer against her. She covered her eyes and her ears. "How can we go home again with nothing but our bare hands?" someone near her said. "We can't go without weapons, without food. They even took our kettles to use to feed the soldiers."

Mehije tried to remain calm. She did not want to hear any more.

The family stayed in the forest for three days, and her labor began. The temperature dropped to freezing. Then the same Serbs who had ordered them out of their village came to the forest and told them to march up the mountain and over the border to Albania. The walk would take another three days.

The Serbs jeered at the refugees in the forest, pointing their guns at their heads and their chests, driving them away with more fear. "Go back to your country!" they shouted. "Your village is burnt! You have nothing left." They told the frightened people to leave, or they would cut their throats like pigs.

Mehije had never been to Albania before. As long as she could remember, her family had lived on land in Kosovo. They thought of themselves as Kosovars. But they did not argue. She and Abdullah and the six children began to walk, slowly, moving in the snow. Her contractions were arriving closer and closer together. She began to time them. Her son came while they were wading through snow up to her waist. Her feet had become so cold she could no longer feel them. The icy slush had frozen her legs, bare except for her socks and her long skirt, and the children were so shocked that they did not cry anymore. Mehije knew she must keep walking, and so she did, pushing herself through the resistance of the snow, until she could walk no more. Then she dropped to her knees, calling her husband to take the children away.

The men cleared a space for her on the snowy ground, and she lay on a pile of twigs. Sedjeije—with an eighth-grade education and no nursing experience—acted as midwife.

"I had never delivered a baby before," she said, "but I had three children, so I knew what to expect." There was no water, no blankets, no food, no privacy, but the baby came quickly, in three hours. Sedjeije cut the cord with a knife given to her by one of the men and wrapped the infant in a man's shirt. Afterward, when her sister-in-law handed her Leotrim, Mehije remembers thinking that this last child of hers came into a world of confusion, of terror, born under a strange, foreign sky.

"I couldn't think of much happiness when this boy was born," she said. "When he was born, when he came into this world, we were hearing shots and bombs."

She looked down at her hands, naked without their rings, because the Serb reservists—her neighbors—had wrenched her gold rings off her fingers as they made her leave her home. She wondered, out loud, if Leotrim would ever know his home, or if he would be destined to wander, a refugee, for the rest of his life.

In the factory, days later, still weak from the birth, she tried to tell herself that this small bundle, her son, would not remember any of this. She was actually only 50 kilometers from her home, but for someone who had never left her village, she could have been on the other side of the earth. She was separated from her husband, whom she had somehow lost on the mountain, and she was still in shock from the birth. The pupils in her eyes looked black, they were so dilated, and she had had only sugar water and some bread for nourishment.

She had the look of a beaten animal. She kept repeating—as if she believed that by repeating something over and over she could make it reality—"He won't remember any of this."

The baby had nothing, not even diapers or cream for his skin. The other children wandered through the factory wordlessly or whimpering. She was worried about Duka, who cried all the time for her father. She was worried about this baby, whose first understanding would be fear. And she was worried about her husband. One of the other women, who was with her in the forest, told her, "We heard they were taking away men and boys." People in Mojstir do not know politics, but they heard what happened in Srebrenica, in Bosnia, in July 1995, when the Muslim men were taken away and never seen again.

That morning, a dimly lit Montenegrin morning, the people inside that factory did not know where their fate lay. Everyone sat placidly on their blankets, holding the paper bag each of them might have brought with them containing a few small items: an apple, a pair of socks, a razor. Or a wedding photograph, a birth certificate. Or a phone number of a relative in Italy, Germany, America, who may or may not have been able to help them.

On the way out of the factory, trying both to find Abdullah—who might be in another refugee center across town—and to buy some supplies for the baby, I passed old man with a bloody stump instead of an arm. He had a beret clapped on his head at an angle, and was sitting upright in a wheelbarrow, smoking. He spoke to himself, unintelligible things, muttering over and over in Albanian. No one listened to him.

This is what it feels like to watch someone else's agony: no matter how many times you listen and record someone's story, no matter how many refugees you see crossing over a mountaintop wearing plastic bags on their heads to protect themselves from the freezing rain—you do not get used to it.

And still, when there are so many, an army of misery, it is easy to dehumanize them. They become cattle sitting on their blankets, waiting for someone to tell them where to go. They have the same faces, the same stories; they come down the road with their lives in two carrier bags. Then you think of the carnage in Bosnia, of the villages and mosques razed, of the streets in Sarajevo wasted in punishment for their stern defiance. At least the Kosovars are living. There are very few male Muslim survivors of Srebrenica.

These people are living symbols of Milosevic's plan to destabilize the Balkans. By expelling the Kosovars, he believed he would have a maximum impact on the region: Albania, Macedonia, and Montene-

gro, each littered with its own internal problems, could not withstand the influx of hundreds of thousands of people. Adam LeBor, in
his biography of Milosevic, painted a gloomy scenario of what could
happen if the Serb leader succeeded with his expulsion policy:

> Albania barely functioned as a state and could not cope
> with the massive refugee influx. Macedonia was under pres-
> sure from its own ethnic refugee arrivals. If enough Albani-
> ans poured across its border, the country could explode, as it
> very nearly did. Greece, although a NATO member, refused
> to recognise Macedonia and Athens cast a covetous eye on
> the territories of the former Yugoslav republic. As soon as the
> air strikes began, Serbs living in the Macedonian capital
> rioted. If Macedonia and Albania collapsed, Greece and pos-
> sibly Bulgaria would get dragged in, and there might even be
> conflict between Greece and Turkey, both NATO members.[3]

The refugees weren't thinking of political gains or territory, or
Milosevic's ultimate game plan. They were thinking of survival. By
the time these people get herded into abandoned schools or ware-
houses, factories or hospitals, all with the same smell of misery and
poor sanitation and dirty bedrolls, they forget that they once had
lives. That they had birthdays, wedding anniversaries, love affairs.
That they had a favorite television show, a dog or a cat that they
loved.

Ethnic cleansing is defined as a comprehensive, systematic, premeditated program to rid, to cleanse, an area of its residents. If it
works effectively, it means that it drives an irreversible hatred
between the victim and the aggressor. During the Bosnian war, the
ethnic cleansing was reinforced by concentration camps and rape
centers. They were instruments of fear. The end result, if it worked,
was that the victims would be so terrified and traumatized that they
would never go home again.

But what it really felt like, for those people walking through the
snow in their slippers, was that they could lose their history, their
identities, their sense of belonging. Nothing would be safe anymore.

Even if they went home again, nothing could guarantee their
safety. If something so catastrophic can happen to you once in your

lifetime, what is to guarantee it won't happen again?

Arrival:
Croatia
March 1999

Now I am going back to the beginning of this journey, the starting point. On March 25, 1999, the day after the first NATO bomb fell on Serbia, I caught a flight from London to Zagreb, the Croatian capital. Flying over Italy's Adriatic coast, passing the port city of Ancona, which had been a U.N. air force base during the Bosnian war, the pilot announced we would be diverted to Slovenia. Airspace in Croatia was already closed because of the bombing.

It was the first tangible evidence for me that the war had actually started. The small planeload of passengers, mainly Croat businessmen going home after a few days' work in London, stopped eating their *prsut* sandwiches and stared out the window as though they could already see the bombs falling.

The electrical engineer from Zagreb sitting next to me said, "It's started. It's really started." His face looked waxy. He sat back in his chair and slid the seat belt over his large stomach. He complained loudly, "My country does not need another war."

We did land in Zagreb. Despite the pilot's warning, we passed over the Slovenian airspace, hovered over checkerboard farmlands, the patchwork of narrow, winding farm roads. In the autumn, the most beautiful season in the Balkans, the colors on those roads become muted and hazy, the fog drops low, and the area is populated by storks before they follow their migration route down the Danube Valley, crossing to Asia Minor and further on to the Great Rift Valley. Now it was earliest spring: still, wet, cold, mud brown.

Ours was the first plane to arrive in two days. The Zagreb airport was deserted. The arrivals hall, which was usually packed with U.N. soldiers, journalists, families returning from Germany, was oddly quiet; the café that sold stale sandwiches and cartons of rancid orange juice was closed. A bored passport control official waved me through, barely glancing at my documents.

Outside, I changed my roll of Deutsche marks into kuna. In the early days of Croatian nationalism, Franjo Tudjman, independent Croatia's first president, replaced the Croatian dinar with the kuna, a currency that had been used by the World War II fascists, the Ustashe. To further stir up nationalistic sentiments, Tudjman gave additional prominence to *sahovnica*, the red-and-white checkerboard flag that was both the emblem of the medieval Croatian kingdom and the wartime NDH (Nezavisna Drzava Hrvatska, or Independent State of Croatia), which had been set up with the help of the Germans and the Italians. He removed the red star that covered the checkerboard design in the Communist era, signaling to some that he wished to return to the nationalistic 1940s. In the 1990 election campaign, he had blurted out, "Thank God my wife is not a Jew or a Serb."[4]

World War II and the Ustashe was an open wound in Yugoslavia. The NDH, under the leadership of Ante Pavelic and with the support of the Catholic Church, encompassed Croatia and Bosnia-Herzegovina. The regime had a specific strategy for dealing with the more than 2 million Serbs who lived within their territory: "Kill a third, expel a third, and convert a third."

Many Serbs whose families suffered under Ustashe brutality came back to fight in the next series of wars with equal brutality. Those wartime atrocities and memories had been suppressed and laid to rest under Tito's mantle of a new Yugoslav identity: Brotherhood and Unity. Now Yugoslavia was gone, and the wounds were as bloody as before. The Croats knew that.[5]

In Zagreb, a taxi driver pounced as soon as I came through the sliding doors, yanking my bag from my hand. He had a desperate look on his face: that look that signaled everything was about to explode and maybe it was time to start stockpiling tins of food again.

The wars in the former Yugoslavia between 1991 and 1995 had left an indelible print on the country. Out of a prewar population of 23 million, 3.5 million were displaced. In the Croatian conflict alone, which ran from 1991 to 1995, 15,000 died and half a million refugees were created. The Croats, for a brief period following the end of their war, thought they were being given a respite. With Kosovo looming, they feared the worse: that they would be dragged in again.

The driver said little on the road to the Esplanade Hotel. He broke the silence by turning up the radio. When I asked him whether the road to Belgrade, the Highway of Brotherhood and Unity, was open, he snapped. "You can only get so far," he said. The border with Hungary was open, but I needed a Serbian visa, which was virtually impossible to get. I had applied and been turned down twice. The road to Montenegro from Croatia was also difficult. As the driver told me, no one in her right mind would make the journey. "It wasn't so long ago that the Montenegrins shelled Dubrovnik," he said. He dropped me at the hotel and screeched off, as though my desire to get to Montenegro was contagious.

The fin de siècle lobby of the Esplanade was empty. I walked across the hallway and peered through heavy velvet curtains into the dining room: silent. I saw a seven-year-younger version of myself sitting at a round table eating caviar with another reporter who had just come out of Sarajevo. It was a few weeks before Christmas; I was on my way to Bosnia, waiting for the airport to open so I could take a U.N. flight. The restaurant had been full. I remembered the scent of pine trees, and imminent snow.

The concierge gave me the key to my room, and I walked behind a porter, who carried my satellite phone and my bags. I was the only person in my wing. When I woke up in the morning, the waiter brought breakfast on a tray with a pink rose in a silver vase.

"Where is everyone?" I asked as he poured the coffee.

"Afraid of war," he said, and closed the heavy wooden door.

I sat by the window, looking out onto King Tomislav Square, near the train station. People were walking to work, moving slowly in the morning fog, carrying umbrellas and wearing hats and scarves. There was still, decades after the collapse of the Austro-Hungarian Empire, a lingering sense of the exploitative Habsburgs. I had always found Zagreb passionless, and the nationalism in Croatia—the songs, symbols, beer-drinking slogans, and grotesque nostalgia for their fascist Ustashe past—was far harder to endure than the Serbian version. At least the Serbs were honest about it. The Croats tried to pass themselves off as democratic.

Down the road in Belgrade, the Serbs—some of whom were standing on bridges with targets pasted on their foreheads shaking their fists at NATO planes—defiantly bore the stigma for all the evil in the recent wars. Milosevic—who had imposed his will as far back as 1986, when he was sent to Kosovo to meet fellow Communist officials and ended up taking up the cause of the Kosovo Serbs—had been blamed for causing the breakup of the former Yugoslavia. Franjo Tudjman was rarely mentioned in the same breath, and the Croats had collectively convinced themselves they were blameless. They managed to absolve themselves not only of their shortcomings in the most recent wars, but of the atrocities they committed in World War II.

In part, they got to hide behind the cloak of Catholicism, as though the fact that they were Christians excused them from the savagery they had committed. The fact that they had massacred an estimated 600,000 Serbs, Jews, Gypsies, and nonfascist Croats in Jasenovac, just down the road from Zagreb, and then managed to cleanse more than 100,000 of them from the Krajina region in 1995, did not cause as much of an outrage as the Serbs marching through eastern Bosnia.[6]

Most of the Yugoslavs, except the Slovenes, spoke a variant of Serbo-Croatian, but the were divided by culture, religion, and ethnic identity. The Croats pined for their Austro-Hungarian past and resented being grouped with the Slavs. "The Croats are Germans without the efficiency," Renzo Cianfanelli, an Italian journalist, once remarked.

Essentially, before the creation of the Kingdom of Serbs, Croats, and Slovenes in 1918, which eventually became Tito's Yugoslavia, the southern Slav people had never lived together in one state before. Yugoslavia had been divided between the Habsburg and the Ottoman empires, with Istanbul claiming most of present-day Serbia, Bosnia-Herzegovina, and Macedonia. Vienna ruled Croatia, Slovenia, and the northern Serbian province of Voivodina. The Ottoman territories were regarded as Turkey-in-Europe, with Belgrade being the northernmost point.

Religion also divided the territories: after the schism of 1054, the Eastern Orthodox Church was based in Byzantium and the western Catholic Church in Rome. Thus, the Ottoman Empire was reflected in the East, the Habsburg in the West. From the sixteenth century until 1878, the western frontier of the Ottoman Empire was roughly the current border between Croatia and Bosnia-Herzegovina.[7]

Karl Marx once called the Balkan people "ethnic trash"; the former *New York Times* correspondent C. L. Sulzberger described the Balkans quaintly, as "a gay peninsula filled with sprightly people who ate peppered foods, drank strong liquors, wore flamboyant clothes, loved and murdered easily and had a splendid talent for starting wars." This colorful image was exactly the sort the Croats did not want to promote. They were not really Balkan people; they were southern Austrians. The Croat denial fostered a sense of mixed identity in Zagreb. The people dressed in Armani but lived in apartments without central heating. They carried the latest Nokia phones but had no money in their bank accounts. While the Serbs and the Bosnians never tried to be anything but what they were, the Croats hid behind a faux and decrepit Habsburg mantle.

Their biggest grievance was belonging to a Balkan group they didn't want to be part of. They saw themselves as a Western democracy. Now the air strikes meant that their tourism would not function this summer—all because of Kosovo, a grubby Muslim province in the south! The Italian tourists were just beginning to come back to Dubrovnik, to eat the fine shellfish and dive off the rocks into the sea. The summer season was two months away, and if bombs were falling on Belgrade and NATO troops were moving in on Pristina, no one was going to spend their holiday in Dalmatia.

But worse than the effect on the economy was the one on their collective psyche. If war was next door, it meant Croatia risked being thrown back into the Balkans, a place from which it had tried so hard to distance itself. Instead of neat little Austrian squares, they were going to get messy Serb fallout. Six years after the cease-fire with the Serbs, they were just beginning to recover, and so were their victims. They had no use for the past—it was a murky place.

In the name of their fight against communism during World War II, the Catholic priests insisted that the Serbs convert or be slaughtered. In 1941, in a town called Glina, which fifty years later would come under attack by Serb paramilitaries, 97 Serbs were locked in a church and burned alive. An Italian captain who served with a regiment in the Dalmatian hinterland during World War II told me he was still haunted by the viciousness of the Croats. They did it, he said, then went home and prayed to God.

The Croats' role in the Bosnian war was also highly dubious.

Tudjman had his own Radovan Karadzic—a thug called Mate Boban who operated out of the hard-line town of Grude—and they had their own concentration camps, where they tortured, killed, and beat men senseless. Tudjman committed his own gruesome atrocities, and if he had lived, it is certain he would have been sitting alongside his old friend Slobodan Milosevic in The Hague court. For him, the Bosnian war was an opportunity to carve out a mini-Croat state within Bosnia, and he connived with Milosevic to cheat the Bosnian Muslims out of their land.

In the autumn of 1992, the Croats launched an offensive in central Bosnia largely around the Lasva Valley region. When Jajce, a strategically important town, fell to the Serbs in October, front-line soldiers said that the Croats, then fighting alongside the Muslims, had abandoned their positions because their commanders had already made a deal with the Serbs. The Croats left thousands of Muslim refugees to make their way through the mountains to Travnik to seek protection from the Bosnian Army.

Controlling many of the roads leading from the Dalmatian coast to central Bosnia, the Croats also blocked arms from reaching Sarajevo, confiscating the best for themselves, or charging exorbitant "taxes." In April 1993, a Croatian paramilitary unit calling itself the Jokers led a raid on the village of Ahmici, killing 116 Muslims. It razed the village, destroying every building. Among the dead that the British troops later found were 33 women and children.

In January 2000, five Bosnian Croats were sentenced to prison terms ranging from six to twenty-five years for their roles in the crime. Antonio Cassese, the presiding judge at the International Criminal Tribunal for the Former Yugoslavia (ICTY), compared Ahmici's infamy with that of Dachau, Katyn, Soweto, My Lai, and Sabra and Shatila. "Today, the name of that small village must be added to the long list of previously unknown hamlets and towns that recall abhorrent misdeeds and make us all shudder with horror and shame," he said.[8]

But the five who were sentenced were, in effect, only five among hundreds of Croatian Defense Council (HVO) troops who stormed Ahmici and attacked dozens of other villages in the Lasva Valley beginning in the early hours of April 16. That operation opened up a second front in the civil war, as the Croats turned against their former Muslim allies.[9]

During the siege of Mostar in May 1993, the Bosnian Croats—with the help of Tudjman—laid waste in an inhuman and exceptionally violent way to the eastern strip of the city where the Muslim civilian population lived. From one side of the Neretva River, they attacked the largely underarmed Muslims, shelling them relentlessly with rockets, mortars, and sniper fire. They prevented humanitarian aid from arriving, leaving the people to subsist on cherries. There was no water. The hospital, in a former library, had no supplies and no staff.

But their greatest act of hatred came on October 9, 1993, when Croat forces destroyed the ancient Ottoman bridge Stari Most. They demolished it not because it was strategic, but because the Muslims loved it. Shortly after the bridge came down, overpowered by the force of a rocket, I saw an old man wandering through the east side, weeping. He loved that bridge. He said, "It survived two world wars. It took this much hatred to bring it down." A Croatian soldier I knew in Mostar who had grown up on the east side but was forced to fight against his neighbors and friends told me he had watched the bridge come down. "They didn't have to do it," he said. "It was a psychological thing." They did that after they had wept over the destruction of Dubrovnik.

Franjo Tudjman was never satisfied with the way the war ended. Following the fall of Srebrenica and encouraged by the Americans, the Croats launched a new offensive in the Krajina on August 4, 1995, brutally cleansing the region of Serbs who had lived there for generations, killing elderly civilians and burning houses. The civilians, who had been abandoned by Milosevic's army and their local defense force, were overpowered. By the time they finished their spree, only 8,000 Serbs—mainly the elderly and the sick, who could not move—were left. The United Nations protested against the looting, intimidating, and indiscriminate killing, but the Croats were mainly left to do what they liked.

The aftermath was pathetic. Centuries of Serbian culture was erased. The Krajina Serb refugees fled on carts with plastic bags, as pitiful as the Albanians later arriving in Montenegro, Albania, and Macedonia. In Banja Luka, a place that had been viewed as the heart of darkness during the Bosnian war, tens of thousands of people slept on the pavement, and waited for hours on clogged roads to travel east to Serbia.

And how many people knew of the suffering of the Serbs? The strongest images of the war were of the ancient walls of Dubrovnik being pierced by shells, not Croats torching villages like Srb or Kistanje. And who cared? In Belgrade in the autumn of 1995, I found my friend Zoran living in a filthy refugee camp outside the city. The place was full of Krajina refugees, old women in head-scarves and old men playing cards. There was the usual smell of refugees, of misery, of a communal toilet for hundreds and a commu-nal kitchen where one pot cooked everyone's food. The only real dif-ference was that these were Serbian refugees; there were no television crews or reporters writing about their plight.

The Croats, of course, did suffer, and the Serbs were undoubt-edly brutal. The vicious battles in Eastern Slavonia, the air raids in Zagreb, the massacre in Vukovar—400 men taken from a hospital, 260 of them executed and dumped in a mass grave—were hideous. So was the psychological trauma. "When I wait at a tram stop near my house in Zagreb," the Croatian writer Slavenka Drakulic wrote in 1991, "an ordinary-looking man, a civilian in a light summer suit, opens his jacket for a moment and I see that he has a pistol tucked into his belt. The tram comes and we get on. But I have this uneasy feeling that my future is in his hands and there is no way to step down off the train anymore."

In Dubrovnik, where people had withstood a nine-month siege, there was still bitterness. Restoration was being carried out, money pumped in by European foundations and grand families with Croat-ian ties. Food was abundant, restaurants and boutiques were open, and construction was beginning on new resorts. A property devel-oper told me there was a surge of interest from the Europeans—mainly Germans—wanting to buy land to build villas and turn it into another Mallorca.

But people had not forgotten. Vesna Gamulen, an interpreter who lived through the siege in 1991, said no one had yet reverted to his prewar mentality. "It's not yet returned," she said, glumly, staring out at an early spring Adriatic, wintry and steel-colored. "We haven't had a normal tourist season. As for normal life, it is low. Low. Low."

Vesna has Serb friends that she grew up with and spent summers with at the beach. She is not happy they are getting attacked, even if their country once attacked hers. She says that it is shocking to see a nation being bombed and that its people can't be blamed for what happened. Then she pauses. "I would still love to see Milosevic disappear." So would Miso Mihocevic, a former commander in Dubrovnik who became a director of the Dubrovnik Festival after the war. He had watched the Montenegrin ships fire on the city. But he also blames the Serb people for allowing Milosevic to continue for a decade. It still makes Mihocevic angry to walk through the town and see the mortars that punched through the ancient stone buildings.

"We are not bellicose people," he said one night at dinner overlooking the harbor. "But this bombardment in Serbia comes as the justice of God. It comes as a puncture in this awful balloon of evil." He said he could not rejoice that another bridge was blown up in Novi Sad, or that a farmer's cow in Nis was killed. The suffering of individuals was one thing. But he could not forget the scenes of battle in Dubrovnik. The Serbs, he said, did so much evil that his own mother, a gentle woman, watched images of Belgrade under the bombs and said, "Now they know what we felt."

"People are indifferent to their suffering," he said of his former tormentors. "During the war, I hated them, but now I just feel indifferent." As for his neighbors, the Montenegrins who were now trying to break with Serbia, he smiled. "They married the Serbs back in 1991," he said. "They have to pay the consequences."

Later, over coffee, he said he realized that even if he wanted no part of Montenegro, of Serbia, the fact that their border lay less than an hour away would undoubtedly affect this new postwar Croatia.

"It's like having a beautiful family," he said. "But you have an alcoholic upstairs fighting. You feel it. Whatever unhappiness they have will be reflected here. It's only a matter of a few miles."

Beginning the Journey South to Kosovo
Zagreb to Sarajevo
March 27, 1999

At the start of the war in Bosnia, in April 1992, former president Alija Izetbegovic watched his country descend into madness. "I felt as though the gates of hell had opened," he would say later. "I expected war, but I did not expect genocide."

He also did not anticipate the repopulation, the map of his country being redrawn. Bosnia today, created after the Dayton Peace Accord in November 1995, consists of two parts: a Serb entity and a Bosniak (the reinvented word for Muslim) and Croat Federation. The Serbs, who numbered 1.5 million before the war, about one-third of the population, have 49 percent of the country. The Croats and Bosniaks have 51 percent.

All this means that in an attempt to stop the fighting, lines were drawn through towns and villages, cultures erased, people divided. Sarajevo, for example, is meant to be an open city, but in fact many Serbs fled in 1995, following Dayton, and some of them left after they burnt down houses and their neighborhoods in fury. It was Slobodan Milosevic, in fact, who gave Sarajevo to the Muslims at Dayton, telling the Bosnian prime minister, Haris Silajdzic, "You deserve Sarajevo because you fought for it, and those cowards killed you from the hills." Perhaps it was a cynical way of ensuring that without an integrated Sarajevo, Dayton would fail.[10]

Srebrenica, which was a mainly Muslim town, is now in Serb hands. And Mostar is divided between Muslims and Croats who loathe each other. When you crossed the Neretva River, you used different currencies depending upon whether you were on the east side, where the Muslims live, or the west side, where the Croats are. From opposite banks of the river, where they once lobbed rockets at each other, they now wage a psychological warfare: since Dayton, the Croats ring their church bells louder and the Muslims have a longer, higher-pitched call to prayer.

Dayton did stop the fighting, but in many ways it simply did not work. Between the two entities, there is even more division: the Republika Srpska (Serb Republic) has its own army, its own parliament, its own capital. The Serbs still feel no one understands or accepts them. Tito's Brotherhood and Unity has disappeared.

In the early morning, on the third day of the bombing, I got a ride through the RS with a Danish U.N. worker who was headed for Sarajevo. We drove toward Belgrade. There were no other cars. Very quickly, the urban landscape faded, and the countryside grew flat and wide, with pretty villages dotting the edge of the road. Fields were full of high grass, the same fields where the Serbs and the Croats had slaughtered each other with tanks and snipers. We stopped for coffee. The Dane ate a greasy omelette; I had thick slices of white peasant bread with cheese. There were truck drivers trying to get to Belgrade.

We asked for some news. One threw up his hands. "Bombs," he said.

Outside the restaurant, I tried to phone Belgrade, but the lines had fallen. I had tried to call the night before from the hotel, and the line had faded as though it were a cable running under the sea and not to a destination just six hours away by train. A friend I had spoken to before I left London said spirits were high. Everyone was going to parties, united by the fact they all felt like Iraqis: "Everyone hates us," she said cheerfully.

Why did NATO not launch air strikes eight years earlier, preventing the entire series of wars that would engulf this region? Why did 200,000 people have to die in Bosnia before the air strikes, while only 2,000 Kosovars had died before Brussels did something? It was because of geopolitics: by 1999, nearing the millennium, NATO had had enough. Effectively, it was because this time Milosevic's ethnic cleansing could trigger an entire destabilization of the region, but it was also because NATO's credibility was on the line.

On March 26, NATO issued a repetitive statement which said it was bombing Serbia to avert a humanitarian catastrophe. Without its intervention, the Kosovo crisis would escalate. This crisis could lead to bigger things: continued fighting could reignite chaos in Albania; destabilize Macedonia; exacerbate rivalries between Greece and Turkey, two NATO allies. It went on to say that the crisis could create thousands more refugees and a breeding ground for international criminals, drug traffickers, and terrorists.

"No one should forget that World War I began in this tinderbox" the press release read. "If actions are not taken to stop this conflict now, it will spread and both the cost and risk will be substantially greater."[11]

I felt bitter as I read it. In the late spring and early summer of 1993 in Sarajevo, there was talk of U.N. air strikes around Serb positions. The word went around the city like Chinese whispers, and people began to get excited. I remember attending a rehearsal of *Waiting for Godot*, which was being directed by the American writer Susan Sontag. Every morning, Sontag brought bread that she swiped from the Holiday Inn in her handbag to give to the hungry actors. They were a talented but depressed bunch. One day, hearing that there might be relief for their city, the actors gathered around her. Was it true? Where had she heard it? When would it happen? Something akin to life came back into their eyes.

Across the Miljacka River, near the Egyptian battalion and the old mosque, an entire street had hung handmade red, white, and blue American flags. When I walked down the street, small kids came out and pulled on my jacket. They asked me if it was true, if the Americans were coming. Of course nothing happened. It would not happen for years. Because of that hiccough on the part of the international community, because of that hesitation, Srebrenica, Europe's worst massacre since World War II, happened. Gorazde, Mostar, Jajce, Bihac, Sanski Most happened. Entire communities were picked up, shaken around, and replanted somewhere else. I doubt if NATO's actions were ever for humanitarian reasons. It was more about a crumbling post–cold war institution that had been humiliated.

In the autumn of 1998, NATO, threatening force, was decisive in getting Milosevic to agree to a cease-fire in Kosovo. It established the OCSE (Organization for Security and Cooperation in Europe) and NATO verification regimes. In January, NATO warned Milosevic again that it would respond if he did not reach an agreement at the peace talks, or come into compliance with the October agreement.

Milosevic, true to form, did not stop, and the repression continued. Forty thousand Serbian security forces, military, and police were positioned in and around Kosovo, poised for a military offensive. His belligerence was rooted in a deep-seated belief that the Serbs were victims of history, and now history once again was proving itself. It was not one nation, but nineteen under the guise of NATO, turning on them. The Serbs felt themselves backed into a corner. They refused any offer of a peaceful solution.

The day after Richard Holbrooke walked out on a Belgrade

meeting with Milosevic, wondering if he would ever see his old sparring partner again, NATO launched a war. It claimed three objectives: to demonstrate its seriousness; to deter Belgrade from initiating an all-out offensive against civilians; and to seriously damage Belgrade's military capability.

The war, sold to the public as high-tech, low-risk, began on March 24, 1999. NATO governments had ruled out a ground war in March, even though most senior military men thought airpower alone could not crush the Serbs. The split over ground troops became one of the major division points between the political forces operating in the background. In Britain, the Ministry of Defence drew up a scheme for NATO forces to sweep first through the Presevo Valley, east of Kosovo. They would then carry out a left hook into the province, in the hope that most Serb forces would be waiting for them to arrive through the narrow Kacanik Gorge, up the road from Skopje in Macedonia.

But Milosevic's advisors were alerted to this risk. Just before the bombing began, American spy planes noted about 6,000 Serb troops had dug in to form a classic Soviet-style defensive wall across from the Presevo Valley. The NATO rockets fell on military installations, on soldiers, on trenches. But they also fell on people who wanted nothing to do with the war, on people who opposed the Milosevic regime and who had dedicated themselves to stopping his insatiable appetite for power.

The mistakes that would later occur were appalling. On May 7, two pilots aboard a B-52 dropped a trio of 2,000-pound bombs that were allegedly meant to hit the Serbian Arms Export Agency. Instead, they fell on the Chinese Embassy, the first time the United States had struck a foreign mission since Tripoli in 1986, when a U.S. Air Force F-111 dropped bombs on the French Embassy. The disaster was blamed on an old map. Intelligence apparently put the right target address at the wrong building on a Pentagon-drafted 1997 document. The logistical mistake cost 3 people their lives, and 20 were wounded.

Later, a convoy of civilians got hit. Houses and farms got hit. A factory that produced vacuum cleaners on some floors and missile and rocket parts on others was hit. It was located in Cacak, a town noted for its resistance to Milosevic. Children were maimed. I saw a small boy in a Belgrade hospital who had been walking his cow in a field when he became a statistic in a file in Brussels: collateral damage. He was blinded.

But that was in the future. For now, we were driving into Bosnia on the first day of the war, and two hours out of Zagreb, before we reached Osijek, we turned south off the highway and crossed the River Sava into Bosnia. We weren't so far from a farmhouse where I had stayed with a group of soldiers from Brcko in 1993. The inhabitants had long fled, but they left jars of pickles and preserved peppers on the shelves, which the soldiers ate. We lit candles at night so the Serbs did not see our position. During the lull in the shelling, we sat outside in the farmyard. The early spring flowers were trying to push through the earth, and one of the younger soldiers was playing with a dog, kept as a mascot.

What happened to that village? I tried to find it on the map, swallowed up somewhere in the redrawn lines of Bosnia. Was it Serb? Bosniak? Croat? Did any of those soldiers live? Had they been resettled, reintegrated, any of the new postwar terms that had sprung up?

Across the river in the Republika Srpska, the mood changed. If Zagreb was stoic and stiff, here everyone was angry. There was no money, no empathy, no aid, no understanding. We drove through villages where people shook their fists at the white U.N. vehicle. When the road leading toward Sarajevo split, we drove through smaller villages, shacks selling Romanian videos, bottles of whiskey, cartons of cigarettes. By afternoon, a radio report came in from Kosovo. In Goden, a remote village, 20 ethnic Albanian men were lined up and shot in the head by Serbian paramilitary. Cleanly, methodically, like Prekaz, like Racak.

We stopped to eat later in the day. A lamb turned on the spit, tended to by a Serb who splashed it with oil from a tin. His son brought plates of the cooked lamb, the fat congealed inside the meat, with bigger plates of roasted potatoes, thick slices of white bread and Slivovica (slivovitz), a plum brandy.

We heard about another massacre later that day as we passed through Olovo, or the ruins of Olovo, where the front-line battles of 1992–93 took place in the snow. I turned on the radio as we drove by a destroyed hotel where soldiers had lived. There were prewar signs pointing in the direction of Srebrenica and Gorazde. I listened to a report about a town called Mala Krusa, near Pec, where around 100 men were executed by Serb forces. Their bodies were later burned to conceal the evidence. Several of the men, young men, were shot as they were trying to run away.

One of the survivors, Milaim Bellanica, hid for seven days. When he finally crawled out, he recorded the aftermath, using the small, hand-held video camera that he had used for family videos. On this camera, he now captured images of mangled bones and bodies thrust together with their arms and legs at odd angles.

Bellanica later reported what he could remember, what he could see from his hiding place. The Serbs were positioned on top of a hill. After the Albanian villagers were shelled, some were captured. Some were killed one by one. Bellanica testified that the young men who died were farmers, and the Serbs who killed them knew some of them. Some of the Serbs kept masks on their faces as they worked, he said. Others let their victims see them, and Bellanica said a few of the victims cried out to their murderers, pleading with them by name, before they died.

We listened grimly, saying nothing. Finally, the Danish U.N. worker turned off the radio.

"Nothing has changed," he said. "It just goes on and on and on."

"And passes on to generations," I said.

Bellanica, the survivor, had said that he had recorded the massacre precisely so that no one would forget. He said he did it so that "my son and my grandson, the next generation, will never forget what the Serb people have done to the Albanian people."

Sarajevo, Bosnia-Herzegovina
March 27, 1999

There was a cold mountain drizzle in Sarajevo. Gray chill from the hills. The cold dug into bones. People still wore their winter coats, their fur hats, their high boots. They trudged to work, unsmiling, through the gray slush. The Miljacka River was still dark and forbidding. The greenness of the Bosnian spring had not yet come.

I stayed in a place that had not existed during the war, a pension run by a couple who owned a hyper Dalmatian. The breakfast had imported cheeses and meats from Germany, coffee from Italy. From my room at the top of the house, I could not see the hills where for three years Serb gunners dug themselves into the trenches high above the town. In the morning, in those days, the soldiers were usually sleeping off their hangovers. They would not be awake until lunchtime, when they would start shooting, and drinking, again. The morning was the time to find water, food, firewood. Or to go to the black market where a tin of Coke sold for DEM 50, or the hospital, or the morgue. Look for a dead relative or go to the man who held a cigarette and sold people puffs. What was it that the Serb General Mladic had said, all those years ago, to his gunners? Shell the Presidency and Parliament buildings, at slow intervals. Target Muslim neighborhoods. Shell them until they are on the edge of madness.

There was traffic now in Sarajevo. Strange to see cars instead of frightened huddles of people gathered together to run together across dangerous intersections. It was a ploy that was meant to deter snipers, but it never worked. Someone would be too slow, too old, or having an unlucky day. The crack of gunfire, a scream, and one would fall to his knees, wounded. Then the trip to Kosevo Hospital where the wounded lay in hallways. An amputation with limited anesthetic performed by exhausted doctors who had not slept in days.

It was four years after Dayton. Cars with license plates showed that their owners came from outside Sarajevo. Buses of Muslims arrived from the Bosnian-Serb border, fleeing the NATO bombing and the anticipated wrath of the Serbs. Strange to see them taking refuge in Sarajevo, thinking it a safe place. During the war, people crossed minefields and risked sniper fire to escape across the airfield. If they were lucky, they broke free via the secret tunnel which ran between Dobrinja and Butmir, underneath the airport runway. If you reached the other side, there was a signpost for Paris.

Wartime Sarajevo was like the underworld, an apocalyptic nightmare. Burnt-out buildings, evil yellow fog, crashed buses, skeletons of shot-up cars, kids with glazed, dulled expressions and gray faces, graffiti spelling out WELCOME TO HELL. Three years of siege.

Now, Sarajevo had become Geneva. It had Benetton shops,

French cosmetic stores, cafés which serve daiquiris and piña coladas, Internet cafés. In a Mexican restaurant, I met an old friend, a former defender in the Bosnian Army. "The war," he said over a Corona beer with a lime stuffed down its neck, "is quickly becoming a bad memory. Or more like a dream that didn't really happen."

At night in my hotel, I watched television, still finding it strange to be able to switch on a light and get electricity. The old war was finished; the new war was starting. A U.S. Air Force Stealth F-117 Nighthawk fighter-bomber was shot down over Yugoslavia. The Pentagon refused to confirm the incident. But in Belgrade, in Republic Square, people held up signs which read SORRY, WE DIDN'T KNOW IT WAS INVISIBLE.

In the morning, I walked through Sarajevo, past the market which had fresh flowers and fruit and bottles of perfume, through the city park, up the hill toward the Kosevo Hospital. The hospital was strangely clean and white, with kiosks selling magazines and Swiss chocolate. The rooms where I sat talking to doctors, blowing on our hands to keep them warm, discussing the difficulty of operating without enough antibiotics, were freshly painted. The windows broken by sniper bullets had been repaired, the sagging furniture replaced. The office of a psychiatrist who had made a survey of the city during the siege—and who finally decreed Sarajevo an open lunatic asylum—was gone. The ghosts had all been cleaned out, swept away.

But still I could not forget, five, six, seven years before, the lines stretching around the block as people waited in the snow with their plastic bottles and buckets, their empty wine bottles and jugs, for water to drink and wash, near the old Sarajevska Pivara brewery. Or running up the hill to check if a relative was in the morgue. Dodging the shooting at a particularly exposed corner near the entrance to the hospital. Or standing in the freezing cold, not knowing who was watching them from the hills, and whether or not he was going to shoot them that day. Or let them live, for some reason or another.

Montenegro
March 28, 1999

Day Four of the NATO Bombing

Maja was waiting for me on the other side of the Montenegrin border, past the customs booth. Montenegro, Crna Gora, Black Mountain. I had walked from Croatia, where my driver had deposited me with my bags, passing Croatian customs and then a short way beyond the checkerboard flag, the entrance to Montenegro. Little Yugoslavia.

Maja was smoking and picking at her nails. "There's soldiers on the streets in Podgorica," she said, grabbing one of my bags. "It's not good."

Maja had just arrived in Montenegro from Belgrade. She had run away from the bombing with her mother, who was waiting for us in Cetinje, the old Montenegrin capital. She got in a car and dialed her mother's number. Her voice was small. She was holding back tears.

"The problem is, everything is so uncertain," she said. Her sister, who lived in Washington, D.C., was calling her every hour, telling her about the NATO planes bombing Belgrade.

Maja's friend Nikola was driving us. He smoked harsh Balkan cigarettes and had a gun under the seat. He said the president, Milo Djukanovic, had given an interview the night before, to calm everyone. It did no good. The only thing that did any good was to load up your shotgun, he said. Montenegrins love guns. There are jokes about houses catching fire in Montenegro and everyone running for cover because of the gun explosions. Even Maja knew how to fire a gun. It was the one thing that made her smile: talking about her guns.

Besides, she said, politics in this country was useless. Djukanovic can't make up his mind whether or not he wants to be a European or a Serb, she said.

She was twenty-one, a Serb student of psychology. She was soft and pretty and tired of politics, of backyard wars, of neighborhood wars. She had moved three times in a week and was weary of living out of a suitcase. She wanted to be back in Belgrade with her friends, sitting in a coffee bar talking about her boyfriend, or clothes. She was worried about her father, who stayed behind.

I left Belgrade because it's a mess, she said. Now Montenegro is a bigger mess.

Montenegro was tense: the government was split between those loyal to Milosevic and his Montenegrin henchmen—chiefly Momir Bulatovic, former president of the republic, who later became prime minister of the Federal Yugoslavia—and those who wanted a return to an independent Montenegro. Serbia's little sister republic was being dragged unwillingly into the war.

On the radio, Djukanovic sounded spent. He said, "There is a serious and genuine danger that even our state could disappear . . . in the violence." It had happened once before—in 1918, in the aftermath of World War I, when Montenegro was annexed to Yugoslavia and ceased to exist with the signing of a treaty. It could easily happen again.

Then, the royal family was sent into exile. Montenegrins had proudly said they would never be subjugated by the Turks, so to be swallowed up, their identity swept away, their possessions left in their palace in Cetinje to gather decades of dust, was painful.

Serbia needed Montenegro. Without it, Yugoslavia would consist of one entity—Serbia. The Serbs needed the coastline. The Yugoslav Navy was based at the Bay of Kotor, in addition to an estimated 12,000 troops, 80 percent of whom come from Serbia. The police force, which was largely loyal to the republican president, had 10,000 members, including a 2,400 Special Force division. In addition, nearly all Montenegrins had their own weapons and were capable of forming a territorial defense.

In early April, shortly after the bombs began falling, Milosevic replaced the popular Montenegrin Army chief, General Radoslav Martinovic, with one of his own, General Milorad Obradovic. It was an effort to undermine Djukanovic, to humiliate him for his Europe leanings. It was also a way to show that Milosevic, though wounded, was still in control. Since then, every morning, there were more troops from the Federal Army—loyal to Belgrade—on the streets of Podgorica. Snipers from the special police forces, loyal to Djukanovic, were positioned on the rooftops of buildings.

Everyone was getting ready to wipe out his neighbor, to burn down his church, to claim his field and his cow. But this time, it would not be a question of burning down mosques or burning Orthodox crosses into the skulls of the losers—this time it would be Serb against Montenegrin.

There is something dark about Montenegro. In the center of the country, the landscape is barren and harsh, and the coastline is winding and rambling. The history too is twisted: by war, by fate, by geography. Bound by the Adriatic to the southwest and the southern end of the Dinaric Alps, the name comes from the Venetian variant of the Italian—Monte Nero (Black Mountain), its historical center and stronghold in the centuries of struggle with the Turks.

Of all the Balkan states, Montenegro was the only one never subjugated by the Turks. While it was incorporated into the Serbian empire in the late twelfth century, Montenegro retained its independence following the Turkish defeat of the Serbs at Kosovo Polje in 1389. At the Congress of Berlin in 1878, Montenegro's size was doubled, and it was internationally recognized as a state. This is what you get told, over and over—history, countries being pushed aside, maps being redrawn, fate and destiny. Even if you hear it for the first time, it all sounds familiar.

In the small northern Montenegrin villages that are Milosevic's strongholds, Kosovar Albanians and Bosnian Muslims are still referred to as "Turks." In 1389, the Serbian Prince Lazar attempted to halt Islam in Kosovo, to save Europe from a Muslim onslaught, and today the Serbs think they are still fighting off the Turks.

Rebecca West once remarked that if you took a peasant in Yugoslavia and shook him, and he turned into his father and his father and so on, you could ask him the same question—Have you ever known peace in your life?—and you would always get the same answer. Now it was not the Turks but NATO that the Serbs were holding off. Soon it would be the Serbs that the Montenegrins would have to hold off.

And there are no more royals on Montenegrin soil. On August 1, 1910, when Prince Nikola 1 of the Petrovic dynasty declared Montenegro a kingdom, he declared himself a king. Two years later, King Nikola fired the first shot during the Balkan wars of 1912–13, in which Serbia and Montenegro cooperated against Turkey. As a result of the war, Montenegro gained territory, extending to the north and the east, giving it a common frontier with Serbia.

Montenegro supported Serbia during World War I, and when the Austro-Hungarian forces were withdrawn early in November 1918, their place was taken by Serbian troops and irregular bands.

Under new control, a "national assembly" met at Podgorica. On November 26, Nikola I was dethroned. He fled with his family into exile, and Montenegro was absorbed into Serbia. The Petrovic family, who had ruled for 222 years, were erased.

During World War II, Italian troops occupied parts of Montenegro. In July 1941, in Cetinje, seat of the Petrovic dynasty, the Italians staged an unrepresentative "national assembly" which declared Montenegro independent, elected an executive body, and requested the king of Italy to nominate a Montenegrin monarch. But rebellion broke out, and until late 1944 when the Communist Partisans arrived, armed with British equipment, there was continuous fighting.

The 1945 federal constitution of the new Yugoslavia led by Josip Broz—Tito—made Montenegro one of the six nominally autonomous federated units of the People's Federal Republic of Yugoslavia. Each of the six had administrative and budgetary authority over its economy, education, and cultural matters. But in 1992, following the dissolution of Yugoslavia and the secession of Slovenia, Croatia, and finally Bosnia, Montenegrins voted in a referendum that they should remain within Yugoslavia. Along with the Republic of Serbia, it formed the Federal Republic of Yugoslavia (FRY).

While technically the constitution said that each republic would maintain its independent authority as a sovereign and equal entity, the reality was somewhat different. Montenegro's coastline later proved useful to bombard the Croats in Dubrovnik. Milosevic was holding on because letting go of Montenegro was letting go of the last of Yugoslavia. In March 2003, Yugoslavia was officially dissolved. Now the federation consists of Serbia and Montenegro, and the latter still hopes to achieve independence.

While a proportion of the population, most notably in the south, wanted to break free of Belgrade, Montenegrins loyal to Milosevic vowed they would never concede. The NATO war only exacerbated the divisions between the pro-Djukanovic, pro-West faction and the hard-core pro-Belgrade contingent.

"There is a splitting of the consciousness which is good for the people," said Bobo Zekovic, chairman of LSCG, the Liberal Party of Montenegro, on a particularly tense day in Podgorica when pro-Milosevic demonstrations were announced and people were told to arm themselves. "The thought of independent, free, and democratic Montenegro no one can deny. It doesn't matter what force or what power people have, they cannot take away the thought of our freedom, our independence. Our democracy."

But the idea of democracy was one thing and the will of Slobodan Milosevic another. Even as Zekovic spoke, three projectiles fell on a hill outside Podgorica, and military hardware from the north, the pro-Milosevic region, was spotted moving down the road, toward the capital.

After the Communist victory in 1945, the capital was moved from royalist Cetinje to Podgorica, a modern, Soviet-style city with grim concrete apartment blocks. However, in 1992, in accordance with the new constitution, Cetinje once again became the national capital, while Podgorica continued as the administrative capital.

For those who remained loyal to the idea of an independent Montenegro, Cetinje, founded in the fifteenth century around an isolated monastery, never ceased being their spiritual center. For five centuries, it was the seat of power for a series of popularly elected Orthodox bishops. A mythic sense grew around the place: that it was impregnable, surrounded by the holy Black Mountain, Mount Lovcen. The Turks had invaded Cetinje three times, and defenders of the local monastery ignited the place, destroying it but scattering the Turks.

Old men in cafés still spoke of Nikola, of the traitors in Belgrade, of the war that would happen if the Serbs tried to impose their will on Montenegro. By the time we found Maja's mother in a dim café in Cetinje, wearing a neat blue suit but nervously smoking cigarettes, the sense of apprehension was very real.

"The fear is based on what could happen here," she explained to me, ordering tea and soup. "This is a tiny country, but it is explosive."

But other Montenegrins were defiant. In the Yellow Moon Café, bad Serbian rap blasted out of old Soviet speakers. Two members of Montenegro's most popular comic band, the Book of Knjige, sat drinking coffee and reading the papers. Rock music from the former Yugoslavia is predictably dreadful: Croatian rap, Bosnian heavy metal, Serbian turbo-folk. But Aleksandar Radunovic-Popaj and Goran Vujovic were loved because they were intelligent and had a sense of humor. Maja described them as Monty Python, with music, with a political edge.

"Sit down! Sit down!" Aleksandar barked. He kicked out a chair and said, "I expect you want to know about the bombs." He then began to ramble. Milosevic was a scumbag, he said brightly. But hadn't anyone learned any lessons from Iraq? Bombing just makes people stronger.

"His madness is spreading like measles," added Goran. "But if the bombs continue to fall down, eventually he will fall down."

Maja, stirring the froth on her cappuccino, asked if Montenegro was in danger.

"Of course!" said Goran. "Anyone that comes in Milosevic's path is in danger!"

The waitress, with long hair and dark brown lipstick, brought more coffee, flirted, then went inside and said she was putting on their new CD.

"It doesn't matter if we are in danger," Goran added over the sound of the bass. "Montenegrins love their country too much to give it up."

The music droned out of the speakers. The waitress came outside again. "I'm going to turn it up!" she said brightly. The music got louder, spilling across the cobbled courtyard. It was a love song to Montenegro, something the band wrote before the bombs started.

"My country, my homeland!" wailed Aleksandar, sounding very far away. "This is all a bad dream!"

Nikola Petrovic was a dreamer, a poet and writer, although he never reached the acclaim of his ancestor, Petar Petrovic Njegos, with his epic poem *The Mountain Wreath*. Nikola loved his country, but he died in exile, far from Montenegro, in Paris in 1921, in Neuilly-sur-Seine. His body was taken to Italy, and he was buried in San Remo in the family tomb. But in 1989, his remains, along with those of his wife, Queen Milena, and his two daughters, Ksenija and Vera, were transferred back to Cetinje.

From the fall of the Serbian Kingdom in 1355 up until the fall of Zeta in 1499, the territory which today is Montenegro was ruled by the Crnojevica dynasty. From 1499, most of Zeta was controlled by the Ottoman Empire. The Petrovic dynasty led Montenegro from 1696. There were seven rulers. King Nikola was the last, ruling from 1860–1918.

His palace, his family home, still stands in Cetinje, but during the bombing it was shuttered and dark, the windows covered in webs and dust. I was peering through the windows, like a child who had discovered something in the woods, when a Montenegrin historian, Aleksandar Brkuljan, came behind me. "I have a key," he said, holding it up. He was a gloomy character who did not look directly into my eyes, but he said he guarded the palace, and he opened the door and led me inside.

There were creaking shutters, large French windows, which, when opened, brought in the weak spring light. We entered the great hall. Then he began: "Montenegro," he said, in a practiced schoolteacher voice, "of all the areas around the Black Mountains, was the only area in the Balkans not to be invaded." He held up a tattered, bullet-ridden flag of Montenegro, the oldest national flag in the Balkans.

"We want to live freely, as all other people in the world live, to choose our own destiny," Brkuljan said, folding the flag. "And to have choice. We don't hate anyone—least of all Serbs. We just have to make some other choice."

He flung open the doors to the dusty rooms, the parquet floors worn and scuffed, the walls dingy. In the bedrooms, the grand drawing rooms, the dining room, Nikola's family had left their possessions, their imprints. Nikola's library contained his leather-bound books, his diaries, his notebooks with his sketches for poems. There were his collection of Turkish weapons; a medal given to him by Queen Victoria. There were faded, slightly sad sepia-printed photographs and his wife's silk and lace dresses, beautifully made and only slightly worn. Their polished Chippendale dining-room table, their elegant, thin china, their stem crystal glasses. A polar bear rug. Tureens which once held soup.

Around the table, there were chairs with the letters *N.I.* monogrammed. I could envision the tureen, now full, and the state dinners, his wife bending gracefully to check the *placement* before an important function; the parties; the children laughing and singing around a piano imported from Leipzig. The children who would grow up and marry: one daughter to the king of Italy; one to the king of Serbia; one would become the mother of the future King Alexander of Yugoslavia; one a German princess; another married the Russian Grand Duke Peter.

All gone, faded, erased. Once they fled, communist followed. Then a regime of cunning nationalism, run out of Belgrade, crushing the last remnants of the Petrovic dynasty. Whoever is alive from the family is exiled. Nikola's grandson, Prince Nicholas Petrovic-Njegos, an architect in Paris, returned to Montenegro during the bombing. He said he was there for solidarity. He loathed Milosevic. What happened in Belgrade hurt the Montenegrin people.

"For ten years, we have been in a dictatorship that has prevented Montenegrin society from doing its democratic duty," he said. "It has forced the entire former Yugoslavia into absurd wars and it has locked them into a system of fear."

I told Nicholas I had been inside his family home in Cetinje, had seen the medals, the ribbons, the photographs of the royal houses of Europe. He did not want to come back, he said, as a "dictator prince."

"I want to come back out of love," he said. But even he admitted how difficult the prospects of that would be. President Djukanovic should have been given more Western support. "Thanks to the mistakes of the international community, Milosevic has managed to unite the Serbian people around him," Nicholas said bitterly. "Everyone is taken as a hostage."

Outside, in the sun in Cetinje, music spilled out of open windows from the former British mission, opened in 1879 and closed in 1916 at the height of World War I. Inside, the old rooms had French doors, chipped tiled floors, and peeling terra-cotta paint. The mission, abandoned by the Brits, had been converted into music practice rooms for the university. Students shuffled through, carrying their oboes and violins. One of them, a twenty-year old named Zoran, played a tarantella on his double bass, stopping briefly as we passed the door. He had no strong feeling about the war, he said. He dropped his head and kept playing. The music drifted, flowed across the faded terra-cotta rooms. There was no trace of the old world, only the new.

As he locked the front door of the Petrovic residence, Aleksandar said no one visited the place anymore. "Sad," he said, "but that's the way it is." No one went to the British mission, with the sign still on the gate. Or the French Embassy, where there had been garden parties. No one saw Montenegro as a kingdom, either, but as an adjunct of Serbia. The country would never return to its former state.

"We do not have a romantic history," he said. "We have a tragic one. We have no freedom to choose our own destiny."[12]

Rozaje
March 30, 1999
Day Seven of the NATO Bombing

Pec, seat of the Patriarchate of the Serbian Orthodox Church, was burning.

It was bombed by NATO and simultaneously torched by Serbs, who made the ethnic Albanians pay for the bombing campaign by running them out of their villages. All around Pec, all around Kosovo, they were fleeing. Four thousand people an hour pouring over the border of Kosovo into Montenegro, Albania, Macedonia, leaving behind a blackened country. Sadako Ogata, the U.N. High Commissioner for Refugees, told an international emergency meeting in Geneva that the enforced "evacuation" from Kosovo was an attempt to "destroy its collective identity."[13]

From Pec, it's thirteen, fourteen, fifteen hours of walking in the freezing cold, over passes of the Prokletiga Mountains, Mountains of the Damned, to Rozaje. The weather snapped, turning icy with deep snow, bitterly cold in the mountains. The refugees were not dressed for it. They wore bedroom slippers and hand-knit cardigans with no jackets, no warm coats over them. There were few with hats or gloves or scarves. They left without time to grab what they needed.

What do people take with them when they are forced to abandon their homes? Documents, baby pictures, animals, blankets, loaves of bread and slabs of meat. Some carry nothing, having had just enough time to grab a jacket, a coat.

On the border position on top of a windy hill near Rozaje, on the Kosovo border three hours from Podgorica, a woman named Anna waited for her brother. She had gotten separated from him in Pec, and now she was searching the faces of the refugees who passed, climbing higher, trying to reach the top of the hill which would lead them into Montenegro. As they passed, they called out stories: "They're burning the hospital in Pec!" "They killed all the cows!" When Visar, a twenty-one-year-old student, got to the top, he sat down for a moment on a rock and held out his hand. It was shaking. "I can't close my eyes without seeing all those terrible things," he said.

Anna had been waiting for four hours. "Where is he? Where is he?" she cried. She stamped her feet in the snow to keep them warm. Tears rolled down her cheeks. "Where is he?" Her brother was young and of fighting age. She knew what the Serbs were doing to men and boys. Why were there so many women passing, so few men? Maybe they had stopped him from leaving.

We climbed into a car on top of the mountain and drove down the road to look for him. A woman passed, pushing a pram with a baby inside, surrounded by three small children, all holding hands. A man rode a bicycle in the snow, falling over every few minutes, but picking it up stoically and continuing. He'd fall, get up, brush off his clothes, and get back on the icy seat. Then he would fall again.

In the crowd, moving with a group of others, was Anna's lost brother. He was a teenager, pale-skinned, dark-haired, wearing a jean jacket. His eyes were teary. Anna shouted and raced to him, hugging her brother, kissing his face and his hands. She kissed me. "He's alive," she said, "he's alive."

A woman walked alone, hysterical, crying. No one was holding her hand or helping her walk. She was a teacher from Pec. When she left, the flames were climbing. "A lot of people are passing, but a lot of people are dead!" she screamed, unable to control herself. Her chest heaved and she waved her hands in the air. "They are dead! Hospitals are burning! They are killing teachers, doctors, anything alive. They are animals!" She dropped her head and began to cry, uncontrollable sobs that came from deep within her. "No, not animals," she said suddenly. "Animals do not treat one another like this."

When she stopped crying, she moved on. There was a horrible stillness in the snow. In the middle of it, an older woman, heavy, wearing a head scarf and a cardigan, walked with a determined stride, slowly plodding up the mountain. She could not speak. She was in shock.

A colleague put her in his car and we drove her to the top of the pass. She was alone, with no bags, no remainders of her former life. "Who are you?" we asked, using an interpreter. "What is your name?" The woman said nothing.

We let the heat run and she sat in the car for hours, saying nothing, watching out the window at the scene of madness. A man carrying a mattress over his shoulder; another carrying a shaving brush. A child with Down's syndrome stumbling through the snow, laughing in a high-pitched, maniacal way. Falling, face-first in the snow. His mother, chasing him with tears running down her cheeks. Nearby, watching him, was another mother with four small children, all huddled close to her body, all shivering.

A man who lived in Italy as a child, who spoke Italian, who wore a thin overcoat, said he did not understand why he had to leave his home. A boy, about nine or ten, was crying because the Serbs had killed his cow. Every morning, his mother made him milk the cow. "Why kill it?" he sobbed. "Why kill a cow?"

In the warmed-up car, I found some hardened bread. I held it out to the old woman, but she only looked at me and did not take it. She sat straight, with her headscarf still on. She did not push the bread away, she only stared ahead. "You must eat," I coaxed, but she did not answer. Outside, the cry of the boy who had lost his cow shattered the silence.

She ignored the bread. She seemed dead already.

Kula Pass, on the Montenegrin-Kosovo Border
March 31, 1999

French Mirage planes bombed Belgrade. Montenegro grew tense. There were rumors of an army-led coup against the pro-West government.

But on the pass, there was clean, fresh snow. It had fallen overnight, and was still falling, as more refugees from Pec passed silently, in single file, walking toward the lights of Rozaje. They stepped carefully, trudging, one after the other.

The sky was darkening slowly, changing from the hazy, gray sunless day to black. There was the scent of pine coming from the forest. Row after row of fir trees. The smell was sharp, and reminded me of a clear lake in Maine, a place from my adolescence. Unedited memories came back. Far from Montenegro, no refugees carrying mattresses and shaving brushes, but Maine, early summer; a secret lake in the mountains; the stillness, the quiet, the flat gray stones on the edge of the water.

The pictures came back, as though I had left a gate open: a strawberry festival in Southwest Harbor; a woman holding a freshly baked pie; a white fence and a house with a front porch beyond it; my father, still alive, sunburnt, sitting happily in a great big wicker chair looking out over a long lawn toward Frenchmen's Bay. The sea rolling north, to Nova Scotia and New Brunswick. The scent of pine. The fir trees lined up in a row.

"Why are you smiling?" It was a friend, a colleague.

The gate was snapped shut. The scent of pine now came from the forest, beyond the mountains leading to Kosovo. Mountains of the Damned.

"I was . . . thinking. It was nothing, a memory."

He said, "I'm going back to Podgorica. You coming?"

I looked at the darkening sky. "No," I said, "I'm going to wait. See if more people come over that hill."

He got in his car and waved. In an instant, he was gone.

The Serbs came from nowhere. From over the pine ridge, from Kosovo. They were drunk. They swarmed over the hill where we waited, two colleagues and I, like dark bees. I sat inside the car and watched as though I were watching a movie.

As they were moving, guns banging against their legs, I realized I had seen them before: earlier in the day, they had crossed the ridge. Paramilitary, unshaven, wearing sunglasses on a cloudy gray day. Yelling to the refugees to move faster. Hitting them with the butt of their rifles. Spitting on the ground. I wondered why they had crossed the Kosovar border into Montenegro.

"They're drunk," a refugee told me, dropping her voice. "Don't speak to them, don't go near them. Don't look at them."

We thought they might be Frenki's Guys, part of a paramilitary unit from Nis, in Serbia. They did not look like MUP or military police. We did not know why they were there, but as I bent down to talk to another refugee who said he had fled Kosovo because his Serb neighbors arrived with guns and told them the paramilitary leader Arkan was coming to slit their throats, the soldiers vanished.

Now it was later, darker. The mountain was empty except for me, two French TV journalists, and their car. Everyone else had left the mountain, gone down to the village.

There was a strange scream. From my window, I saw one of my colleagues on the ground, the Serb soldiers, their guns swinging, surrounding him. There were about ten of them, some very young.

One kicked him, and he curled up on the ground to protect himself. Then they pushed him, and half falling back into the snow, he raised his arms above his head. An instinctive act of surrender.

One of the soldiers took his Kalashnikov, cocked and aimed it at his head. My friend called out, "No!"

The soldiers dropped their guns, laughed. One saw me.

"Get out," he said. They dragged me out. They stunk of brandy. Once, in Bosnia, leaving the Sarajevo checkpoint near Ilidjza, I had been stopped along with two other colleagues and strip-searched by Bosnian Serb soldiers. They separated us, questioned us, robbed us—in my case, of 3,000 British pounds stuffed down my trousers—finally released us after hours of tears, pleading, and threats. As a final humiliation, they gave us receipts, saying we could reclaim the money after the war, in Belgrade.

Then, arrogantly, I said to them, "You can't do this."

A man, leering, spat out, "We can do anything we want. We're winning the war."

But the present situation was different. These men were losing the war and they were out of control.

"Give me your documents."

"British! Spy!"

"French! You bombed Belgrade!"

Their voices, raised to a hysterical high pitch.

"Are you English?"

"American?"

I said nothing. My passport said I was born in America. One of the soldiers, who spoke Italian, took the passport in his hands. "Okay, you have Italian blood. You get arrested. But the French, who bombed us, we kill."

He turned to me again. "Isn't that fair? France killed Serbs today, so we kill them. Fair?"

I didn't notice the refugees passing behind us, but they were there: walking with their heads down, seeing us, but unable to help, terrified they would be taken out of the line. A young Serb with red hair, a cowboy hat, and acne pulled out his pistol, aimed it at them.

"Move!" he screamed, raising his gun to an older man's head. "Move! This has nothing to do with you."

Then they confiscated our things: phones, passports, computers, and documents. They took the armored car belonging to the French TV. They told us to walk with our backs turned to them, toward Rozaje.

Don't ever turn your back if someone is pointing a gun at you. Who had told me that? "Move!" they shouted.

We ran. They fired over our heads. We ran, down the icy hill, slipping, but moving toward the lights at the bottom of the mountain. How far was Rozaje, the Red Cross? Two, maybe three miles. In the dark, we could reach it in an hour.

Then a Serb Army jeep, coming up the mountain, blocked our way. Another soldier got out, with a gun, and ordered us to go back up. He took us to the snowy spot on the hill. He told us to wait in the armored car and not to turn around. "Look in front of you," he says, and slammed the door. He turned to speak to the other soldiers.

There were shots. They were not fired in the air, but into something, I remember thinking, like an air bag. When I turned around, I saw they had lined up refugees and were stealing their possessions, rifling through their bags.

"Don't turn around," my French colleague said to me in a quiet voice. "Look forward."

"They're paramilitary, definitely paramilitary, they've got no chain of command," the other one said.

From the corner of my eye, I saw the soldiers beating a refugee boy I had spotted earlier in the day, one who was using his truck to ferry the older people, the children, and the women up and down the mountain. Over and over, they hit him with their guns while he made noises like a whimpering, hurt dog. One hit him hard, and he fell to the ground like an empty sack.

There was another shot.

"What will they do to us?" I asked, knowing there was no answer. "They can't kill us."

"You think so?" said my friend, dubiously, next to me. The other French reporter quietly said something about his family.

The Italian-speaking soldier returned. He was eating an apple and told us to drive, to follow them into Kosovo. He told us to stay between his jeep and the other jeep on the narrow icy road. "You're going on a nice long trip to jail in Pec," he said. "Now you'll know what it feels like to be bombed."

Through the snow, through the icy banks, to Kosovo. Toward the bombing, passing more refugees. There was another jeep behind us, watching us with a gun pointed at the back of our vehicle. We could not turn around.

"I've got to get rid of my notebook," I said.

"Oh, shit," said the French reporter. "What's in it?"

Names, testimonies, phone numbers of relatives, information about massacres and mass graves and farmers shot in the head and buried near their homes. Names of KLA fighters and their bases. Maps.

Very slowly, I ripped it up. I handed the shredded pages to my colleague who sat in the front passenger seat, and very slowly, he opened his door and dropped them low, into the snow. Finally, when all the pages were gone, I gave him the spine of my black notebook. He dropped it underneath the moving car, carefully so that the soldiers did not see it, and it landed somewhere in the snow, in the middle of the road. When I turned briefly to look back, I saw it left a black mark in the whiteness.

It wasn't so long, or so many kilometers, but it seemed endless. We drove on, past abandoned farmhouses, past frightened refugees, past snowdrifts. We drove 30 kilometers into Kosovo before the soldiers got a radio call. We watched a man stop the jeep, get out, light a cigarette. Slowly, he marched to the car, a rifle in his hand, a pistol at his waist.

The cars rested at an isolated bend of the mountain. When I peered over the ridge, over the cliff, I saw nothing but trees—pine trees—and snow. Maybe that's where they will kill us, I thought. No houses, and only the darkening sky above us.

"Get out," he said, his cigarette in his mouth. "Get out of the car."

He told us to follow him, toward his jeep. "Wait," he said. I stared down at the snow, at my feet, at my blue Gore-Tex hiking boots buried in white. It seemed better not to look.

He finished his cigarette and crushed it in the snow, under his boot. Then he opened the back of the jeep and handed back our things. "Get out of here," he said. "There are terrorists everywhere. Albanians. It's not safe for you." He began to laugh. He kissed me on both cheeks and hugged the Frenchman he had earlier beaten. "It was a joke!" he said. "A joke!" Happily, he passed us our equipment that he had taken earlier: satellite phones, computers, IDs, passports.

"Goodbye!" he said like an old friend, climbing in his jeep and waving frantically as his jeep sped off.

We turned and drove but did not speak. Later, in Montenegro, an aid worker said that Serbs on the Macedonian border with Kosovo had captured three American soldiers at around the same time they caught us. "Why would they want three little reporters when they got the big fish?" he said, not unkindly, adding, "You were lucky."

By the time we reached Rozaje, time-delayed fear hit. My French colleague said to me, "Now I will tell you. It was you we were worried about." I set up my satellite phone on the roof of their car, shaking slightly from cold and nerves. There was not enough light. A man approached me, heavy and solid, with a tweed cap and an overcoat. He looked familiar. He spoke good English. He touched my shoulder. "It's you, thank God," he said, his voice deep. He looked at me with kindness, with concern. "We saw them march you off. We saw them take you at gunpoint. We saw you go into the woods. I never thought I would see you again. You were very lucky, God was with you."

The man, who was called Mustafa, said that he and his wife tried to go to the Red Cross to report it.

"Thank you," I said quietly. We left to have a coffee. He said he was a professor of Engineering at the University of Pristina. He spoke English, French, Italian, and Danish, and had been living in Denmark with his family for several years. He was visiting his family in Pec when the air strikes started. It was more than bad luck; it was a death warrant for him to be in Kosovo. As a dissident intellectual who frequently entertained Westerners in his home, and who spoke out against Serbian repression, he was on a hit list, targeted by Serb paramilitary. He was worried that Arkan—the paramilitary leader responsible for atrocities in Bosnia and later indicted as a war criminal—along with his squad, the Tigers, were coming to Kosovo to join their Serb brothers.[14]

There was a blare of hip-hop music in the small café. Mustafa asked if I would help get him and his family—his wife and four children, who were hiding in a cave in the mountains—out of Montenegro as soon as possible. It was not a request. He begged me, taking my hands in his.

"If Milosevic marches into Montenegro, which everyone says he will do soon," Mustafa said in a soft voice, "I will be killed. All our lives hang on very little here."

The cold went through the plastic chair I was sitting on and reached my back. I kept seeing the faces of the laughing soldiers, the refugee boy falling into the snow after he had been beaten, whimpering.

"God was with you today," Mustafa said again. "Usually, the Serbs just shoot. They don't have a change of heart."

In the morning, I phoned the Italian Consulate in Bar. Mustafa and his family got out, crossing by ferry from Montenegro to Italy, then flew to Denmark.

He phoned me, often, after that. He said that I was forever a part of his family, that all his family sent blessings to me. He said I was like their child, and they would never forget me. He said he would probably never go back to Kosovo.

Near Race, a Serb Stronghold in Montenegro

April 4, 1999
(Easter Sunday in the West)

There were Yugoslav soldiers on the barren, desolate road east out of Podgorica, leading to Kuce and Race. There were trucks of military hardware coming from the north. The headline in the hard-line Serb newspaper, *Dan*, showed pictures of the war under the headline HERE'S TO A BEAUTIFUL APRIL.

One year before the Serb offensive and the NATO bombing began, the British historian Noel Malcolm wrote, "Quite simply, Serbia had already lost Kosovo—lost it, that is, in the most basic human and demographic, terms."[15]

But Malcolm did not foresee, as NATO did not foresee, the die-hard feelings of the Serb people, solidified by the bombing campaign. The NATO war had only fortified their view that they were victims. Because they felt victimized, it was easier for more of them to unite under the mantra of the World War II Serbian royalist Chetniks, whose symbols were misinterpreted to mean Only Unity Can Save the Serbs. The emblem was usually painted on burnt-out houses in Bosnia and Kosovo after they were ethnically cleansed.

More than ever were the Serbs unwilling to give up Kosovo, their Jerusalem. It was more than a political stronghold; it was sacred, containing the remains of their most revered saints, the monasteries, the holy battlefield of Kosovo Polje.

During the Balkan war of 1913, which reclaimed Kosovo from the Turks, one Serb soldier wrote:

> The single sound of that word—Kosovo—caused an indescribable excitement. This one word pointed to the black past—five centuries. In it exists the whole of our sad past—the tragedy of Prince Lazar, and the entire Serbian people. . . . Each of us created for himself a picture of Kosovo while we were still in the cradle. Our mothers lulled us to sleep with the songs of Kosovo.[16]

Milosevic had said, at the start of his political career, April 20, 1987: "Yugoslavia does not exist without Kosovo! Yugoslavia would disintegrate without Kosovo! Yugoslavia and Serbia are not going to give up Kosovo!" His words united the Serb people again. Two years later, to make his point clear, he revoked Kosovo's autonomy within the Yugoslav Federation and fired Albanians from state-run institutions.

Race was a village carved out of a mountain: hard, gray, forbidding. There were about twenty houses, all hard-core Serb supporters, many of them related to Momir Bulatovic, Milosevic's Montenegrin lap dog. In Race, there were no NATO TRAITORS, no SERVANTS OF NATO, the graffiti criticizing the Djukanovic government spray-painted on the rocks leading to the town. This was Slobodan Milosevic's sphere of influence, full of simple farming people who before the war supported him, who would now, unified by the new tragedy, go to their graves for him.

There was other graffiti on the rocks that chilled me: a Serbian unity symbol with the name ARKAN. Then there was a tank ominously parked outside the entrance to a small café where some families sat, a portrait of a youthful Milosevic hung on the wall.

Inside, men sat drinking beer, laughing, their blond children eating sweets and drinking Cokes. At first, the men—mostly farmers whose families had lived in Race for generations—were hostile. Anyone foreign, anyone from a NATO country, was the enemy. Then Rajko Rajkovic, one of the men, pulled a chair away from a table and motioned for me to sit. He ordered a black coffee and pushed it toward me, moving the sugar bowl and a spoon. He wanted, he said, to put forth the position of the Serbs in Montenegro.

His family had lived within these dark hills forever and ever. And yet he did not consider himself a Montenegrin, he considered himself a Serb. Greater Serbia, or the dream of it, was as important to him as God. If the Montenegrin separatists—led by Djukanovic, that NATO traitor—tried to separate, tried to follow the pattern of the former Yugoslav republics, he would die fighting. If the Serbs were attacked, he said, they would fight. There were already tanks on the Border with Montenegro.

As for this war, it was propaganda. Ethnic cleansing in Kosovo did not exist; what was happening was that the people were running away from the bombing, which was natural. It was NATO that was guilty—this morning, in Serbia, they had bombed bridges, making it impossible for civilians to move around, get to work, continue their normal lives. But despite that, his family in Belgrade were singing and dancing, not afraid at all.

"This war has to end eventually," he said. "And someone's got to stay here. And it will be the Serbs. They can't shoot every single one of us." He did not believe a coup d'état was coming, or that the government would change. As for the tank sitting outside, he regarded it and shrugged. "They are preparing for a long war," he said.

His friend, sitting at another table and listening to Rajko's words, suddenly looked up from his early-morning beer. He pointed to the tank, "Fuck Milo Djukanovic," he said.

In the evening, there was a concert in Ivan Milutinovic Square for Milosevic supporters. She was a great Partisan fighter, and the concert was billed as a peace effort, a show of unity for the civilians being bombed in Belgrade. But there was a strange atmosphere all day in the city, and foreigners were advised not to go, to stay in their hotels, out of sight. My friend Momo said he would take me, but he made me promise not to speak English.

As the light faded from the sky, more than 10,000 people gathered to listen to Yugoslavian heavy metal bands called Katapult and Columbus' Mistake, perform. "Sometimes," Momo noted drily of the latter's name, "you have to give it to the Serbs for their humor."

Gula, the lead singer of Katapult, took to the stage and began belting out at the top of his lungs, "Serbia! Serbia!" while the crowd swayed like a wave and shouted along with him. It was terrible music, off-key, repetitive, and too loud, but the metamorphosis of the crowd was extraordinary. By the time a young singer named Sara Vujosevic took to the stage, the people were primed, an angry vigilante mob.

"Let's go," Momo said quietly, and took my hand. "Let's get out of here." He led me across the square, pulling me when people looked at my jacket, my shoes, my face, suspiciously, speaking to me in Serbian. When we finally reached the edge of the crowd, we found a way to climb on top of the roof of an apartment building which looked out high over the square. In order to get to the top, we had to pass through one apartment where a couple sat watching television, oblivious that we were walking through their living room, and oblivious, for that matter, to the terrible noise outside.

"That's right, go right ahead through our window to the roof, everyone else does," the husband said good-naturedly.

There we could see everything. The heaving crush of people, the faces twisted with rage and frustration. The waving pictures of targets. The placards that read YES FOR YUGOSLAVIA.

Momo, watching, said quietly, "This is not good."

Afterward, we climbed down the steps, through the window of an apartment, and down a set of ancient stairs, and Momo walked me home, back to the hotel. We passed a crowd coming from the concert, still singing, "Serbia! Serbia!"

I did what he said. I did not speak; I looked away from the passing faces. But even doing that, I still felt naked antipathy, a surging sense of anger, suspicion, and hatred from the crowd.

"This is my generation," said Momo when the street had cleared, as if reading my thoughts. "You can't blame them. This is what ten years of losing war after war after war has done to them. They feel as though they have nothing left to lose."

Podgorica, Montenegro
April 7, 1999

I sat in the cold late-winter sunlight, in a café outside the Hotel Crno Gora, drinking milky coffee with an old Montenegrin general. His hands were unsteady. He took a spoonful of sugar from a silver dish, balancing it carefully before dropping it into his caramel-colored coffee. He stared out onto the street, where soldiers from the Yugoslav Second Army lingered, men from Nis and Novi Sad and Belgrade, joking among themselves, not quite sure what good luck had brought them to Montenegro, where the weather was good, the women beautiful, and they were not condemned to the trenches of Kosovo.

It was two days before Serbian Orthodox Good Friday and the day after the anniversary of the devastating German air attacks on Belgrade in 1941. Ironically, Serbia at the time was aligned with the Western powers, the West choosing first to back the Chetniks, led by Colonel Draza Mihailovic. But the Americans and the British forces criticized the Chetniks for not standing up to the Germans the way the Communist Partisans, led by Tito, did. They eventually switched sides.[17]

In Belgrade today, President Milosevic called for a cease-fire to respect the upcoming Orthodox Easter. It was a joke. A cease-fire in the Balkan meant nothing more than playing with time. The refugees were still crossing the mountains, arriving with more stories of mass graves and burning houses. In Montenegro, the tension between the pro-Milosevic and the pro-Djukanovic factions was palpable. NATO bombs had fallen on Serb Army targets.

"We are expecting a civil war or a coup d'état," the General said quietly, staring into his coffee cup. "But nobody knows. It depends on our strength, our ability to defend ourselves."

The General, who had served under Tito and fought against the Germans, pinning them down in central Bosnia during a cold winter that remained embedded in his memory half a century later, could not give his name. He had spent all night driving south, from Belgrade to Podgorica, when he first heard rumors of an imminent coup d'état. He had come to fight against the Belgrade regime, against Milosevic, leading Montenegrins who wanted freedom into battle as he had done with his ragged bunch of Partisans. "I am old," he said. "But I can offer advice, I can be of some use."

I had watched the General for several days, moving, with great dignity in his elegant Italian-made suit and tie, between the breakfast room and the café of the Crna Gora, always surrounded by Montenegrin dignitaries and politicians. His posture was so correct, his manner so patrician, that even the normally surly waiters who slapped half-cooked eggs and slabs of greasy meat on the dirty tables treated him with respect. They called him General and brought his food quickly, while it was still hot. They opened bottles of Vranac red wine with a flourish; they piled plates with bread and pickled vegetables.

The General was eighty years old, born in 1919, in the days when Montenegro was part of the Kingdom of Serbs, Croats, and Slovenes, when Prince Nikola I was still alive, living out his last days in sad exile in France. He was born in Naples, the son of a theologian, but was brought to Montenegro as a child, raised in Cetinje, where he was steeped in legends of Montenegrin freedom.

"For centuries, people from Cetinje were proud people, people who were willing to fight for their freedom," he said.

At seventeen, he moved to Belgrade to study medicine, and shortly afterward began moving toward communism. He believed, as the revolutionaries in Russia believed, it was a way of ridding Serbia of the stifling poverty, of the vast division between the peasants who could not read and write and died in the slums, and the bourgeosie in Belgrade who took tea at the cafés in Knez Mihailo Street. Four years later, the war began, and he joined the Partisans. In another world, he would have been barely old enough to sit in a bar and order a drink. He smiled shortly. "It was a time when people became older," he said.

He was twenty-one years old in April 1941, when he hid for two days during the German bombing raids that smashed Belgrade, destroying the fine white buildings of his adopted city and interrupting his studies. After the bombings, he said in some ways his own fate was sealed: his dreams of becoming a doctor faded and were replaced by war, vengeance, dreams of freedom.

He made his way down to Montenegro to his family, and to attempt to organize an insurrection. Three months later, on July 13, 1941, the Partisan insurrection was born. His first action was to ambush Italian tanks on the road from Cetinje to Budva.

By December, he was promoted to battalion commander, and led a Partisan battalion of 341 men into guerrilla warfare against the Germans and Italians near Sandjak, in the tip of Serbia that stretches toward Bosnia and today has a largely Muslim population. His battalion fought "from early morning until early night," ambushing tanks and engaging in hand-to-hand combat. By daybreak, his men were exhausted. When the sky lightened, it was his job to move across the battleground, counting the casualties: 180 wounded, 82 dead.

"And that," he said somberly, fifty years later "was the saddest morning of my life."

He continued fighting throughout the war, moving wherever Tito called him—Montenegro, Bosnia, Croatia, Serbia. He slept in caves, in fields, on freezing mountaintops. When it was finished, he became a National Hero, the highest decoration given by Tito. He was declared a general after the liberation. He was twenty-six years old.

"At that time, we were living so close to death that we became older and more clever with double speed," he said. "Events made us older."

In the new Yugoslavia, he became undersecretary to the minister of the interior, and later, the Yugoslav ambassador to Hungary and then Sweden. He was a member of the Senate, the Federation Council, and was renowned for his extreme Montenegrin views. Despite Tito's years of Brotherhood and Unity, despite communism, despite Milosevic's nationalism, he yearned for an independent country, the way it was before he was born, when Cetinje was capital, when Nikola ruled.

Now, after all the destruction he had witnessed, after watching the birth and the death of communism and of Yugoslavia, after watching Bosnia's hills burn twice, after Milosevic's ascent to power and nationalism grabbing Serbia by the throat, he was now seeing Belgrade bombed. The memories flooded back: of himself at twenty-one hiding during a German air raid, of leading his young soldiers into battle, of the aftermath, the sea of bodies.

He had come to offer his services to the Montenegrin separatists who might have to fight against Milosevic. The young man who had fearlessly ambushed Italian tanks, who had grown up to be a general, was suddenly frightened at what he was witnessing.

His hands shook as he spoke of the bombing raid the night before. His wife, an invalid, his son, his two grandchildren, were waiting in a bomb shelter in Belgrade for the all-clear to go stand in queues and try to buy milk. He looked once again to the Podgorica street where Yugoslav Army soldiers stood in their Soviet-style uniforms, faces razed of any expression. "Nationalism is poison," he said. "They hate everybody and everything."

Suddenly, the General looked old. His posture remained stiff, his shirt was as neatly pressed as the day before, his tie at a perfect angle. But his face appeared to sag with sorrow. This war in Kosovo was a mystery to him, the Milosevic forces pushing the country he loved deeper and deeper into destruction.

He did not understand.

"Everything is ruined!" he cried. "Everything is ruined. There is no more fraternity and unity! The last ten years, everything is ruined." He put his cup down with force, pushing himself away from the table. His face crumbled, he was close to tears.

"I lost so many friends during World War II, so many young people who were trying to create a new country," he said. "Now everything is falling down because of ideas. Who are these people? Are they insane? Why are they cleaning out Kosovo?"

I returned to Montenegro several times, most notably during the September 2000 Serbian presidential elections. President Djukanovic had boycotted the elections and had made contingency plans to prevent violence. But it was still tense in Podgorica, and many of my friends had left, fearing that there would certainly be a coup. There were roadblocks on the way to the coast, and one cold morning I drove north to Berane, an industrial city known for paper mills and Milosevic supporters.

The town was sullen and paranoid. The landscape was remote and rugged, dotted with sheep and pigs. At a small mountain café, the only food available was a broth in which something gray floated. "Stomach," the waitress said cheerfully. A farmer who sat drinking coffee at the next table explained that this was hard country, and that it was known as "Raska"—land that would always belong to Serbia.

The federal deputy of the municipality, Milos Bojovic, met me for coffee in a chilly Soviet-style hotel with orange swivel chairs. A television set in the background blared American soap operas, and Bojovic told me about thirteenth-century Serbian saints who came from the region. "We won't turn brother against brother," he said, "but this is Serbian land, and we want to remain part of Yugoslavia." He warned me, not unkindly, not to attend the pro-Milosevic rally that day. More than 80 percent of the north supported Milosevic, he said, and he was expecting a turnout of around 120,000. "I don't think they will be happy to have a member of a NATO country there."

On election day, only 24.8 percent of the people came out—essentially those loyal to Yugoslavia—and voted. Vojislav Kostunica, a relatively unknown academic researcher, collected enough votes to be the new president of the Yugoslav Federation. Milosevic, after a decade of war and misery, was officially out.

But he did not go easily, and it took what would eventually be called the October Revolution to topple him. In Montenegro, his supporters were also resilient. Some of his soldiers, members of the Seventh Battalion of the Military Police, were still on the streets, taking orders from his generals to launch an insurrection. To counteract them, Montenegrin nationalists were put on alert. "We are ready to mobilize in a second," Bojica Vusurovic, who was part of a militia called Kantunjani in honor of their clan, told me from his base in a remote national park above Cetinje. He had refused to meet in the town, instead gave me elaborate instructions to drive high in the gray, stony hills to a closed-down resort hotel. It was cold and dusty. There was no water in the taps. He sat in his ski jacket and woolly hat, talking aggressively. "If someone attacks," he snarled, "we are ready to defend the sovereignity of Montenegro with whatever means."

Katunjani was typical of small, local, but potentially dangerous territorial militias. The group of nearly 100 men, most from the Cetinje area, had formed in 1993, and began launching attacks on then Republic President Momir Bulatovic. In one instance, in front of King Nikola's palace, Vusurovic flung himself at the president, wounding his bodyguard. He was sentenced to three and a half years in prison. He served and was granted amnesty in 1995. The time in prison had given him the opportunity to recruit more men for his militia. Now, he said, should Milosevic set his Seventh Battalion against the people, small militias like Katunjani would counter the attack. "The people will fight back!"

Shortly before the elections on September 24, I met Dino, a Serbian soldier who one year before had burned houses and chased hundreds of Albanians out of Prizren. He had spent twenty days getting bombed by NATO near Gorozup, in an open place with nowhere to hide. He was angry about the end of the war. "We started the war in Kosovo and we won the war against the Albanians and NATO. But political leaders stopped it," he said.

We met in a secret location, in a house outside the city. He had changed out of his fatigues into jeans and a T-shirt, and warned me that he would find me if I told anyone where I had met him. "I know where you live," he said. "Don't think I won't find you." He seemed drunk or stoned. He wanted money to talk and sat in a chair nervously drumming his fingers against the frame.

He was twenty-two, heavy-set, with close-cropped hair, and said he had joined the VJ (Yugoslav Army) because he was unemployed, and they paid him around DEM 500 a month—more than the usual VJ soldier. Members of the VJ were recruited in a different way than conventional soldiers (who were members of the JNA, the Yugoslav National Army), but he would not go into detail. Before that, he had worked as a bodyguard for a shady underworld character. He claimed there were around 2,000 other Serb soldiers scattered around Montenegro, in Podgorica, Berane, and Bijelo Polge, and they were training others, twelve hours a day.

"If Montenegro chooses to leave Yugoslavia," he said, "we're told to prepare for the worst." It was a possibility, he said, and if it happened, it would be violent. The West lied, he said; they lied about Albania, about Kosovo, and now they were interfering with Montenegro. "It's not their thing," he said. "This is the country of my forefathers."

Then he took my notebook and drew a map of Montenegro with marks for the locations of the Yugoslav soldiers. "We are ready," he said. "We are being told by Belgrade to be in our positions by Saturday night."

But by Saturday night, their plans had changed. The coup was off. Despite the fact that in a town like Herceg Novi, which had the highest percentage of ethnic Serbs, came out in force to vote, and that special units of Milosevic's Second Army, known as Gepards (Cheetahs), patrolled polling stations and harassed voters, Kostunica had taken the vote. The chain of events which would eventually lead to Milosevic's downfall had started.

A few days later, I drove toward Cetinje, to Archbishop Mihailo Dedeic's makeshift white church nestled in grove of pomegranate trees. It was a strange oasis in the middle of the madness: quiet, tranquil. Archbishop Dedeic, the metropolitan of the Montenegrin Orthodox Church, stood in the doorway, shielding his eyes from the sun.

"Are you looking for me?" he said softly. He was white-haired, tall, slender. "I think you are here to talk about my church." He smiled, moving away from the door to let me in.

Archbishop Dedeic's tiny church is a microcosm of the divisions that are tearing Monenegro apart. Like the Katunjani, he wants an independent Montenegro. But Dedeic is not so interested in politics as in the spiritual. He wants an independent Montenegrin Orthodox Church—separate from the traditional Serb version.

"In fact, we don't want to see the Serbian church split," said the priest. We sat in his office, decorated with two enormous national red and white flags of Montenegro and with wooden icons of St. Michael and St. George. It was hot, a fly was caught in the window. He tried to swat it away, then disappeared and came back with two glasses of ice water, which he set on his desk. "Because two separate churches have always existed."

It is a controversial view. Pre–World War I, the Montenegrin church was not recognized by the Patriarch of Constantinople. Following the war, when the Kingdom of Montenegro disappeared, the smaller church was amalgamated by the Serbian King Aleksandar Karadjordjevic into the Serb church. The Orthodox Church of Montenegro lay dormant until 1993. Father Dedeic wants to resurrect it.

His detractors are many. "I don't care," he says. He insisted that his church is growing, and that the 75 percent of the Montenegrin people who boycotted the Serbian elections and are in favor of independence are all his followers. "There are many people who want to see their own church, on their own soil."

The church schism mirrors the political schism. Father Dedeic and his followers—who he says constitute around 610 churches and 48 monasteries across the republic—no longer want to take the lead from Patriarch Pavle in Belgrade. "In every eastern country—Russia, Bulgaria, Greece—they have their own church. So why not Montenegro?" he asked. "The Serbian church wants to keep us so that they can have their Greater Serbia." He talked about his dreams for this separate church. He talked about the rights of the Montenegrin people. He talked about the saints in heaven. He became so passionate that his face grew red and he had to pause and drink water.

I left a few hours later, nearly driving over a cat asleep under my car. The heat of early autumn was fierce. Not far from Father Dedeic's start-up church was the grand fourteenth-century monastery of Cetinje, headed by Metropolitan Amfilohije. At the door, two young monks, Father Jovan and Father Ambrozije, burst out laughing when they heard where I had been.

"But now you must come have tea with us!" they said. "Because you have just had tea with a defrocked priest."

This was a very different place than the Montenegrin church with its simple white lines. The Orthodox Monastery of Cetinje was founded in 1484 and housed the first printing press in the Balkans. There were 61 priests and 150 sisters and nuns. Inside the monastery, along cool stone hallways, there were alcoves dimly lit by candles that illuminated ancient icons. Old women, Orthodox sisters, sold slender yellow candles, lit for intentions of both the living and the dead.

"Time passes slowly here," Father Jovan said. "But we do have the Internet."

"We are very modern," said Father Ambrozije. "We have a Web site, a radio station, we read everything we can get our hands on."

When the tea came, they talked about Archbishop Dedeic. "This Montenegrin Orthodox Church is a purely political concoction and should be treated as such," says Father Ambrozije, who spoke a strange, formal English that he learned in England when he converted to the Orthodox faith at St. Michael's Church in Essex. "The American Bill of Rights, the First Amendment, states that church and state should be separated. We believe the same thing."

Father Jovan took a biscuit. "Archbishop Dedeic is a Raskolnic, a breakaway heretic," he said faintly.

"He's only using religion as a smokescreen for a political agenda," added Father Ambrozije.

"First of all, Mihailo is not a priest. He was defrocked by the ecumenical patriarch of Constantinople for criminal deeds," Jovan sputtered. "And second, they formed this church on the street. It's the invention of two political parties. He doesn't have a following of the faithful; he has a following of supporters—like a football club."

The two monks fell silent.

I said, "You sound like politicians. Even religion is fractured."

"No, but it's true!" protested Ambrozije. "If someone in Britain declared themselves the Archbishop of Canterbury, would you believe them? There are nowhere near six hundred ten Montenegrin Orthodox churches. It's ridiculous. They don't legally exist. They have no churches, they have four priests. They have no power!"

The Montenegrin Orthodox Church is officially registered under law in Montenegro, while the Serbian Church never applied for registration. Except for a period during the NATO bombing when Patriarch Pavle guided the Serb people to take a stand against Milosevic, and urged them to seek a more peaceful solution, the Serbian Orthodox Church has refrained from politics. But they have always the backing of the wealthy, the influential.

Father Jovan and Father Ambrozije loathed Milosevic. "Right from the beginning, we backed Kostunica," Father Ambrozije said. "He was here, two weeks ago, giving a radio interview."

"It's not that we're against Montenegro becoming independent," added Jovan. "If the people of Montenegro want to go of their own will, we would not stop them. But it's an irrelevant question. All over Europe, countries are uniting. Here, they are trying to become these little statelets."

"Father Dedeic said most people who support free Montenegro support his church," I said.

"Well, he can believe whatever he wants," laughed Father Jovan. "If he makes up a church, I'm going to make up cartoons." He threw his hands up in the air in exasperation. "Monty Python's Flying Circus doesn't exist anymore, but if it did, this is it. What a country!"

He led me down the dark hallway, past the nuns and a woman on her knees with a lit candle in front of an icon, silently mouthing prayers for the living and the dead.

Chapter Four

I had come to Yugoslavia to see what history meant in flesh and blood.

—Rebecca West, *Black Lamb and Grey Falcon*

I am a Serbian, born to be a soldier
My brothers are numerous as grapes in the vineyard
But they are less fortunate than I, a son of free Serbia!
That I may hasten to help those who wait for me!

Ancient Serbian folk poem, taken from John Reed,
War in Eastern Europe

Serbia is badly wounded, physically and emotionally. It will last and last, this pain, because Serbs like to suffer. But this is the beginning of the end. The real end. Maybe something will finally happen, with an army or with civil war. Or Milosevic will finally go.

Ivana, 22, student at Belgrade University, June 24, 1999, the day after the Serbian Parliament declared an end to the war

The Road Between Pristina and Nis
June 12, 1999

The war has been over for three days. It's raining an oily rain which makes the road more slippery for the Serb tanks. They're steaming up the road, toward Serbia, camouflage still hanging off the sides. Some of them have flags—red, white, and blue—sticking out of their turrets.

The war lasted seventy-eight days. On June 9, against the wishes of the hard-line Serb element, Milosevic—who had once said, "Kosovo is not a part of Serbia. It is the very heart of Serbia"—capitulated to NATO. He signed a military agreement, and now the tanks and the soldiers are heading back to Serbia, along with a lot of confused and baffled Kosovar residents who fear the Albanians.

From where I sit, the war does not look over. The tanks still carry surface-to-air missiles, rockets, mortar launchers. The column stretches for miles north—through the flat roads, past fields of lavender just now in bloom, and peonies, the red flowers sprinkled all over Kosovo in the summer. The Serbs say these traditional flowers are symbolic of their spilled blood.

The soldiers are exhausted and angry. A young one jumps down to talk to me and take a cigarette. He tells me not to follow a retreating army: "There is too much disappointment." He climbs back onto the tank and waves, motions me to look south.

The village behind us is burning. The houses were torched as the army pulled out. Crater-size holes were punched through the walls. We drive through, slowly, and see the destruction: shops looted, a small grocery store with the windows smashed and the goods grabbed, an old kerchiefed woman sitting in front on top of shards of glass, quietly weeping.

Milosevic tried to pretend the end was not entirely humiliating. It was clear from the beginning that the Yugoslav Army could not win against NATO. Only 2 NATO planes were lost while more than 100 of the Serbs' aircraft were destroyed. More dangerous was the fact that NATO's air force had become the KLA's air force, and as the war progressed, the KLA gathered both strength and numbers. Its bases in northern Albania grew; the Serbs could not destroy them.

But the Serbs' biggest fear was a realistic one. They believed NATO would invade them, and in fact, NATO's military planners were drawing up plans for an invasion which would be launched either from Greece, Albania, Macedonia, or Hungary. When NATO began to turn its sights from an air war to a ground war, Milosevic realized he had to back down. There was no way he could withstand a ground war without thousands of civilian casualties.

And so the Serbian leader consoled his nation with the words "We did not give up Kosovo." His men had fought bravely. And by leading this extensive column of tanks and hardware out of Kosovo and back into Serbia, he was also showing that NATO had lied about the damage the Serbs had suffered. A minimal amount of hardware had actually been damaged.

To the Serbs, a retreat did not necessarily mean the end of their fight. They had retreated before: In Kosovo Polje in 1389; from Kosovo again in 1690; from Serbia in 1915; Western Slavonia in 1991; the Krajina in 1995; and in Serb-held Sarajevo in 1996. Lazar's martyrdom in 1389, rather than humiliating and debasing, inspired the Serbs. The poem that depicts the battle, in which the prophet Elijah, disguised as a falcon, offers Lazar the choice of either winning the battle and taking an earthly kingdom or losing and opting for heaven, is a Serb classic. Lazar chose the latter, erecting a church instead of urging his army forward.

> The Tsar chose a heavenly kingdom
> and not an earthly kingdom
> He built a church on Kossovo
> Then he gave his soldiers the Eucharist
> Then the Turks overwhelmed Lazar
> And his army was destroyed with him,
> Of seven and seventy thousand soldiers.
>
> All was holy, all was honorable
> And the goodness of God was fulfilled.[1]

In 1999, the Serbs saw the retreat from NATO as another noble sacrifice. "My troops protected the rights of all minorities inside Kosovo," General Nebojsa Pavkovic—who had commanded the 180,000 troops of Yugoslavia's Third Army during the campaign, overseeing all the military campaigns inside Kosovo—would later tell me. "We saw ourselves as peacekeeping forces, preserving peace and guaranteeing safety for all nations."

Pavkovic said his men had fought bravely given the circumstances, that they were being pounded by thousands of planes. The Serb losses, he said, amounted to 161 casualties; 13 tanks; 8 transport vehicles; 3 cannons; 10 antiaircraft weapons; 5 or 6 army vehicles. More important, he said NATO expected them to surrender within "two or three days, and that all the Albanians would rise up, and NATO would slip into the country easily." "That was their plan," Pavkovic said, "But we held back. We managed to prevent attacks from northern Albania. We organized ourselves. My men fought well."

Therefore, signing the military agreement—which from the Serb point of view guaranteed the sovereignty of Kosovo, the protection of Serb civilians, and promised there would be no referendum in Kosovo—did not necessarily mean the Serbs had lost the war. "We did not lose," he said. "I am convinced we had a moral and military victory. Signing the military agreement is our way of handing a domestic problem over to the U.N." The UCK, he said, were an unruly, disorganized bunch of fighters who were no longer the Serbs' problem, but NATO's.

"We'll be back within a year," Pavkovic predicted somberly. "They won't be able to handle the Albanians."

Pavkovic also said there were no paramilitary units inside Kosovo. What was there, he said, were special police forces or antiterrorist units. Whoever they were, they were not retreating like noble soldiers. While the younger men in the Yugoslav Army were already thinking of how quickly they could get to the beach in Montenegro, the paramilitary were angry.

Pavkovic had effectively ordered them out. They went home in vans and minibuses with painted grafitti like BORN TO KILL on the side. For them, it was no NATO victory. They said they would be back as soon as NATO left the region. To make sure people got their message, they began to burn, loot, and gut buildings.

I drove through a string of villages along the path of retreat. Each one was different, all of them eerie, almost apocalyptic. There were no commanding officers, just soldiers who had lost and were running wild. In Glavnik, there was a stereo shop displaying Tito-era radios and phonographs. The glass was cracked by a rock and three soldiers yanked out equipment. Near a café, blackened and hollowed by fire, glass was splattered like blood. Outside were four young soldiers, wearing bandannas and faded combat trousers. They smoked cigarettes and drank from a cloudy bottle of loza, a plum brandy that is a common peasant drink. One pulled out a tin of lighter fluid. He doused a baby pram someone had left behind. The carriage was empty, but it shot up in flames, the blue baby blanket catching fire and sending a column of smoke up toward the sky. The soldiers laughed and laughed, passing the loza bottle.

In Podujevo, a town close to Serbia renowned for its Albanian resistance, four NATO jeeps crawled through the town trying to convince Albanians to come out of their hiding places, from the cellars and closed rooms where they had hidden for weeks. When they emerged, emaciated, cheeks sunken, they blinked in the sunlight. Then they began to cheer the NATO jeeps, scratching in the dirt for wildflowers and throwing them at the soldiers.

The buildings were still smoking from the fires that had been lit, and every window of every storefront had been broken. There were no leaves on the trees in the central square. They had been burnt. The only shop that had not been completely looted was a hairdresser's, where the pale-skinned mannequin was modeling a brunet wig.

One hour before NATO arrived, a blue-uniformed Serb policeman had smashed the window with a brick, then pulled all the hair dryers from the sockets. While the town was burning, NATO representatives stood outside and argued with Serb soldiers about the time that they were allowed to enter. Every time the NATO commander mentioned "freedom of movement"—allegedly part of NATO's mandate—the Serbs burst out laughing.

Jeva stood back from the crowd cheering NATO. She was not throwing flowers, laughing, or calling out to the jeeps. Were these people completely stupid? she whispered. She had come down from the mountains, where she had slept for four weeks. Her clothes were ripped and her face was dirty. "They're still here," she said in a voice so low that I had to lean closer. "The policemen. Serbs."

Jeva led me above the town, up the hill, to a position once inhabited by the UCK. Now, instead, a Serb tank was still dug into the forest and several soldiers sat behind a sandbagged machine-gun position. The muzzle of their heavy machine gun pointed toward the mountains, the direction they were looking. They did not see us.

Around the tank, the houses were smashed. There were no people, only a starving dog on the dirt road.

Jeva found her house, near Lapastica, a few kilometers away. It was destroyed. As she looked at the shattered windows and broken-down door, she spoke quietly, giving her own catalogue of the war: a story of a twenty-year-old girl who had been abducted by Serb soldiers the day before; of an alleged massacre in Koliq in which 90 people were killed; of her son, a UCK fighter, whom she had not seen in days.

"Can we go to his command?" she asked. We drove to the top of the village, past the tank, in the direction where the machine gun was pointing. The site was abandoned.

"He was here a few days ago," Jeva said, climbing out of the car. She did not seem to be aware of any personal danger, of mines, of snipers, or booby traps. She kicked a pile of rotted leaves, a few tins of food that had been opened. "He was sleeping here, living here. Where is he?"

I told her we had to leave. The position was not safe. She argued that she would stay behind, this was the last place her son had been. We convinced her to get in the car, but she sat silently, staring out the window. At the bottom of the hill, a Serbian policemen stopped the car. He peered inside.

"Get out," he said, seeing Albanians. He grabbed my arm and yanked. Jeva shrank deep into her seat. Her face visibly paled under the dirt. Our interpreter, Dejan, who came from Belgrade, calmly climbed out of the car. He took the policeman aside. Dejan offered a cigarette. They quietly smoked and talked about how ineffective NATO was. They talked about football.

Jeva did not listen. She turned her face away from the window and tried to bury herself in the seat. Dejan came and tapped on the window.

"Everything's cool," he said. "Nothing can happen."

Jeva shook violently. "Everything can happen," she said.

After twenty minutes, the policemen was given a pack of Marlboro Reds and $20. He let us pass. We dropped Jeva back at the place where her house had been. We asked if we could leave her with a friend, a neighbor, rather than here, alone. We offered to drive her back to Pristina, if it was easier.

She shook her head. "Leave me," she said. Her quiet voice had already gone dead. "My son will be home soon. I have to make him his dinner. There are so many things I have to do."

In Belgrade, there is a canvas depicting Patriarch Arsenije Carnoje-vic, flanked by a Serbian flag, leading an exodus of tens of thousands of Serbs. The year was 1690 and the Serbs, along with the Austrians, had just been crushed by the Turks. In the painting, their leader is guiding the mothers, the children, the fighters away from their homes in Old Serbia—Kosovo—and into exile. Some three centuries later, during the Balkan wars of 1912–13, hundreds of thousands of Serbs would also flee across the southern Balkans. The pattern of migration would continue, in 1995, when the Croats drove more than 100,000 Serbs into exile from the Krajina.

Six months before the new millennium, the Serbs were again fleeing Old Serbia. They were packed inside their Yugos and Volks-wagens, their oxcarts and their farm tractors, with things they loved crushed inside in boxes or strapped to their roofs. Pets, washing machines, satellite dishes, baskets of produce. Some of them draped Serbian flags from their cars.

They were trying to reach Belgrade, a four-hour drive, by night-fall. The NATO commander, Sir Michael Jackson, had given a speech to the Serbs in Kosovo Polje, promising to protect them. No one believed him. Whether or not they had been there when their Albanian neighbors' houses were torched or looted was irrelevant.

"We are no longer safe there," Irena, a forty-two-year-old secre-tary, told me. "It is no longer a place for Serbs."

Most of them did not get to Belgrade by nightfall. Milosevic, fearing an uprising if the population saw these refugees as symbols of his defeat, ordered the capital cordoned off and police checkpoints set up to keep them out. *Politika*, the largest Serbian newspaper—and Milosevic's unofficial mouthpiece—and Tanjug, the state wire service, claimed the refugees were safe and the situation in Pristina was under control. But it was far from that.

Meanwhile, Belgrade was swiftly moving into a postwar euphoria. Nobody seemed to care that they had lost. The STOP THE BOMB signs were coming down and a concert with the British violinist Nigel Kennedy was being planned. Everyone was fed up with war and hardship. The sight of the Kosovar Serbs sleeping in the park and protesting in front of the Parliament building was a toxic reminder. Milosevic feared the explosive effect they could have and chose to ignore them.

"The government is afraid of their appearance," Slobodan Vuksanovic, a member of the Democratic Party, the Serbian political opposition, said grimly.

Outside Prokupje, as the military hardware gathered, more than 200 Kosovar Serbs also assembled, waiting in the hot sun for police to check their documents, open their suitcases, and search through their baskets of food. After several hours, they were told to go home to Pristina, Prizren, or Pec, cities that had just been taken by the KLA hours before. When they protested that they were going to families in Belgrade, they were told to shut up. When they tried to buy gasoline to finish their journey north, they were refused.

Vuksanovic believed there were 6,000 Serbs from Kosovo trapped somewhere on the road. It was these displaced people, not NATO, he said, who were the "the main enemy of the Milosevic regime." One of the enemies was a middle-aged mother from Prizren clutching the hand of her teenage daughter. Another was an older man with a straw sun hat held by a string around his neck. A third was a young family—father, mother, and three children—silently staring at a police officer who was supposed to be on their side but who told them to go back to Prizren.

"Do you know what is happening in Prizren now?" the mother said, her voice beginning to grow shrill with desperation. "Serbs are being marched on the street. They will be *killing* them tonight."

"NATO will protect you," the policeman said sarcastically. "Go home."

"Milosevic said he would protect us," the woman shot back. "Where is he now? Safe in Belgrade. *We're* the ones who are in danger."

"You're not getting past this line," the policeman said. "Go home."

But the family could not go home. So they stayed, waiting, until the sun ceased being so hot, and they put on nylon anoraks that they had brought; until it was past the time for the children's supper, and they gave them some apples and some cheese; until it was time for bed and the children were whimpering quietly. Then, like the other people lined up by the side of the road, they put their heads down on suitcases as if they were pillows and tried to sleep.

No one was sure how many displaced Serbs were coming over the border. In Kraljevo, the council counted nearly 2,000 sleeping in the local park. The Red Cross, trying to determine the number that had left Kosovo, counted roughly 30,000; the Democratic Party—which had a vested interest in shaming Milosevic—claimed it was 50,000. The United Nations High Commissioner for Refugees (UNHCR), who could not really get involved because it was not a cross-border displacement, could only account for 17,000 Serb civilians who had tried to cross into Montenegro since June 9.

An exhausted U.N. officer said she had no idea how many had followed the retreating army, but knew that they were not getting the care, the food, and the protection that they should. "They're Serbs," she said. "The world never feels the sympathy that they should feel for them. Look what happened to the Krajina Serb refugees. No one gave a damn. They're still in refugee centers."

These were Serbs, losers, defeated. But the smell in Kraljevo, the miserable smell of too many people camped in a place with not enough water or sanitation, was the same as that of the Albanians in Kukes or the Bosnians in Travnik. The sound of wailing kids separated from parents and shell-shocked mothers sitting in a corner unable to speak.

So what if they were Serbs, if they had believed that Kosovo was theirs and that Milosevic would never leave them? Just yesterday there was a war, but they were the safe ones, the protected ones. Now they were part of the largest refugee population in Europe: during the course of the ten-year war cycle, 600,000 Serbs from all over the former Yugoslavia had flocked to Serbia for protection.

Kosovo was the last stand. A long time ago, Milosevic had told them that no one would ever beat them. But sleeping outside, unable to go home or to go forward to Belgrade, they were beaten. They were the enemy. Overnight, the country that they lived in had ceased being theirs.

Pristina
The First Week of Peace
June 10–17, 1999

The generals had officially declared peace, but the Serbs still had eight more days to withdraw. Eight more days to get a last bit of fighting in, eight more days to do some collateral damage.

"Every (Serbian) peasant soldier knows what he is fighting for," John Reed wrote during World War I. "When he was a baby his mother greeted him, 'Hail, little avenger of Kossovo!'" But the avengers of Kosovo were pulling out, and the ones who stayed behind were armed. At night, they began shooting: in front of Pristina's Grand Hotel; in the western suburbs; near the wooden stalls that had formerly housed tailors and cobblers.

It was a strange time, between war and peace, in Pristina. The early-summer weather shifted. Sometimes a pale and listless sun came out, but mostly it drizzled, and then it was cold and the fog made the darkness fall quickly.

It was not a bad thing, the darkness, because it shrouded the damaged city, the bombed sites, the gangs of tattered people who roamed the streets either looking for their houses or relatives, or looking to rob someone. Even before the bombing, Pristina had been gray and ugly: dull, dirty, uninspiring. A Tito-inspired cubist design gone mad; the Grand Hotel with its dark lobby usually inhabited by Serb secret police; the ugly, sprawling sports complex; the Eastern-block-style university.

Unlike Sarajevo, Belgrade, Zagreb, even Podgorica, Pristina has the feel of an unloved, unattractive stepsister. It has the same sense of forlorn misery that Kosovo's western neighbor—and for all practical purposes, their *patron*—Albania does. Shqipena, Land of the Eagle, as its called in Albanian.

Whether or not the KLA want to admit it, they share blood and history with Albania, in much the same way the Bosnian Croats living in Herzegovina have a certain loyalty to Croatia, or Bosnian

Serbs do to Belgrade. Descended from Illyrian tribes, the Albanians allegedly came to the Balkan Peninsula before the Greeks did, more than a thousand years before the Slavs.

By the time the Great Power intercession in 1913 resulted in the creation of an independent Albanian state—without the Muslim province of Kosovo, which the Serbs took for themselves—the Turks, the Serbs, the Greeks, the Bulgarians, had all invaded Albania. The land and the people have the air of a country that has been over-run and dominated to the point of surrender.

Following the invasion of the Serbian troops into Albania proper in 1914, the Albanians welcomed the Habsburg Austro-Hungarian troops, seeing them as friends. When they were defeated, and the Austro-Hungarian Empire was carved up and dissolved, the Albanians were once again alone and at the mercy of conquering armies. Fascist Italy invaded them in April 1939, and one year later the Greek Prime Minister Ioannis Metaxas announced that his forces would fight to regain parts of Greece and conquer Albania.

After Mussolini fell, Nazis controlled Albania, and the mainly Communist resistance, led by Enver Hoxha, fought them. Following the war—with 7.3 percent of the population either dead or crippled—Hoxha took over a starving, broken country and guided it into a period of isolation, fearing not only the Americans and Europe, but the Russians, the Bulgarians, and anyone else vaguely threatening. The result was a paranoid and terrified population that had no knowledge of the world outside Albania.

Next door, Tito had placed the neighboring province of Kosovo, with its largely Albanian population, under the jurisdiction of the Republic of Serbia, one of the six states of Yugoslavia. But the ethnic mix was often fractious. Throughout the 1960s, '70s, and '80s, tension between the Serbs and the Albanians increased, and finally erupted when Milosevic revoked Kosovo's autonomy in 1989. It was only a matter of time before it spread to all-out war. Throughout the Bosnian conflict, Muslim commanders frequently remarked that the next conflict would be further south, in Kosovo.

By the end of the second millennium, the war everyone had predicted had happened, and it had left the country empty and dark, wounded and defensive. Pristina, seething with revenge, had a stale smell to it. People locked themselves inside. Everyone was warned to stay off the streets until the last armed men had left. The air seemed thick and yellow, unhealthy to breathe.

Houses were booby-trapped by the retreating Serbs, and units of British soldiers were sent to deactivate them. "Do not go into your houses until we have checked them," they shouted in Albanian through bullhorns to the crowds of people who watched them go in and out of the destroyed shacks, and emerge with grenades, home-made bombs, and guns.

People did go out to shop, but hurried home quickly with their eggs and their thick white bread under one arm, the other clutching their handbags for fear of robbery. Gradually, there were more chil-dren on the street; the Zenel Hajdani primary school, named after a World War II hero, opened, even if the windows were broken and someone had crossed out the Serbian symbol and replaced it with UCK. But parents walked their children to and from classes, clasping their hands tightly, making them wait until the teacher arrived before leaving them alone.

As people waited for the arrival of the UCK in Pristina, their sta-tus as fighters and visionaries seemed to grow to mythic proportions. In Vranjevac, a suburb, teenagers who had just returned from Mace-donian refugee camps wore red armbands that spelled out GURILJA along with odd baseball hats from McDonalds that someone had dis-tributed in the camps. They spent hours, first picking, then spread-ing, pink rose petals to spell out in enormous letters UCK on the street pavement.

Although none of them had actually seen the UCK in action, they had heard stories every night in the camps. To them, the sol-diers took on vast dimensions and heroic forms. They were capable of destroying entire platoons of Serbs with just a few units of brave men. They could blow up indestructible tanks by dropping grenades down the turret. Or, the planes that dropped the bombs that eventu-ally crushed the Serbs were in fact secretly flown by UCK command-ers. My interpreter, Xevi, who had seen the UCK in action in northern Albania, smirked. "They're in for a big disappointment when they actually see these losers," he said.

A few days later, the illusive UCK drove into town. One morning the rumor circulated among the crowds loitering near the Grand Hotel, and by afternoon, they had arrived, from Tirana, Geneva, and

Germany. Jakup Krasniqi, the KLA's political spokesman, who had been virtually invisible in the past, set himself up in a freshly painted hilltop villa with an iron gate and bodyguards.

That same day, KLA fighters who were supposed to be disarming surrounded a Serb monastery in Prizren, where 200 to 300 Serb civilians, including the town's bishop and monks, were hiding. One of Krasniqi's bodyguards, a heavy-set man with a cracked leather jacket, idly kicked a soccer ball while we waited to speak with his boss. "The shoe is on the other foot," he said snidely, referring to the Serbs.

"But they're civilians. They're inside a church."

He said, "We had civilians too. They put them in graves."

Krasniqi kept us waiting for a while with the now silent and angry bodyguard. When he emerged from his new office, he looked weary and apprehensive, older than his forty-eight years. He had spent ten years in a Serbian prison, and it showed.

He led us inside a room full of unpacked boxes and a hand-painted sign that read UCK (KLA) in black and red, and said he was waiting for his chief, Hashim Thaci, to arrive. The walls smelled of fresh paint. The whole place, like the KLA itself, which was trying to turn from a fractured guerrilla operation into a legitimate governing body, seemed embryonic.

Krasniqi sat down at his bare desk. His new chair creaked under his weight. A bodyguard brought coffee on a tray, along with packets of sugar and cookies from Turkey. "Everything is new," he said. "And challenging. We are very young."

Even if Krasniqi's presence was an attempt to show that the KLA wanted to move away from its shadowy origins, he was still evasive. He would not answer questions directly. He had no explicit vision for the future. He dismissed Ibrahim Rugova, the former Kosovar Albanian leader who had been under Serbian house arrest during the war and then exiled to Rome by Milosevic with his entire family. "He is out of the picture completely. We don't want to work with him or the people around him," he said shortly.

As for divisions within the KLA, such as the rival faction led by Bujar Bukoshi, Krasniqi had no comment. Then he spoke. "He lost credibility," he said. There was another awkward pause. He would not elaborate on how the KLA planned to turn a group of freedom fighters into a government. Or how they were going to work with NATO or the U.N.

"We will work in accordance with them," he said. Then he dropped his voice. "We *will* make it work." He sounded desperate and, for the first time, more human. "We have to make it work."

But exactly how they were going to do it remained unclear. The KLA had fought for an independent Kosovo, not for an autonomous Kosovo. While Krasniqi said they would settle for something in the middle—a two- or three-year protectorate—it was clear that the people would eventually want to choose their fate in a referendum.

"It's a long way from peace," he said as he showed me to the door.

Eighteen months later, when I would return to Pristina, the KLA would have shiny new offices, fax machines, and e-mail addresses. Hashim Thaci, who during the war and for a few months after had given himself the title Prime Minister of the Temporary Kosovo Government, was now leader of his party, the PDK, or Democratic Party of Kosovo. Local elections had just taken place. One year later, they would be followed by general elections.[2]

But the U.N. Mission to Kosovo (UNMIK) was running the country. And Krasniqi was right, peace had not yet come to Kosovo. That winter, KFOR (international peace-keeping forces in Kosovo) was working with the Serb military to curb activities of a new ethnic-Albanian militia, the UCPMB, the Liberation Army of Presevo, Medvedja, and Bujanovac, which claimed to represent 70,000 ethnic Albanians living in southern Serbia, near Kosovo. This was a new conflict, not to be confused with the old one. In this battle, there were nearly 2,500 heavily armed UCPMB fighters who had declared war on the Serbs and KFOR, who were sent to disarm them.

The new Balkan flashpoint was the remote Presevo Valley southeast of Pristina, largely inhabited by Albanians. The area technically lay within the boundaries of Serbia, but the sovereignty had been contested since the 1999 United Nations Security Council Resolution 1244 declared it a buffer zone and out of bounds to Yugoslav forces.

But the Albanians had been building up arms for months—believed to have come from old KLA supplies—and attacking Serb civilians and burning them out of their houses. The lightly armed Serbian police, the MUP, who were allowed in the buffer zone, had shown restraint until November, when Albanian rebels killed four Serb policemen and seized several villages in the area.

General Pavkovic's warning to me at the end of the war—that the army would return—was becoming more and more prophetic, even if they had not stormed back one year later. The new Serbian president, Vojislav Kostunica, growing increasingly frustrated with the Albanians' hit-and-run tactics against Serb civilians, was demanding that the buffer zone be narrowed so the area could be "cleansed" of Albanian rebels.

The concern was that the Serbs, who had conceded during the NATO war, would not sit tight and allow KFOR to do their job. The fear was that the VJ—or worse, paramilitary—would move in if there was compelling evidence of atrocities against Serbian civilians.

The Presevo Valley, which lay between Nis and Macedonia, was an important supply route for the Serbs, and they needed it. They also had to protect their civilians for purposes of morale. The Serbian people, so recently humiliated in Kosovo, were furious. At the same time, the West was urging them to restrain themselves. Zoran Djindic, the new Serbian prime minister, grimly admitted that "the situation in Southern Serbia had potential for a new Balkans war."

For Kostunica, only two months into his new role and facing midterm elections, it was a delicate time. The last thing he needed was a conflict with the West that he had so recently drawn to his side, but he had to reassure the Serbs that they would not be pushed around by the Albanians.

"We face problems," Kostunica said on Serb television, attempting to calm the public. "Before our domestic public, and even before history, whether or not the Albanian terrorists will remain in the ground safety zone or not. We cannot let them stay."

In December 2000 the British KFOR forces, the First Battalion of the Princess of Wales's Royal Regiment, were deployed in the area. Technically, this place was under American KFOR control. But the Americans had been criticized for their earlier heavy-handed handling of the situation: roughly searching civilians at checkpoints and trying to cover their insecurity in a foreign country with an aggressive cowboy stance. Most of the 150 Brits had come from serving in Northern Ireland. They were skilled in difficult terrain, and their confidence was reassuring to locals.

"It's nothing drastic, it's just that we have a sensible approach," explained Lieutenant Colonel Stephen Kilpatrick, who was leading the operation and trying to avoid a potential conflict with the Americans.

The Brits were efficient, and it did not take them long to defuse the situation. From their base at Camp Sobroan in the Ostravica Hills—a few freezing-cold tents scattered with hay for a bit of warmth on top of a windy hill—they broke down into teams of four to monitor trails and set up observation posts. They flew a Union Jack and called the miserable place "Camp Bastard." The rebels were believed to be less than 1 kilometer from their base, and the roads and trails were heavily mined.

Within days of arriving, the British had cut off the rebels' food and arms supply. One freezing night close to Christmas, they caught 13 Albanian rebels moving down mountains roads in cars and tractors near Draghibac Mahala, and intercepted uniforms and a cache of weapons that included AK-47s, grenades, rocket launchers, anti-tank mines, and machine guns. The Americans, who had been unable to control the situation and had been caught in a skirmish along with Russian KFOR troops a few days earlier, were deeply embarrassed. They tried to claim some of the credit.

The front line, a village called Lucane, had the two sides, Albanians and Serbs, separated by sandbagged positions only 100 yards apart. They were fighting from the same broken-down villas, from the same sniper positions with the same packs of unfiltered cigarettes lying around, with the same rusty guns that I had watched eighteen months earlier. But this time, they were fighting over three towns in a three-mile demilitarized zone.

"We got some of the rebels, but in the big picture, Kosovo hasn't really gotten very far in terms of peace," said a Brit one night near Camp Sobroan, setting up a gas cooker to make tea. "It's not that people don't want it; it just seems too far out of reach."

In Pristina, the other KLA commanders I had known on the front lines were not so concerned with Presevo as with jockeying for power in their petty administrative jobs. Their police forces were littered with corruption, and with Albanian thugs returned from living abroad for years, where they specialized in stealing cars and smuggling cigarettes. Worse, Serbs in Pristina were still in fear for their lives, and it seemed as though the damage that had been done during the war would take generations to heal. It was clear to me that these people could not live together.

One morning, I visited the Illeria School in southeast Pristina, which was being guarded by a group of British soldiers. There had been reports of Albanian children being kidnapped, and there was still violence in the area. We arrived in an armored personnel carrier. KFOR had recently installed fencing around the school, and inside, the director of the school, Mahmut Breca, told me that the boiler was broken and that until they got DEM 75,000 the children would not have heat.

Before the war, the school had been divided between Serb and Albanian children, both of whom studied under the Serbian system. In 1990, the use of the Albanian language was banned, and while it was taught privately, or spoken at home, the children and teachers were beaten if it was used in the schools. Now, of the 280 children, none were Serbian, and classes—biology, mathematics, literature—were taught in Albanian.

Nearly all of the children were deeply traumatized. Breca went through the classrooms, picking a few of them out to be interviewed, and led them and me into his cold office.

"The problem is, if they see a soldier in a uniform, they get very upset," he said quietly, closing the door. "It took a while for them to get used to KFOR. Now they feel safer with them here. They are still afraid of the Serbs."

The children's stories were predictably horrible. Some did not want to talk, although Breca urged them to speak: "The world has to know what happened to the Albanian people," he said. A British soldier and I grew more and more uncomfortable as one of the children, twelve-year-old Osman, grew visibly upset. He lost his mother in the war. Another boy had hidden with his mother while he saw his father being killed. Another, Ramsi, eleven years old, was witness to his mother and grandmother being "massacred." A thirteen-year-old girl named Donika had lost her beloved brother. So did Blerim, along with other members of his family.

It was a disturbing experience, mainly because all of the children had expressed fear and hatred for Serbs while at the same time desiring a free Kosovo "cleared" of Serbs. For years, I had worked with children in the West Bank and Gaza, listened to their stories and watched them draw pictures of Israeli soldiers leading away their fathers in the middle of the night, or of being bombed by helicopter gunships. The difference was that usually there was some redeeming factor, that no matter how much fear they expressed, they—or their mothers—usually had some story of an Israeli friend or a desire to live in a peaceful land where all could have their own homes.

These children were different. They had been so badly beaten, they said, that they never wanted to see Serbs, good or bad, again. In the afternoon, the British soldiers took me to the center of town where four of them were guarding the Orthodox church the Albanians had frequently threatened to burn down as a symbol of their past repression. Inside, the interior of the once-grand church was freezing, damp, and musty. The Brits were living in a tent in a corner and had rigged up electricity from a generator and installed a small gym with free weights. They had a small Christmas tree in the corner and were watching *Good Will Hunting* on a small video machine. Nearly every night, they intercepted Albanian vandals who had come to destroy the church. The week before, a building 150 meters away had been set on fire. Had the soldiers not been there, the place would have been demolished.

Before the war, there were roughly 45,000 Serbs in Pristina. By December 2000, there were between 600 and 700. About 180 of them were moved to a ghetto, a grim apartment complex known as Dardanija.

The British soldiers from the Royal Marines 415th Commando Group were trying to set up programs so that the Serbs could live safely and securely in the city, but it was an impossible task. The Serbs needed to be guarded twenty-four hours a day and escorted by soldiers if they wanted to buy a pint of milk or visit a doctor.

Their lives were hell. Going to a club or bar in downtown Pristina that they had frequented most of their lives would now be suicidal; their children had to be bused to Gracanica to go to school. If they fell ill and went to an Albanian hospital, "they would either be ignored or harassed," said one of the British soldiers. There had been a rocket attack the week before, two minutes after a guard changed shifts.

"The Albanians know this is where the Serbs live, and we are a target for extremists," said Diana, a geological engineer who had moved to Dardanija after her flat in the center of town got targeted one too many times by Albanians. The electricity didn't always work in the complex, but at least there was water, and she felt safer than she had in downtown Pristina. She would leave, she said, but she had nowhere to go. "I am staying," she told me miserably, "because I have to feed my children."

The Brits were trying hard to get a dentist into the compound, and had installed a $55,000 closed-circuit television, mainly as a psychological deterrent. "It's not one hundred percent," said one, "unless you put an entire brigade in here to protect them." That clearly was not going to happen, and the Dardanija residents were vulnerable.

"We have to be lucky all the time. The bad guys only have to be lucky once," Major Dave Wilson from the 415th Commando Group said. But the Dardanija residents were luckier than the rest of the Serbs, who were scattered throughout Pristina and had to be checked every forty-eight hours to ensure they were not massacred. Here, at least, the crime rate had been reduced by 55 percent since the British troops arrived.

Diana had a pretty nice life as a Serb in Kosovo before the war. She took it for granted that she had a job, money, a decent apartment. At Coalfields, the mining company, she had a senior position and a good salary. For someone who had been independent and had worked all her life, she was finding the situation increasingly impossible, mainly on the psychological level. She could not work, and had to rely on NGOs to feed herself and her family.

There was a small community center in Dardanija where she spent part of the day trying to help other Serbs. The Brits had tried to make it cheerful and had set up a satellite TV, a pool table, and a stereo. But the Serbs sat listlessly, drinking coffee, staring at the walls and waiting for the next attack. And it pained Diana to see that the director of the center was her old boss at Coalfields, Radomir Kovatic, a man who was a highly skilled engineer and manager. Now his job was making sure people did not argue over the satellite television channels.

One of the soldiers said he would drop me at my guest house. I had chosen to stay there to avoid the Albanian creeps at the Grand

Hotel, and also the gloom which never seemed to go away. But my guest house was no better. There were no mafiosi, but there was only intermittent electricity and heat. One minute I would be reading a book on my bed; the next minute I would be plunged into freezing darkness. Like everything in Pristina, light and heat were casualties of the broken-down system.

On the way to the guest house, the soldier had to stop and make a delivery of medicine to an Albanian family. He said it would take five minutes. They were living in an underground bomb shelter.

We climbed up a hill and down a rancid passage, and there they were, five of them. They had left their apartment in Pristina during the bombing and driven their car to Macedonia. When they got back, the apartment was gone. Torched.

Underground, they lived like rats, with no air. They got water in buckets from the nearby Catholic church, and the smell inside was unbearable: like old clothes, like vomit, like damp, putrid air.

The father, Rexh, was fifty-seven and a former engineer in Pristina's energy plant, so he had rigged up some primitive lighting that hung from the exposed pipes overhead. But he was ill with a liver condition and spent most of the day lying on a cot under a damp duvet. His two daughters, who were twelve and seventeen, sat nearby with their mother, Nepe, a former teacher, and stared at their hands.

They had a radio, which was like a ray of hope inside their cave, and had somehow managed to drag their refrigerator from their burnt apartment. They had no electricity, but they stored their few provisions inside it. The twelve-year old showed it to me proudly, as though it were the last symbol of their old life.

Her mother, having a lot of time on her hands, said she thought back often and remembered the old days of repression and misery under the Serbs. She did not think the two groups could live together again. "It's too hard."

Her husband coughed from his bed. She glanced over, concerned. Almost as an afterthought, she said, "But still we have to try."

Suzanna had come to Pristina as soon as she heard the Russians were at the airport. She woke up thinking, The war is over. She came from the refugee camp where she was living with her mother and her little sister, never thinking she would be so happy to hear that Russians had invaded her city. When she was young, she was forced to learn Russian at school. She hated the fact that she lived in a Communist country that looked east, not west. She wanted to live in Europe and buy Levi's and CDs. She didn't want to study boring Marxist ideology.

Suzanna didn't have much to pack. She drove over the Kosovo border, the same one she had passed over nearly three months before. On the road, driving through valleys, she thought she smelled death, thought she smelled bodies everywhere in the villages that she passed. But she was still joyful, she was going home. She wanted to enter her old apartment. She did not know what she would find, or how she would get in. She went with a friend who had a hammer.

But before that she went to the café where her friend had died. She walked there slowly. As she got closer, she felt her head pounding. She pushed herself to go faster.

The café was still there, still a wreckage of glass, blood, and broken, overturned furniture. No one had touched it. In one corner was her handbag, left behind when the rescue workers pulled her from the scene. And next to her bag was her hair. Clumps of her long hair that she was so proud of. She stared at the pools of dried blood that no one had bothered to remove, at the clump of her scalp. Then she began to scream.

Suzanna grabbed whatever she could, and smashed it. It was the only thing that made her feel better and made the rage subside. She thought of her friend, of the professor who had met her that night to talk about theater, about the other people who had died just because they wanted a cup of coffee. She screamed so hard that her stomach hurt. She was hurling pieces of brick when a NATO soldier passing by grabbed her.

She screamed at him, "Leave me alone! You don't know why I'm doing this! My best friend died in here!"

The soldier held on to her and spoke softly. Later, Suzanna would say that he seemed like a kind man. She started to cry, to really cry, for the first time since the war began. She sat on the ground in the middle of the rubble while the soldier tried to calm her. Finally, she got up and began to walk home.

"I didn't want to calm down," she said later.

She did not want to forget the rawness that she felt. If she did, if she lost her anger, the whole act of evil that had killed her friend would be justified.

She was still crying when she reached her apartment. She did not need the hammer. The lock was untouched, and even though she thought she might need her gas mask, the one her cousin gave her in Kosare, to go inside, the place was clean. Her Serb neighbors had watched the place, making sure no one looted it.

"They were good neighbors," she said. She couldn't hate all the Serbs.

Inside, everything was exactly as she and her mother had left it on March 25. In the corner was the Versace dress, the one she loved and that she had been wearing the night of the attack. It was in a heap on the floor. She picked it up. It was covered with blood, rust-colored blotches that would probably never come out. She threw the dress back on the ground.

The war had passed, but nothing was touched in her apartment. The jewelry and old books she and her mother had hidden were still intact. The food in the refrigerator had gone bad when the electricity had been turned off. It was a little bit dustier, but it was fine.

She turned and went out the door, locking it behind her. She caught a ride back to Tirana. She didn't want to stay there, to sleep in her own bed. She did not want to stay in Pristina, not yet. It doesn't feel right, she thought. It doesn't feel safe yet.

Those initial postwar mornings were the same: misty, gray-colored, confused. Crowds of Albanians gathered outside the Grand Hotel either searching for someone or looking for work or money. In the first few days, there were a few Serbs. Later, they disappeared.

On the anniversary of the battle of Kosovo Polje, June 28, the day that Serb knights had marched onto the Kosovo plain with armor engraved in gold, ready to take on the Turks, there was not one single Serb civilian attending a celebration. In Kosovo Polje, the dusty, hot streets of the town were empty. It looked like the film set of a Western that had been cleared by Clint Eastwood. The cafés, the restaurants, the bars, were locked up. Some dried brush flew down the road.

A few weeks before, I had driven through, and the single vehicle I saw was a car jammed with suitcases, the driver veering down the road as though he could not get away fast enough. The only people I could find were an elderly couple, Stava and Rado Pavic, who ran a small food shop on Tsar Dusan Street and were too old, too sick, to run away.

The shops on either side of them, which had been owned by Albanians, had been looted and vandalized. The local garage, owned by an Albanian friend of the Pavics', had been burnt out.

"We helped each other all the time," said Rado, who had a voice wizened by decades of smoking harsh Balkan cigarettes. "They were our friends here. I honestly don't know who burnt them out."

"I never had a bad word from them, or them from me," his wife added. "We never had problems with them, never."

Before the war, Kosovo Polje had a population of 18,000, mainly Serbs. Now most of them had followed the retreating army, and the Pavics were left guarding a ramshackle shop that sold soap, toilet paper, stale cookies in large plastic sacks, and chocolate. The shop, with its open door and a few people lingering near the entrance, stood out in the midst of all the rubbish and broken glass.

"We are the last Serbs in town." Rado made a thin joke without smiling. But seeing his wife's anxious face, he stopped.

The night before, the last of the Serbian troops had pulled out of Kosovo Polje, and with them went most of the population, including six of the Pavics' eight children. The seventh, thirty-seven-year-old Svetisan, was packed and ready to go, trying to make his way to Serbia, where his nine-months-pregnant wife was waiting with their two other children.

Only Velibor, forty-five, was left behind. He decided he could not leave his parents alone. "They are too sick to travel," he said. "And even if they weren't sick, they wouldn't go."

But Velibor's wife, Sofia, wanted to go. "I don't want to stay here anymore," she whined. "We will be made to pay for what happened, even if we did nothing."

Stava and her husband arrived in Kosovo Polje in 1964. Before that, she had always lived in villages in the area. She did not like change. She did not know anything else, did not know what it was like to live in Belgrade, for instance. She did not want to leave her rose bushes.

At lunchtime, Stava locked the shop—"There's no one to buy anything, anyway"—put the key inside her apron, and led me down a trail behind the shop to their small cottage. Rado stopped outside and stared at his house. "My children were born in this house. My daughters got married in this house. We welcomed our grandchildren in this house. We are such a close family that when my sons got married we built houses for them behind ours."

Inside, it was dim and quiet and smelled faintly of wax. Everything came from another time, the Tito era: ancient electrical equipment in the kitchen; the overstuffed sofa; damp out-of-date magazines. One of the grandchildren, now somewhere in Serbia or possibly stranded in no-man's-land, had left behind a doll, another an accordion. There was a Soviet-style transistor radio, their only source of information, on which they listened to Serbian Voice of America.

They did not have a television and had no idea what "ethnic cleansing" or "mass graves" meant. "What are these things?" Rado said, confused.

Velibor left the room, but Rado listened to the descriptions of mass graves, rape, looting, killing. His long face sagged. "We never heard about this," he said. "People who do this kind of thing can't be human. It can't be true."

At lunch, there was pork and thick slices of bread, bowls of tinned vegetables. Rado opened a bottle of loza and passed the plates. Stava said, carefully cutting her pork chop into small pieces, "We *are* going to be the last Serbs in Kosovo."

In the weeks that followed, the Serb population in the Kosovo province—once 180,000—dwindled to 50,000. Further north, Pec—Kosovo's second city and the traditional seat of the Serbian Orthodox Church, seen by Serbs as the cradle of their civilization—came under siege.

Albanian fighters tried to torch the symbol of their oppression, the fourteenth-century Monastery of St. Dmitri, which is tucked in a gorge in the hills, surrounded by lush rose gardens. Inside, thirty priests and monks attempted to continue their daily routine, the same routine that had been followed for hundreds of years. They studied the scriptures, weeded the gardens, and tried to tend to the diminishing Serb community. Outside, the streets of Pec were covered in stinking and smoldering garbage, the ruins of war. The Albanians were returning and finding horrific things: bodies thrown down wells, their houses torched and gutted. They blamed the Serbs.

When the priests stepped outside, they ran into armed and aggressive UCK soldiers who threatened to cut their throats and hang them like pigs. Belgrade demanded the right to send 300 troops to protect holy places. Patriarch Pavle, the head of the Orthodox Church, left Belgrade to take up permanent residence inside St. Dmitri, as a gesture of solidarity.

Stava heard the news of the Patriarch while she was working in her shop in Kosovo Polje. The town was nearly deserted now, and Stava was stacking tins of tomatoes out of habit. She listened to the news on the radio and raised a worn hand to her forehead, as if she were cooling a fever.

"God will protect us now," she said. She almost sounded happy.

Rado, however, sitting nearby on a stool with a friend, smoking a cigarette, looked uncertain.

Near Klina and Glogovac
The Second Week of Peace
June 1999

The war went on in Drenica. The roads were still mined. The tentative peace that had reached Pristina had not arrived. NATO, in the form of French soldiers, was not yet there, so the war continued the way it had for the past three months—small hit-and-run operations, snipers, minefields.

Near Klina, a UCK resistance stronghold, fighters were still in trenches, in dugouts, still shooting with their old hunting rifles, still dodging Serb shells that were getting lobbed over to their side. Nearby, in a small village called Lausa, 30 people had been killed in the past few days.

"All we have now," said one soldier, "is our Kalashnikovs and nothing else."

It smelled of bodies in Drenica, bodies rotting somewhere in ditches or in fields. When you drove by in your car with the windows open, the smell wafted in: rotting flesh, rotting carcasses of animals. Units of Serb paramilitary in the hills said they were not going until they were driven out. When cornered, like trapped animals, they responded with brutality. Two German journalists were murdered by the paramilitary. The Albanians too were often afraid to return home.

So everyone waited for the peace to take effect.

In Klina, 10,000 refugees gathered in the town square, lying or sitting on the ground on blankets, waiting with their children for the UCK to tell them to go home. They crowded together in small groups, holding pieces of paper with telephone numbers of relatives abroad etched on them. When someone appeared who might have a satellite phone, they begged for it, their faces soft with hunger and fear.

The Klina refugees had some hard loaves of bread and some tins of meat—the first humanitarian aid convoy had arrived ten days before. But they had no shelter or water supplies, and they did not know what had happened to their homes. They wanted NATO to clear the way into their village before they went forward.

Most of them came from near Prekaz, the site of a massacre the year before, and had been hiding in the woods since early May.

"I will not go until NATO comes with me," said a woman who had been sleeping under fir trees for three weeks. As for living again with Serbs, she stared blankly: "After the killings, after the massacres?" An eighteen-year old girl called Teuta Muliqi who came from a village near Prekaz said that in May she had watched the Serb police kill five or six people in front of her. Then they marched the boys and men away. "You can see why we don't want to go home without NATO," she said quietly.

The KLA was still in control, its positions well hidden in the hills above Klina. Babaj, a twenty-four-year-old crane operator from Djakovica, now a soldier, had come down from his post to the village to find more ammunition. He took us back to his position, through fields, hilltops, through a forest and over a small riverbed. It took about an hour and a half. Finally, we came to a hilltop stable near

Lausa, where his unit was holed up, fighting the last of the Serbs.

Babaj walked quickly, moving in his worn-out sneakers. He was still dressed in civilian clothes and his gun was hidden under his jacket. Six of his brothers and his father were also fighting in the KLA. His only sister had been wounded by shrapnel. His mother was somewhere in that crowd of 10,000. He had been looking for her that morning.

That morning, Babaj had counted 144 graves in Izbica, 15 kilometers away. He hated counting the dead; he hated seeing the fresh mounds of earth, knowing that underneath were stacked legs, arms, torsos. Sometimes when they killed a lot of people, he said, the Serbs would pile dead cows on top of them to disguise the smell.

He wanted to be back, operating his crane. He never really wanted to be a soldier; he said he felt he was pushed into it, with no choice. It was the same story with the rest of his unit, who met us outside the stable. "There is not one person," Babaj said, "who wants to be here."

What was left of the fighters were a few ragged and dirty men holed up in an abandoned farm. They had a vantage of the dry hills surrounding the valley. Inside, Babaj took off his jeans, his T-shirt, his sneakers, and put on a faded green KLA uniform with loose trousers. He had lost weight over the last few weeks.

There was the sound of machine-gun fire. Someone ran in and told Babaj to hurry, and he grabbed his rifle. "The war appears to be over," he said, "but it is not. NATO can't be everywhere."

Then he was gone, over the ridge.

Somewhere down the road, out of the forest and away from Babaj and his men in their stable position, there was the sound of marching. In Glogovac, the KLA had arrived. As soon as the Serb Army slowly moved out, the KLA in their new black and camouflage uniforms donated by the Albanian diaspora. They carried Russian rocket-propelled grenades, and old machine guns slung over their shoulders.

Women and children followed the fighters as they entered the town. They threw red and pink flowers they had picked in the fields. The fighters moved in formation, marching and chanting.

Asmina was watching them, holding a flower she had found already thrown in the street. Occasionally, she opened her mouth to shout when the soldiers marched by, holding onto her flower. She studied biology before the war. She left all her books and papers in a neat pile on her desk when she left, with her family.

This parade meant something to her. It signified that it was all finally over. "I wonder what I will discover when I get home," she said. "I wonder if everything will be the same. The dishes we left in the sink, the pan we cooked our eggs in. Do you think it's the same? I wonder, but I am not sure I want to know."

The soldiers continued marching, in strange formation, as though they were imitating old war movies they had watched. They marched straight to the old Serb Command Post. They hung their red flag with the black eagle in the same place the Serbs had hung theirs.

Shaban Shala, the commander, had already selected his new office—the former office of the Serbian commander. He took advantage of his new authority and was shouting at a young soldier to move his desk near the window. A young blond girl wearing tight black trousers and a buttoned-down shirt with the KLA insignia hovered near his elbow. He barked for tea.

"*We* are controlling the area," Shala said proudly, fingering his new uniform. "We respect NATO, but at the same time, there is still fighting with Serbs in the villages of Vitak, Citak, and Lapushnik . . ." He drifted off, naming villages, naming places where mass graves had been dug up, where body parts were being pulled from the earth.

No one was turning in his gun yet, he said. As for peace in Pristina, he smiled down at his dark tea. Pristina was a long way away. There were secrets in these hills, and the war was not over yet.

Chapter Five

Dear citizens, the aggression is over. Peace has prevailed over violence. Dear citizens, I wish you a happy peace!

Slobodan Milosevic, June 10, 1999

Belgrade
June 10, 1999

It was hazy in Belgrade. There were ashes in the air from the bombing, and the destroyed buildings lay open and exposed—naked staircases, and office furniture turned upside down. In downtown Belgrade was a poster of children with the words SERBS HAVE CHILDREN TOO.

The war was over, but the first days of euphoria were fading. A taxi driver, Nikola, took me to the Military Medical Academy. He had just returned from the front three days before. He pulled out a photograph of his unit: at thirty-five, he was the oldest, and said he had no idea who had won the war. But the worst thing for him was coming home and finding his four-year-old son hiding under the kitchen table.

The second floor of the Military Medical Academy was reserved for intensive care, and the beds were pushed close together to accommodate more casualties. General Nebojsa Pavkovic, the commander of the Yugoslav Third Army in Kosovo, told me he had lost a total of 160 men; Milosevic claimed that there were 400 dead from the war. But the doctors told me the real figure was four times that. Another said she believed there were as many as 8,000 civilian injuries alone, and that was not counting the psychological damage.

Dr. Radoslav Svicevic, one of the hospital's directors and a clinical psychologist, was putting together a database about posttraumatic stress following the bombing. He said that already people were suffering nightmares, paranoia, a sense that nothing was safe. The problem, he said, was the anger: people did not understand why they had gotten bombed, killed, injured.

In one room overlooking the wide, green lawn of the hospital was Damir Ivica, eleven years old, recovering from an operation the day before to remove both his legs. He was tiny, with a blond crew cut and some toys by the side of his bed. He came from Vitina, a small town in Kosovo, where he had been working in the fields with his father when a NATO cluster bomb landed. Damir arrived at the military hospital with a note attached to his medical file from the local doctor: "Please do everything possible to try to save one of his legs."

Svecivec lifted the sheet to reveal Damir's torso, his two stumps, a hunk of his shoulder ripped away by shrapnel. There were small, circular wounds on his face, chest, and torso.

Damir was emerging from a morphine haze. The place where his legs had been still hurt, and he tried to move an arm to touch his aching shoulder. He looked up and saw strangers around his bed. "Please don't make me talk about it," he said to the doctor. He began to cry. "Don't ask me. I want to forget that morning, that day."

The doctor calmed him with a softer voice than the one he had used to show me the amputated limbs. "Don't cry," he said. "You will go back to your farm soon."

There were two other boys in the room, older than Damir, soldiers. Both had injuries—one, shredded intestines; the other, a smashed-up leg with a four-inch metal pin and a bullet wound in his chest. Both of them stared at the child as the tears continued to roll down his face in frustration. They said nothing. It was not unkind. They just had nothing to say.

Down the hall was a seventeen-year-old from Prizren. Dalabor Dravic had a friend, a best friend, an Albanian called Agem, whom he had known since childhood. On April 29, Dalabor opened the door and saw that Agem had become a KLA soldier. He held a gun.

"What are you doing?" Dalabor said, trying to keep his tone light and friendly. He was scared, but he thought, He's my friend, he won't hurt me.

Agem pointed the gun at Dalabor's sixteen-year old sister, who was standing behind him in the doorway. He shot her. Dalabor did not have time to catch his sister before she slumped to the floor because Agem pointed the gun at him and shot him in the gut.

There's a ten-inch scar running down Dalabor's body. It's angry and pink, but the doctor tells me it's a good incision. It will heal, as will the hole in his stomach, and he can use the bag attached outside his body. Dalabor is not complaining, but he is still confused about what happened that day.

"I'm alive," he said. "My little sister is dead." He does not know why Agem did it. As Dalabor lay bleeding on the ground, believing that his soul was passing out of his body and joining his little sister, Agem said, "Get out of Prizren. Leave your home."

Dalabor gets angry when he thinks of that. It supersedes the pain in his gut. "All my good friends were Albanians," he said, shivering in the hospital bed. "I still don't get it." He shivered some more, and the doctor shook some yellow and green pills into his hand, which Dalabor dutifully took with water. The pills helped him forget, he said, everything about this useless war. He rolled over to sleep.

Belgrade had adjusted to an uneasy peace. The Writers' Club opened. The tables and chairs were set out on the piazzas. The shops got more food, more cigarettes. Concerts started. On June 24, 1999, all but two members of the Federal Parliament voted to lift the official state of war. The weather was cold, gray, with low-hanging clouds.

Not everyone was happy about the end of war. There was an air of discontent, from the wounded soldiers coming home; from the drunk reservists, who had not been paid, blocking the road near Kraljevo; from the scores of refugees from Kosovo who had managed to get inside the capital, sleeping in the park.

The government, embarrassed by the refugee presence, offered them food and money to return to Kosovo. The offer was ignored. Then the refugees were ordered back within four hours, saying NATO had guaranteed protection. Again they refused, and responded by organizing a demonstration in front of the Federal Parliament building. It was broken up by police who said public gatherings were illegal under the state-of-war law, which was oddly still in effect, and moved to Terazije Square. The refugees' leader, Svetozar Fisic, was detained by the police.

The refugees stayed, and the postwar days passed listlessly, became weeks. The weather improved and the cafés became full. But there was anticipation and panic about shortages of petrol, heat, and electricity. No one talked about mass graves or Serbian atrocities committed in Kosovo because most people believed it was Western propaganda. Politically, Milosevic held on. The fractured political opposition called for early elections. A demonstration of 25,000 opposition supporters in the town of Cacak was planned, the day after the 610th anniversary of the battle of Kosovo Polje.

The demonstration was the day after Anna's twenty-second birthday and she wanted to go, but she was too hungover. The night before, she and her friends, all students from Belgrade University, sat up late in her mother's flat in Novi Belgrade drinking vodka and trying to blot out the war.

The next day, Anna and Julia were reading an article in the newspaper that said that in forty years' time, the Serbia economy would be back to the 1989, the prewar, level. According to an independent economic society called G-17, the GDP, she read out loud, was 44.4 percent lower than last year because of the war. The damage caused by NATO was estimated at $29.3 billion. "It's a bore, living like this," says Julia, who has a mournful face like one of the ancient saints painted on the wall of the old church downtown, across the River Sava.

Julia's paternal grandfather was a colonel in the Royal Army under King Peter and King Alexander; her mother's family once owned big houses in downtown Belgrade, which were confiscated under communism. Now, nearly all her father's family have emigrated. One uncle, an opera singer, lives on the Upper East Side in New York City. Her grandfather lives in Washington, D.C. Her mother, dead from cancer, was a painter.

Julia and her friends had the misfortune of being born in 1977. They had just passed puberty when the troubles started: Slovenia, Croatia, then Bosnia, Kosovo. They came of age under Slobodan Milosevic, a life of total uncertainty. They are proud of being Serbs but are ashamed of Milosevic and despise his regime.

Now the war is over and their friends are coming home. They are depressed because their country just lost its fourth war. They are confused about the reports of what Serb soldiers did in Kosovo. They hate NATO for ruining their city, but at the same time, they want to go live in England, America, France, and Germany. They know nothing but war, sanctions and the fact that they come from a country that is an international pariah. They say they are completely fucked up. They call themselves the lost generation.

Julia has strange childhood memories: toilet paper shortages, the shops having only withered apples for sale, and the inflated dinar having a zillion zeros attached to the end of it. Her teenage memories are more vivid: war reports on the radio, dead soldiers, anti-Milosevic demonstrations, and economic meltdown.

She's smart and she wanted a way out, so she studied languages and archaeology, perfecting her English and French, studying classical Greek in her bedroom at night. Then, two years before the NATO war started, her mother got sick. Then she got sicker. Chemotherapy under sanctions was difficult; Julia got her mother a visa to France.

In Paris, she rented a room for three months and put her mother in a clinic. She visited her every day, sat by her bed. Sometimes she wandered through the museums by herself. Once in the Louvre, she met a boy. He asked her where she was from. She replied Serbia. She swears that the boy looked at her strangely, then made his excuses and got away from her as fast as he could.

"We are pariahs," she said.

She met another Serb who had also come to Paris for treatment. She saw him every day. They fell in love. Then he died. Then her mother died. Then Julia packed her small bag and went back to Belgrade, back to the wars.

But she couldn't finish her thesis on early Roman ruins and church restoration, because part of her work was in eastern Serbia and Kosovo, now an off-limits military zone. Her classes were canceled. She aimlessly applied to places like Harvard and NYU, but who was going to take her with no money, and who would give her a visa? She wrote to Columbia University, but even though she had top grades, they never wrote back.

What made it harder was that anyone who could get out, left. No one had any desire to stay and rebuild the country. Julia loved her country, but she said it felt like being in a country full of losers. Still, to be a stranger for the rest of her life was frightening. In the newspaper *Glas Javnosti* one morning, she read that one-third of all Serbian high-school students are desperate to leave the country.

One afternoon, she sat drinking a cappuccino at Ipanema, a downtown outdoor café, with her friend Ivan. The cappuccino is more than they can afford, and the cigarettes they smoke are Marlboro Lights from Romania. Across the street is the annoying grind of a chain saw. The city council is chopping down trees for the upcoming winter. It's not even high summer yet, and everyone is predicting a miserable winter with no money for coal and gas.

Ivan says, drawing deep on the cigarette, "When I graduated from high school in 1990, the future seemed so amazing," he said. "Then, I had hope. The wars hadn't started yet. I was proud of my country. Proud to be a Yugoslav. In those days, you thought, Yes, I'll get a good job and be able to buy a car and get an apartment with my girlfriend."

None of that has happened for him. "Then, it might have been possible," he said, stubbing out the cigarette and lighting another. "Now, it's not."

Julia's little brother, Djordje, is going to America. Her father, Antonio, spent three months getting papers to get Djordje out of Belgrade. A former Yugoslav basketball star living in America charges three months' salary to place young and talented players with suburban American families.

Antonio said that in Djordje's school—Belgrade High School Number Four—seven out of forty-one kids have managed to get visas to go somewhere other than Serbia. "It's a matter of survival," he says. "It's worse now than it was under communism."

Julia wants to go with her little brother too, but she can't. She can't travel. In postwar Belgrade, 1999, a Yugoslav passport has heavy restrictions. If someone wants to apply for a visa, he or she must have the money to get to Budapest first because there are no embassies in Belgrade. Julia had to register with the authorities every six months to maintain her Yugoslav citizenship.

Sometimes at night, as the summer grew hotter and the days longer, we drove down the Danube to sit outside in cafés and eat fresh fish from the coast. We could hear the singing from inside the restaurant; traditional Serbian music and the sound of the *gusla*. Srdjan, who taught film, said that 50 percent of his students had left the country. "The most talented ones," he said glumly. The days when Belgrade was the capital of Eastern Europe for its intelligentsia, film, writers, and dancers was gone, he said. He emptied the bottle of Montenegrin wine and ordered another.

"What will happen to my country?" he said, staring out at the brackish Danube. "The children of Milosevic and Vojislav Seselj [an ultranationalist politician] will be left here. The country will be a shell. Anyone with any sense will be long gone."

No one was looking too deeply at the war crimes issue in Belgrade in those days. People changed the subject. Even mentioning Kosovo got a hostile response. "Look," said one kid in a club, listening to a blues band. "America didn't look at Vietnam for years. The Germans didn't think about the Holocaust until Willy Brandt fell on his knees in Warsaw in 1970. In Chile, they just started talking about Pinochet, and in South Africa people still say it's too early to address apartheid. This is going to take us years to address."

Belgrade was wounded. Hundreds of dead Serb soldiers were being shipped home; a winter was approaching without adequate food or firewood. The Serbs had lost their fourth war in a decade. They had been demoralized by Milosevic for years. The graves in Kosovo, the dead Albanians, the torture, the rape—all were silent topics.

By the end of the war, the international community claimed that 10,000 Albanians had been killed by Serb forces. In Serbia, no one took the figure seriously.

"Maybe hundreds, maybe a thousand, not *thousands*," General Nebojsa Pavkovic, the leader of the Yugoslav forces in Kosovo, told me. It was June 28, the anniversary of Kosovo Polje, a steaming day in Belgrade. Pavkovic had invited me to meet him at the Moskva Hotel, one of the last examples of Art Nouveau in Belgrade.

I saw him in a shabby suite which had not been painted or refurbished for years. Summer heat filtered through the polyester curtains. The general was sitting on an overstuffed sofa eating a melting strawberry sundae. He looked up gloomily when I entered but did not rise. His bodyguards searched my bag.

Pavkovic mentioned the significance of the day as he spooned ice cream into his mouth. "It's hard," he said. "People think we lost the war. It wasn't a loss. But the world must realize that the Serb people are proud and brave; that Kosovo is our holy land."

Pavkovic, a three-star general, would later become Milosevic's chief of staff as well as his close ally. In the final days of Milosevic, it was Pavkovic who had to tell his friend that the army would not protect him during the civil demonstrations which eventually toppled him. It was a difficult role for Pavkovic: he had grown up under Tito's Communist mantle of Brotherhood and Unity, and he believed in the old Communist structures that had brought Milosevic to power.

From his pocket, he removed photographs taken with an Instamatic camera. One showed Pavkovic with his men, standing next to an antiaircraft gun. There was another of him in the midst of a crowd of young soldiers, all smiling.

"We moved all the time," he said, fingering the worn photo. "From Pristina to Dakovica, to Pec, to Prizren, Mitrovica. Close to the Albanian border. The worst day was when we got carpet-bombed by a B-52. It lasted twelve hours."

Pavkovic and his men hid in a cave dug into the mountains. He said he had gotten to know his men during those days, those weeks. He had seen the war "with my own eyes," not sitting at some desk in Belgrade. He knew what he was talking about. There were no atrocities in Kosovo.

"I am certain Yugoslav forces—and that includes police—did not commit them," he said. "They were too busy fighting terrorists and NATO planes. And defending our country."

I asked about Frenki's Guys, the paramilitary unit led by Franko Simatovic, who had formerly headed the Secret Service's Special Operations Unit.

Pavkovic put the photos back in his pocket. "They were not in Kosovo."

"But there were witnesses who saw the paramilitary in Prizren, in Pec, in Pristina—"

"They were not in Kosovo. There were no civilian atrocities."

Pavkovic sighed. "We were forced into this war. We didn't want to fight. We were just defending our country." He moved to the window that overlooked downtown Belgrade. "It's so easy to blame the Serbs," he said. "What's happening in Kosovo now? There are atrocities being committed against Serbs by Albanians. We have witnesses. People who have seen the exodus."

Sometimes this collective denial was due to a lack of information. Many Serbs genuinely did not know. Because of the state of emergency, most of the newspapers—including *DANAS*, the most progressive daily—were heavily censored and published nothing, or very little, about the "so-called massacres." And every night at 7:30 P.M., Serbian State Television (RTS) aired its nightly news program jokingly referred to as "The Holy News" without mentioning the refugee crisis or investigations into war crimes. Every night, two-thirds of Serbia tuned in to it. Very few people could afford satellite dishes to watch CNN or the BBC.

Radio B-92, the one really independent radio station, was closed down at the start of the war by armed police who entered the studios in Dom Omladine, a building in the Old Town. The journalists regrouped as a pirate station, broadcasting on various frequencies and over the Internet in order to prevent the jammers at the Telecommunications Ministry from closing them down again. But the large majority of Serbs outside of Belgrade's educated middle classes did not know how to tune into a pirate radio station. Aside from journalists, not many people had shortwave radios.

"Provincial Serbia is completely in the dark concerning anything not fed them by Milosevic's war machine," said the historian Aleksa Djilas, the son of the late Yugoslav novelist and dissident Milovan Djilas. "And with the political situation so tense, they may never become enlightened."

It was a strange, isolated world. Magazines like *Vreme* were silent. Only private newsletters such as *Republika* or the well-respected *VIP Daily News Report*, which were largely read by internationals—took on the subject. *VIP* was run by Braca Grubacic, a former editor at Mladost, the publishing house of the Yugoslav youth organization, and was delivered to subscribers in various Western embassies and at the Hyatt Hotel. But ordinary people could not afford it. And if they did, would they believe it? "It's very painful for people to hear about war crimes," said Grubacic. Even the liberals—the ones who got on the blocked Web sites on the Internet and who listened to Voice of America or Radio Free Europe on shortwave—still had grave doubts about the extent of the killings.

"They say ten thousand so easily, but there are no facts yet," said Dusan, a twenty-four-year-old who worked for B-92 and who described himself as "left wing." His mother, a journalist, had been blacklisted in 1992 by Seselj, and Dusan had access to the Internet and the BBC. He knew what was going on.

We met at the Sports Café, a restaurant with a huge screen that broadcast never-ending MTV videos, football matches, and haute couture collections. There were never any breaking news broadcasts. The kids at the tables ordered American-style burgers and listened to Puff Daddy, but they had more interest in why Notorious B.I.G., the black American rapper, was murdered than about what had just taken place in Kosovo. It was just easier, Dusan said, to think about music than massacres.

"I know there are massacres in Kosovo, but how does NATO figure ten thousand after only one week? They have a propaganda machine the same way Milosevic does," he said.

Dusan was a student, and he did not serve in the army. But most of his friends did, and that was the underlying reason why he, and Julia and all her friends, expressed such disbelief: no one could imagine their friends committing war crimes. Dusan grew up with his mother lecturing him on liberty and the rights of man, but during the course of our conversation, he got so angry he could not speak.

Later, he relented. "I have a friend who just came back from Kosovo. But he's not here. He's in a hospital in Krusevac after having a breakdown." Maybe, Dusan said in a smaller voice, it came from what he saw. Things might have happened, he finally relented, but it was the paramilitary units, not "the regular army, not guys like me.

"My neighbor was in Prizren," Dusan said. "They say Prizren is full of human rights violations. But would my neighbor—a genuinely good guy—do something like that?"

In his elegant second-floor flat on Palmoticeva, Aleksa Djilas waited out the war and the bombing, surrounded by his books and his papers. Djilas tried to stay in touch with the rest of the world. Friends rang him from America, concerned for his safety. He wrote articles for the *New York Times*.

But as the war progressed and his own city came under attack, as his own children screamed from fright and bombs fell near his own apartment building, Djilas began to question the international community's position that the Serbs were the aggressors. He believed that if the attack against the Albanians was truly systematic and truly planned, why were there not half a million dead?

"You have to ask yourself questions: Who killed them? Locals? Paramilitary? Soldiers?" he said. He was skeptical about the journalists' reports without forensic evidence, of President Clinton's allegations about Serbian rape camps.

"A lot of these soldiers were twenty-year-old mama's boys," he said. As for torture chambers allegedly hidden in the bowels of the secret police headquarters, he cast a disbelieving glance: "Why would the police leave the equipment behind?" he said. "These guys aren't stupid. Why did things happen just the way NATO wanted it to?"

Any grave that was found with more than one body was being called a mass grave, he pointed out. Executions by the KLA of Serb civilians, the KLA using them as human shields, or NATO collateral damage to Serbs was being ignored.

Djilas was not totally one-sided, but he was sick of Serbs constantly being branded the bad guys because they had the most pronounced political will in the region. Most other Balkan nations, he said, went with the tide. And war, he argued, was never pretty. "If there is an ethnic conflict," he said, "there are no good guys."

He was willing to see Milosevic accused of many things—human rights violations, minority rights violations, police brutality, abolishing autonomy, and excessive force dealing with the KLA—but he was not prepared to compare Kosovo to South Africa or Algeria under the French. He argued that before March 23, Kosovo had a great freedom of the press—something that had not happened during either of those regimes.

But others would disagree with Djilas. The former editor of *Politika*, Aleksandar Nenadovic, told a British journalist:

> Even during the war we had foreign papers on sale in the center of Belgrade, and you could listen to the BBC or watch satellite television. But the average man would only have heard about the ugly things being done to Serbs. The simplest truth is to say that "we are victims, look what they have done to us." When you believe that, it is so easy to get rid of any curiosity to find out more. That the Serbs were shooting at Sarajevo for years, shooting at innocent people, that some of our writers went there with a machine gun, the average Serb doesn't know.[1]

Djilas believed the West was littered with hypocrisy, and that, to some extent, Serbia suffered because it was an Orthodox country. Tudjman, for instance, got away with numerous crimes. "There is something so false about European outrage," he said. America and Britain were not dispassionate social workers; they had vested interests. And in the end, their own record was pretty appalling. "Britain, for instance, who made so much of Serbian atrocities, only received three hundred Albanian refugees."

In the end, he concluded, Serbian people were more likely to self-examine than any other people in the Balkans. He reminded me that one of his father's most memorable novels, *Worlds and Bridges*, was about Montenegrin atrocities against Muslims after World War I. During the Bosnian war, there were protests against the siege of Sarajevo, and the film director Srdjan Dragojevic released the controversial *Pretty Village, Pretty Flame*, which was shown widely. Roy Gutman's revelations from the Omarska death camps, *A Witness to Genocide*, was translated into Serbian and sold in bookshops.

But Kosovo was different. The Serbs had suffered under NATO's bombs, which brought on a blind anger.

"The conflict must stop," Djilas said. "But the admission of guilt must not have further loss. . . . Do you punish the guilty or prevent the suffering of the innocent?" The real problem, he believed, lay with Milosevic. It was not easy to accept that the Serb people were being sacrificed for Milosevic's bad policy.

Earlier, at the Sports Café, my friend Irena, a student of mathematics whose classes had been canceled during the war, sat eating a fruit tart. That tart cost the equivalent of most Serbians' daily salaries. The café was full of mafiosi and their girlfriends, and foreigners. Irena, who was a Serb originally from Sarajevo and who arrived with her parents in Belgrade in 1992 as refugees, was troubled by the effect the Kosovo war was having on her friends. "Most Serbians would say it is okay to expel Albanians, not to kill them," she said. "But the bombing made people harsher."

She pointed out that since the bombing started, many of her friends had changed their views on Bosnia: those indicted for war crimes, such as General Ratko Mladic and Radovan Karadzic, were seen by many as local heroes. There were Karadzic T-shirts sold on the street, and several people asked me, "Would Serbia have been bombed if it were a Catholic country?" If anything, the NATO bombing had only contributed to the Serbs' sense of collective victimization, which was spearheaded in 1986 when a small group of intellectuals at the Serbian Academy of Sciences and Arts published an article called "Memorandum." It stated that "in the general process of disintegration which has encompassed Yugoslavia, the Serbs have been hit the hardest . . . this process is directed towards the total breaking up of the national unity among the Serbian people." This, added to the emigration (or genocide, as they called it) of tens of thousands of remaining Serbs in Albanian-dominated Kosovo, led them to conclude: "One cannot imagine a worse historical defeat in peacetime."[2]

There was no sense of unified anguish in Belgrade now, no sense of collective guilt. Djilas doubted it would happen in the near future, at least not while the signs of the bombing were still so evident. The Ministry of Defense building, the Chinese Embassy, the victims of the convoy who had been slaughtered in a single hour; the small boy lying in the military hospital without legs. It was too early, he said gently; it was unrealistic to think that people traumatized not only by the war, but by ten years of Milosevic, would turn inward to examine the violence.

Milosevic was already in his cell at The Hague, in the early summer of 2001, when graves of Albanians were found, not in Bosnia or Kosovo, but in several locations in Serbia, including the Batajnica air force base outside of Belgrade.

These graves were Milosevic's idea of playing it safe. He knew that if he lost the war in Kosovo, NATO troops would eventually find graves there. The bodies had been moved during the bombing campaign, as the story later emerged, from Prizren, where sanitation workers were ordered to an army rifle range. There they loaded corpses into a refrigerator truck. The truck was then dumped in the Danube, which was discovered in April 2000 by a startled fisherman. Police then found 86 bodies, which were moved to the Batajnica. The testimonies were provided by the Serbs who had been forced to take part in the disposal. It was this incident that led directly to the fall of Milosevic.

"There is not a single case in history in which a group of people can express collective guilt during a conflict," Djilas had told me two years earlier. "Especially in front of the aggressor."

But the conflict was over. NATO had gone home. Milosevic would soon be in jail. And it was guilt, on the part of the disposal workers who came out and talked, that would lead to his downfall. The time had come, painful or not, to process what had happened.

But that is fast-forwarding. I am still in Belgrade, in June 1999. I sleep badly, am anxious. When I pull open my curtains at the Hyatt, the first thing I see is an enormous unfurled Serbian flag. I watch the news and dress carefully for tea with Arkan—the dreaded leader of the paramilitary group the Tigers, whom I mentioned earlier as the ethnic cleansers of Bosnian Muslims. His real name is Zeljko Raznatovic, and on the phone he tells me he has old-fashioned manners. He warns me not to be late.

He's in a bad mood when we meet at the Tea Garden of the Hyatt—the Obilic Football Club, a team he owns, just lost a match. But he perches on a sofa and says he likes to be seen in public here, "so people know I'm not in Kosovo." He's heavier than in his Bosnian days, and he orders only a tisane, passing on the Sacher torte. He asks which language I prefer. The former Kosovo deputy—elected on a hard-line Serbian nationalist ticket—speaks four: English, French, German, Italian. "Not counting Serbian," he said.

Arkan is a half-Slovenian half-Kosovar Serb, the son of an air force officer. Born in 1950, he came to the attention of the Yugoslav Federal Secretariat for Internal Affairs (SSUP) in the mid 1960s while he was robbing banks and cars. The SSUP, who ran an espionage network, made a deal with Arkan—who later took his nickname from one of his many forged passports. In exchange for overlooking his multiple prison escapes, he allegedly worked for them abroad, involved in political assassinations.

Arkan robbed banks in Sweden; carried out armed robbery in Holland, Belgium, and Germany; and was wanted in Italy for a 1974 murder. He spent two years in London learning English during "the Summer of Love" as he called it, and four years in Italy. In the 1980s, after a long sojourn abroad, he returned to Belgrade, calling himself a businessman, giving himself a legitimate front as a pastry-shop owner. By 1990, he had emerged as a new force in the growing Milosevic-inspired nationalism.

As the head of Delije, the official fan club of Belgrade's Red Star football team, he found he could manipulate the hard-core nationalist fans. With an overly enthusiastic gang brought over from Delije, he founded the Serbian Volunteer Guard in 1991, otherwise known as the Tigers. Their training camps were in Eastern Slavonia, a region the Serbs had ravaged earlier. From there, the Tigers seized eastern Bosnia in 1992. Arkan's work would inspire the phrase "ethnic cleansing."

In the midst of his paramilitary activities, the Croatian police arrested Arkan in November 1990, for allegedly discussing the logistics of Serbia secretly arming the Krajina Serbs. He was caught in a car full of weapons and ammunitions, tried, and convicted. Once in Belgrade, he taunted the Croats: "You will never catch me alive!"

Now another court had a warrant for his arrest. Arkan feared he would be called to The Hague. It was rumoured that his lawyer had tried to arrange a plea bargain. It never happened. Prosecutors at The Hague would later say that they told Arkan's lawyers they would deal with him when he was standing in front of the tribunal. But he never got there. In January 2000, not long after we sat drinking tisane in the Hyatt. Arkan was gunned down across the street in the Intercontinental Hotel.

That afternoon in the Hyatt, he had two bodyguards who called him Commandant. One guard was called the General. He allegedly had worked for South African intelligence. The other—who often broke into our conversation and once tried to physically remove me from my seat while sneering, "You are insulting Mr. Raznatovic!"—was referred to as "the Security."

"He thinks you're CIA," Arkan said. As he poured apple tea from a small china pot, it was difficult not to think of what Arkan had done in towns like Zvornik, Sanski Most, and Vukovar.

"I am against terrorist actions of any kind that involve innocent people," he said suddenly, stirring the tea.

"And Zvornik?"

"Were you in Zvornik that morning?" he said icily. "Did you watch what I did? No. Then how can you accuse me?"

His version of the ethnic cleansing of the former Ottoman-era town was that it was "a clean, legitimate military job." There were no civilian casualties. This is a claim that goes against hard evidence that he and his men butchered innocent Muslims.

"We only killed soldiers," he said. "Not like NATO wounding six thousand civilians they could not even see—bombing them from the air! Cowards!" The real war criminals, he said spitefully, were Tony Blair, Bill Clinton, George Robertson (Nato secretary-general), and the NATO generals. "All of them."

In September 1997, Arkan was indicted on charges of crimes against humanity, violations of the laws and customs of war, and grave breaches of the Geneva Convention. The indictment was sealed to protect witnesses and prevent Arkan from fleeing. Two years later, the chief prosecutor at The Hague, Louise Arbour, announced that Arkan's name was among those on the wanted list and did not specify the charges.

It irritated him. He said he did not have to defend himself. "Why should I?" he said, growing agitated. "It's a political court."

Arkan abruptly changed the subject. "Let's forget The Hague. Something else. I was not in Kosovo. Neither was my army. I go first and they always follow me. We were here, training for a ground invasion."

"What were you doing while everyone else was fighting in Kosovo?"

He was playing with his children, he said. He had married the pop singer Svetlana Raznatovic, known as Ceca, in an elaborate

Orthodox ceremony in February 1995, wearing an old World War I uniform with a massive cross hanging low over his chest, and they had one child. He also had eight other children with three different women.

But now, he said, he was tired of being a soldier: his new role was as a politician. He was president of the Serbian Unity Party, which had five seats in Parliament. His platform, he said, was once pro-West.

"I actually wanted to be part of NATO before they started showering us with bombs," he said. "I opposed the bombing of civilian targets in Sarajevo, Zagreb, Osijak, and Dubrovnik. Those bombs killed civilians. And I regret every Albanian civilian killed. I was deeply sorry when I saw the pictures of Albanian refugees in Kukes."

He ordered more tea.

"Were there a lot of Albanian civilians killed in Kosovo?"

"How should I know?" he said irritably. "I can tell you that the tea here is good. I can tell you that the milk is fresh. But I can't tell you about Kosovo. I told you—I wasn't there."

His focus was on his family. And money. The wars in Serbia had left a fractured civil order, had spawned a violent criminal class in the former Yugoslavia. Drug smuggling, arms dealing, prostitution, sanctions, created an entire class of people who were loathsome to Belgrade's gentility, their *"finsvet."* But it made Arkan and his friends rich.

"I don't want to talk about business. I'll tell you about my dog." The dog was strictly disciplined. His children, he said, were being raised with moral conviction.

The Security leaned over.

"Mr. Raznatovic wants you to go now."

The other bodyguard, the General, insisted on walking me to my room and giving me his card. The day after Arkan was killed, I found that card and rang the General, who was weepy and in bed with the flu. The illness had saved his life: he was off duty when Arkan was gunned down. "They say Mr. Raznatovic was not surprised when he faced the gunmen," the General added. "He must have known who they were."

Who was behind it?

The General sniffed loudly. "Oh, I don't know!" he cried out miserably. When pressed, he admitted he had suspicions, as did most of Belgrade: someone who slept very close to Slobodan Milosevic.

After the war, the Milosevic question remained. He had lost four wars; how much longer could he go on? His response was not to be seen. He lay low. He did appear on television on June 16, Yugoslav Army Day, standing on a wrecked bridge in Voyvodina, distributing medals to military officers. The expression on his face was of misery. It was one of his first appearances in weeks and his last for some time.

I watched the pale and sweaty Yugoslavian leader on television with Julia. She stared at the screen and said it was a bad sign if Milosevic was making a play for television. He hated cameras. "If he's stepping up propaganda," she said, "it's not good."

Most of the time, Milosevic met with his advisors or stayed behind the gates of his villa in Dedinje, a leafy embassy district with his wife, Mira, while the opposition called for a unified front. His strange family drew closer.

Milosevic and his wife, Mira Markovic, had an unnaturally close relationship. The CIA called her his "mother replacement." A strong-willed sociologist and leader of her own party, the Yugoslav United Left—an alliance of twenty-three left-wing groups attached to her husband's Socialist Party—Mira did more than play an important role in Slobodan's political life, his ideology, and his policy-making. In many ways, she shaped his thinking.

As a couple and a family, the Milosevics were also untouchable. Anyone who threatened or criticized them found themselves either dead or exiled: Arkan; the former opposition leader Vuk Draskovic, whose wife Dana waged a war in print with Mira Markovic; Milosevic's former mentor, Ivan Stambolic, whose remains were found in early 2003, most likely killed by Markovic; or a one-time friend of the family, Slavko Curuvija, owner of the *Dnevni Telegraf* newspaper. Curuvija criticized the family publicly and was later gunned down in broad daylight in downtown Belgrade. The investigation did not produce any evidence but showed that members of Milosevic's secret police had been tailing Curuvija. Most of Belgrade believed Mira Markovic was behind the killing.

Markovic's control of her husband stemmed from the time of

their meeting, as teenagers, in Pozarevac, a gloomy town southeast of Belgrade that was best known for its sugar-beet and biscuit factories before the Milosevic family turned it into their own fiefdom. The encounter took place in December 1958, at a meeting for a Communist youth New Years' celebration. The young couple—both considered oddballs at school—bonded. Markovic noted that their Christian names, Slobodan and Mira, respectively, meant Freedom and Peace.

They had vastly different backgrounds. Markovic, already strong-willed and controlling, was a daughter of the Communist elite. Her aunt was Tito's secretary and alleged lover. As a young girl, Mira was showered with gifts by Tito, which led to the rumors that she was his child. Her mother told her another version: Mira was conceived during the war when she and Mira's father were Partisan fighters. She was born in the forest.

"I was born on 10 July 1942," Mira later wrote in her diary. "In the Partisans, and that fact had a great influence on my personality. When I say 'in the Partisans' I REALLY mean that—I was born in a wood. In my documents, one village, the closest settlement, is written as my birth place."

Her mother, Vera Miletic, was later arrested by fascist collaborators and killed shortly after the birth. Mira was raised by her grandparents in Pozarevac, and her childhood memories revolve around lying on her bed watching the rain and dreaming about how she could change the world.

"I will always be on the left side," she wrote. "I want to help people who are poor and with no rights to fight for human dignity." She cried if she did not get the highest grades in the class. She was obsessed with *Antigone*.

Milosevic was different. His home life was full of grim postwar deprivation. His father, Svetozar, a deeply religious man who wrote poetry and studied philosophy, committed suicide in Montenegro in 1962. His mother, Stanislava, a primary-school teacher and Communist activist, did the same thing twelve years later by hanging herself in the living room with a belt. Milosevic's favorite uncle also took his own life.

Slobodan grew to be a somber and reticent child, a bad athlete. By the time he was a teenager, he already had a reputation as a technocrat. But like Mira, he was a brilliant student and transcended his misery by studying and dreaming of something greater, something better. Together, the couple were insufferable perfectionists. A classmate recalls seeing Mira weeping and Milosevic comforting her because she had only received three fives—the highest grade in the former Yugoslavian school system—and one three.

Staunch Communists, they took on the party elite. At Belgrade University, they saw themselves as beatniks; she read Dostoyevsky and dressed in black. She often placed a fresh gardenia in her hair, a gesture that would become her trademark. He studied law; she studied sociology. They likened themselves to the lovers in Louis Malle's film *Les Amants*. They plotted their future.

They married in 1965. Their eldest daughter, Marija, was born later that year. Marko, their son, came nine years later. In 1969, Milosevic, with Mira's family connections, got a job at Technogas. It was an ambitious move—the company was run by Communist-appointed managers, and it was a training ground for young politicians. He spent eight years assembling political contacts, including Ivan Stambolic, later head of the Serbian Communist Party, whom Milosevic would blithely knife in the back, and who later, just days before Milosevic's ouster in the fall of 2000, would disappear, presumably murdered.

He then went on to banking, making frequent trips to the United States, where he perfected his English and learned how to deal with Americans, which would prove useful when he was courted by the West at Dayton. But banking was not his primary goal. By 1984, Milosevic left his job as president of Beogradska Banka for a full-time position in the Belgrade Communist Party.

Three years later, at the now infamous Eighth Session of the Serbian Communist Party, he swept his former mentor Stambolic aside again by becoming Serbian party chief. He humiliated the older man by securing the backing of the Yugoslav Army and the old Communist apparatus, and purging the party of Stambolic supporters. He installed his own men.

By April 1987, Milosevic—with Mira behind him offering advice—began to drag Yugoslavia into madness. Following the Kosovo Polje speech, where he whipped up Serb victimization sentiment purely for his own political gain, he managed to secure the trust of the Serbian intellectual elite.

In January 1987, the Serbian Academy issued its "Memorandum," which pushed for the expansion of Serbia to include the 2-million-strong diaspora in Bosnia and Croatia. The act came from a long-running sense of grievance and a collective persecution complex the Serbs felt, having sacrificed themselves for Yugoslavia, first in 1918, later in 1945.

By blending the symbolism of Serbian nationalism and Yugoslav communism, Milosevic sought to appeal to all disgruntled Serbs, under all political and religious umbrellas: the Orthodox Church; Communist officials; former Partisans and Chetniks. The common goal was to fight against secessionism or to unite Serbs in one state. It was, essentially, a war cry for Greater Serbia.

Early on, Milosevic's popularity vied with Tito's. At a 1988 rally of Brotherhood and Unity in Belgrade, nearly 1 million people turned up and began singing:

We were wondering
Who will replace Tito?
But now we know that
His name is Slobodan.

His appearance at the six-hundred-year celebration of Kosovo Polje on June 28, 1989, attracted a million. The following year, his Socialist (formerly Communist) Party won the first multiparty elections in Serbia. Milosevic was elected president of Serbia, and his portrait began to replace Tito's in cafés, restaurants and homes throughout Serbia.

But the end of communism brought a sense of despondency to the couple, particularly to Mira. She continued teaching Marxist studies at the University of Belgrade, but she also indulged other passions: clairvoyance and writing. The ability to see into the future came shortly after the speech at Kosovo Polje, when she and Milosevic were on holiday in Dubrovnik. Lying on the beach surrounded by newspapers, she tapped her husband on the shoulder.

"Slobo, I fear the ghosts of nationalism," she said. She told him, in a troubled voice, that she foresaw the death of Yugoslavia.

Markovic was not far off. The wars in Yugoslavia had begun.

Within four years, the Serbs in Kosovo would cry, "Slobo, prepare a salad—there will be meat, we'll slaughter Croats."

Personally, the family was flourishing. They moved from their small Belgrade flat to Dedinje, and later into Tito's former villa, only after Mira had checked under every carpet and in every piece of furniture for bugging devices. Milosevic's Yugoslav Zastava became either a Mercedes or a BMW. He began smoking cigars, enjoying whiskey.

Meanwhile, his son, Marko, used his father's position to become a crook and a thief, in addition to running most of the major businesses in Pozarevac. The family enjoyed their power as shamelessly as the Ceaucescus in Romania: in Pozarevac, no building permits were ever needed to construct Milosevic houses; no tax inspector ever visited Madona, one of Marko's nightclubs, which served duty-free whiskey; and any business competition folded before it even started. It was estimated that the family worth was somewhere around DEM 1 billion—spread among South Africa, Cyprus, and Greece.

Marija also ran nightclubs, a record label, and a radio station, Kosava, that got taken out by NATO bombs. Considerably less high-profile than her thuggish brother, she nonetheless used her parents' power for her own benefit—dating a convicted murderer who was pardoned halfway through his prison sentence. The family was utterly unlikable.

But perhaps what was most startling was their lack of empathy for the Serb people, the *narod*, that Milosevic professed to be saving by raiding what was left of Yugoslavia. Throughout the end of the 1990s, when the Serbian economy was in ruins and life genuinely was Kafkaesque, the Milosevics seemed totally oblivious to the plight of ordinary Serbs. In fact, Milosevic's popularity had begun to fade by 1990, due to the disastrous state of the economy, resulting in the riots of 1991, which were crushed by the police.

In many ways, though, he was addicted to war. Shortly after the Slovenian war began, a precedent was set: every time Milosevic's popularity plummeted, he launched a war to temporarily revive it. This was followed by resentment, disillusion, and more war. The pattern continued throughout the 1990s.

If Milosevic did not actually seem to care about the individual suffering of his people, neither did his wife. Mira, with all of her desire to change the world, was never seen visiting a refugee camp or helping war victims. Marko continued to get richer on stolen money, more flamboyant, more loathsome. And Milosevic, who had just lost his fourth war in a decade, leaving his country so desperate that gasoline was sold in Pepsi bottles by the side of the road, barricaded himself in Dedinje behind his electronic fence at a crucial time in his country's history.

He trusted no one and saw few people. Occasionally, he was spotted wandering aimlessly in his rose garden.

The day after the uneventful anniversary of Kosovo Polje, Julia and I drove to Cacak, a town that had been at the forefront of the anti-Milosevic movement. Cacak lies in the Serbian heartland of Sumadija, where many of the inhabitants were the descendants of peasant outlaws known as *hajduks*, who ran the Ottomans out of Serbia in 1804 and 1815. The people of Sumadija, the Sumadinci, are poor but fiercely proud. Their place in Serbian mythology is as warriors and revolutionaries. They do not fear authority.

On October 5, 2002, Cacak would play an important role in the rebellion that actually brought down Milosevic. It was the miners, workers, farmers, and peasants from the region who constituted a large percentage of the marchers who descended on Belgrade, eventually toppling him. An elderly man and his friend, a baker, used their loader truck to hoist students into the first floor of the Parliament building and later drove, under a hail of bullets from the police, into the Radio Television Serbia building.

Today's rally in Cacak was to be the first of a series that would attempt to loosen Milosevic's hold. It was organized by the Alliance for Change, an umbrella opposition group. Busloads of students, workers, and politicians were heading down from Belgrade to lend solidarity to Cacak. The mayor, Velimir Ilic, had to leave behind his five children and go into hiding after he received death threats.

During World War II, the Sumadinci provided the highest percentage of non-Communist fighters pitted against the Germans. In later wars, many of the paramilitary who murdered large numbers of people in the Croatian regions of Banija and Kordun in 1991 came from nearby Valjevo and Loznica.

"The Cacak region has always had a history of resistance and dissidence," said Verica Barac, a lawyer who had been arrested during the bombing for her involvement with the People's Parliament. "Milosevic sees Cacak as a threat because he sees every democratic change as a threat. He can only rule by police repression. This is a country where everything is banned."

Despite its resistance to the regime, Cacak got bombed by NATO. The bombs hit a vacuum-cleaner factory and leveled it, costing 40 percent of the working population of 200,000 their livelihood. It was later documented that the factory also housed a munitions plant. The other workers were employed in a food-processing plant which produced jam and preserves from the rich orchards surrounding the town.

Even after the bombing stopped, Cacak still suffered for its defiance of Belgrade. The local television and radio stations were closed. Sima Stokic, a member of the New Serbia Party, a small opposition group, was arrested for distributing leaflets. But the people of Cacak still held out.

Milosevic, who was growing increasingly paranoid, wanted to squash the budding rebellion. That morning, the road was blocked on the way to Cacak. About forty minutes out of Belgrade, a newly recruited policemen at a homemade roadblock stopped our car. He yanked open the driver's door, demanded papers, and said we had to go back to Belgrade. "No one's going to Cacak today. The demonstration is illegal. The road is closed."

We turned around, found a map, and took another road. So did the busloads of students and housewives and demonstrators who managed to get through. People who have been repressed for a decade would not let a few policemen stand in their way, which is why some Democratic Party supporters hitchhiked after their bus was confiscated. They arrived in time to hear the chanting from the crowd of thousands in the main square urging an end to Milosevic: "Gotov je! Gotov je!" (He's finished.)

There was electricity in Cacak. Some people, overwhelmed by the emotion of the end of the war, cried. Others stood and talked of the torment of living under Milosevic to anyone who would listen. Speaker after speaker took the podium, demanding an end to the regime. Everyone waited for the police to crush the meeting, but it didn't happen. Outside the television station, closed by Milosevic's police, the protesters carried handwritten signs: POLICE, LISTEN! YOUR PEOPLE ARE AWAKE, PUT DOWN YOUR BATONS!

People called that rally Day One, not only the day after the anniversary of Kosovo Polje, but the beginning of the end of the regime. A small group of women, all of whom had lost children in the war, stood off to one corner carrying a DAY ONE sign. One of them, with a face wizened by sorrow, pushed through the crowd. "This is it! If people come together all over Serbia, we can push him down. We can throw Milosevic away."

"He doesn't have long," said Nada Despotovic, a professor of literature who was in jail with Verica Barac. "How can you have an indicted man leading the country? The West should put him on trial." A man near Despotovic hearing the words "put him on trial" took up the chant. It passed quickly through the crowd until thousands of people were saying in unison, "Put him on trial! Put him on trial!" They clapped and stamped their feet. By the time the mayor of Nis, Zoran Zivkovic, came onto the makeshift platform to say "It's time to choose Milosevic or Serbia," the woman next to me burst into tears of frustration, then began to scream, *"Gotov je! Gotov je!"*

Then she grabbed me and pointed to the stage. Velimer Ilic, the outlawed mayor, was standing there, having come out of hiding at great risk. He looked down at the crowd with an air of victory. "The government has shamed us," he said. "Milosevic resign!"

The demonstration came to a temporary halt when someone threw a tube bomb, harmless but startling, from the bushes. People scattered and started wandering home. But Cacak was not forgotten. The rally had awakened the formerly placid Serbs to rise up against Milosevic, and later, after he was gone, people remembered the demonstration as a watershed.

Toward the end of the day, the summer sun still high in the sky, the mayor of Kraljevo climbed on the stage. The people who had not run from the tube bomb were tired and thirsty and anxious. Still, they listened to him. They were not thinking about how they were going to get through the roadblocks back to Belgrade, but, instead, how they would get rid of Milosevic.

"We once had second thoughts about whom to blame," he said,

looking down at the crowd. "Now we know it's Milosevic. We started the ball rolling. It cannot be stopped."

The end was beginning.

"I never said it before, but I believe this is the end of Milosevic," Aleksa Djilas said. "People are angry. He has got to go. As far as Kosovo is concerned, he is a total loser."

"There is only one subject here—the resignation of Milosevic and his government," added Slobodan Vuksanovic, vice president of the Democratic Party, slumping in a chair in his office. It was the day after the Cucak rally, and he was exhausted, his face gray with lack of sleep. "It's a question of our own survival. With him, we don't have a chance."

It would be the loss of Kosovo, the refugees, and the demoralized military which would ultimately lead to Milosevic's fall, Vuksanovic predicted. "In 1989, he told those people they would never be beaten again, and look what has happened," he said. "The refugees are symbols of that."

The opposition—which would later unite into a coalition of eighteen parties known as DOS, or Democratic Opposition of Serbia—may have known Milosevic's days were numbered, but they were too weak and fractured to do anything about it. One of the leading figures was Vuk Draskovic, leader of the Serbian Renewal Movement (SPO), then the largest opposition party in Serbia. Draskovic was a former journalist, novelist, and hard-line nationalist. During the Bosnian war, he had taken the line that Muslims were treacherous Serbs whose ancestors had converted to Islam.

Later, Draskovic became one of the biggest opponents of the war in Bosnia, although he could never make up his mind whether or not the greater crime was Milosevic the warmonger or Milosevic losing to the Muslims. Just before the war, he became Milosevic's prime minister, but was sacked in the middle of the bombing campaign. Part of Draskovic's problem—and ultimately his downfall—was his political indecision.

Briefly, following the bombings, Draskovic's popularity soared. A report published by an independent Belgrade think-tank, the Belgrade Institute of Social Sciences, claimed Slobodan Milosevic's popularity had fallen by half since the beginning of the NATO bombing campaign. The appeal of Vojislav Seselj, the ultranationalist leader of the Serbian Radical Party, had also diminished. This gave way to Draskovic, whose party had its highest ratings since 1990.

During the bombing, Draskovic—looking more and more like a World War II Chetnik fighter, with long flowing hair and a full dark beard—was featured regularly on CNN. He spoke in halting, careful English, trying to convince the world that the Serbs in Kosovo were simply defending themselves against an attack by nineteen nations. But some technocrats at the Ministry of Telecommunications—who worked hand in hand with Milosevic—must have not liked what they saw, because he was eventually sacked for "public statements which were contrary to government stands." Draskovic was called a "corrupt opportunist" by State Television and viewed as a man who would do anything to be courted by the West.

Though charismatic, Draskovic did, in fact, have a schizophrenic quality. A former Communist who once said he was "Red on the outside, me on the inside," he then turned and said there were "two great evils—civil war and Communism." In 1991, he led the first anti-Milosevic demonstrations in downtown Belgrade. Milosevic sent tanks onto the streets, but Draskovic gallantly led the crowds chanting, "Vuk, Vuk." He was imprisoned and beaten, along with his wife, Dana, but he returned to lead the street demonstrations in 1996–97.

Despite his enthusiasm for justice, Draskovic still chose later to join the Milosevic regime. "I don't regret it," he told me pointedly after the NATO war. "I did it on the condition that Milosevic would agree to an international peacekeeping force in Kosovo."

But when the war ended, Draskovic tried to distance himself from Milosevic. He reminded people of his former role as a freedom fighter. He called for an interim government, early elections, democratic reforms, and a free press to try to integrate Yugoslavia into Europe. But his image was tainted. His final mistake was refusing to align himself with DOS, and he thus fell out of the political frame as new leaders came forward to take Milosevic's place.

The day after Yugoslavians went to the polls on September 24, Draskovic was in his summer home on the Montenegrin coast, disgruntled and exhausted. He was effectively grounded. He had survived two assassination attempts—one in September 1998, which killed his brother-in-law and his bodyguards; the last on June 15, when gunmen opened fire on his sitting room while he was eating a plate of yogurt and cheese and watching television.

He could not go back to Belgrade, where his would-be assassins were still free; nor could he run for office. Instead, the mayor of Belgrade, Vojislav Mihajlovic, was the candidate for the SPO. Draskovic was watching the news of Belgrade from Montenegro.

I went to visit him along with his old friend, the Balkans correspondent Dessa Trevisan. He opened the door of his small cottage, which was guarded by Montenegrin policemen, looking exhausted. The windows were now bulletproof, and there were still bullet holes in the wall and on the sofa where Draskovic had been sitting until he dove under a table.

Draskovic had lost weight, the flesh below his cheekbones having sunk into his face. He spoke slowly in English.

"After tomorrow, nothing will be the same in Serbia again," he said, sounding slightly hollow. While Dessa spoke to him, he got up frequently, seemingly full of nervous energy. He talked of the past.

Draskovic would need a mighty political comeback. His image in Serbia had been shattered by the decision to join Milosevic, and by an earlier photograph of him kissing Madeleine Albright's hand. It was clear that the man who might have replaced Milosevic—and might have done a good job—had fallen from grace.

By the time we met in Montenegro, the attention had already shifted to Zoran Djindjic, the former mayor of Belgrade. An academic who had studied philosophy in Germany, Djindic had a successful business dealing in industrial machinery in Eastern-bloc countries. He was ambitious, smooth, and in many ways ruthlessly focused.

Unlike Draskovic, Djindic had consistent street credibility. Born in northern Bosnia, the son of an army officer in the Yugoslav National Army, he rebelled against the Communist system. At twenty, he was imprisoned in Slovenia for leading a dissident organization during the Tito years. He left, becoming part of the Frankfurt School of philosophy, studying under Jürgen Habermas and writing a dissertation criticizing Karl Marx.

In 1989, he returned from his studies burning with idealism, and founded the Democratic Party. He eventually led the winter

1996–97 demonstrations against Milosevic, alongside Draskovic. He marched with angry pensioners and frustrated students, announcing, "I am the horse the West should back." Instead, they supported Draskovic.

After the NATO war, Djindjic made the shrewd decision to back the cause of the disgruntled Serbian refugees from Kosovo, and presented their leaders at press conferences, which he called frequently. He courted the West, traveling to London and Germany. He met with British Foreign Secretary Robin Cook and announced that "I am confident that this time next year Milosevic will be history."

His party lacked power and had no seats in Parliament, because they boycotted the 1997 election. But his outspoken pro-Western stance and focus on the economy appealed to people. Djindjic's deputy in the Democratic Party, Slobodan Vuksanovic, went so far as to say that he wanted Yugoslavia to join NATO.

However, he made one mistake. During the NATO bombing, Djindjic fled to Montenegro, to escape a warrant Milosevic had issued for his arrest for avoiding the draft. Like Draskovic, he had also received death threats—but so had others, and they stayed put in Belgrade. Djindic's deputy Vuksanovic, for instance, frequently had visits from "these NBA basketball player–types, skinheads with sunglasses and gold necklaces." Vuksanovic and others like Goran Svilanovic, leader of the Civic Alliance, a coalition of human rights activists, stayed in Belgrade during the worst days. Svilanovic actually had been called up for military service and served—despite the fact that his party supported conscientious objectors.[3]

While the opposition in theory was based on intelligence and determination, they lacked power in the face of Milosevic's regime. Yet they knew—as did everyone—that it was coming to an end.

"I'm speaking as a soldier and a member of the opposition," Svilanovic said one afternoon in his office in downtown Belgrade. "It's all over for Milosevic. It's the beginning of the end." It started, he said, with the refugees fleeing Bosnia and Croatia, the devastation of the infrastructure, and now the gloomy prospect of a winter looming ahead with shortages of food and heat. "It could be a month, it could be two months, or seven months, even a year. But this is the final end—of his policy and political life."

In fact, it took a little more than a year. Fifteen months later, the opposition, aided by students, peasants, and blue- and white-collar workers, took to the streets of Belgrade and finally pushed Milosevic out.

Five months after the bombing, I went back to Belgrade to see how quickly the opposition was moving. As soon as my cell phone registered a signal, text messages kept coming up, from Otpor, the resistance group founded by students. There would be a beep, then the words *"Gotov je."*

But Milosevic was not finished yet. It was the beginning of the winter everyone was dreading, and the cold and fog were descending. The nights came quickly and money was scarce. The underworld, however, was flourishing. In restaurants like Villa or Franchet or bars like KGB, the mafiosi lounged in smoky banquettes with their girlfriends, shouting into cell phones. The spirit of Cacak appeared to have faded. People seemed more focused on surviving, on getting enough money to pay their bills, than on getting rid of Milosevic.

Part of it was bitterness and, in many ways, the postponement of the trauma from the war. Suzanna, a radio journalist, told me it was the fault of the West.

"Everything they have done has kept Milosevic firmly in place," she said. "He would be gone if it weren't for the air strikes." Suzanna had been working at the station for five years. She was a good reporter, one of the best. She earned DEM 80 a month and lived with her mother.

"The only reason I stay in this country," she said, "is because of the graves of my ancestors."

Despite the lack of cash, we went out every night. The bars—places with names like Mondo, Soho, and Scena—were crowded with tall and elegant people who smoked constantly.

"Criminals," a friend, Marija, snorted. "If you go to Franchet and you see people eating two-course dinners and drinking wine, they're either criminals or foreigners."

Marija took me shopping. She picked me up at the Hyatt—which had closed several floors due to lack of customers—and we drove to a nondescript house near the Old Town. We passed two bodyguards who searched us for guns. Inside, we met a man with a shaved head and a rottweiler who pointed us in the direction of a room full of young women. Boxes of expensive Italian lingerie spilled across the floor, lingerie that in Italy would cost hundreds of dollars. Women were stripping off their shirts and pulling on lace camisoles and silk nightgowns. The tags had been ripped out, and Marija hissed, "Don't ask where any of this comes from." When we left, the man told Marija that he was getting a shipment of Fendi and Prada the following week.

Then they went home, slept briefly, then headed for work. "Except," Marija pointed out, "most people don't have any work anymore."

She steered her car across the bridge, over the Sava. "But people don't want to think about unhappy things."

At first glance, there did not seem to be a problem. Then, when you talked to people, you realized there was a common thread: everyone spent all their money on bars or restaurants; no one had any dreams of the future, or plans; no one was getting married and having children. University classes were held in an old cinema downtown, and people shared seats and had to write with their notebooks on their knees.

There were few prospects once classes finished. There was just the constant thud of techno music, drugs from Turkey and Albania, and lots of vodka and brandy and scotch. Eventually, though, it was those students and disgruntled individuals combined with the opposition—and backed by American money coming from a shadowy office in Budapest—who toppled Milosevic. Once events started happening, once the wave gathered, it crashed hard.

On September 24, 2000, the Yugoslavian people—minus most of Montenegro, whose citizens followed the call of their president Milo Djukanovic for a boycott—went to the polls. It was clear beforehand that Milosevic would rig the polls by getting the Chinese immigrants to vote and signing up dead people. He tried hard to stay in power. But a count several days later revealed that Vojislav Kostunica, a little-known academic, had won. Predictably, Milosevic refused to accept the count, using a constitutional provision calling for a rerun between the two highest-placed candidates if neither polled a 50 percent majority.

In the interim, Milosevic hoped he could find a loophole that would give him another term in office. At the same time, he was planning his counterattack to the revolution he knew was coming.

In Pozarevac, the people began to take down the posters of Mira Markovic's YUL Party the day after the elections and scrawled fresh graffiti over the ones that were left. *HE'S FINISHED*. In the center of town, in a place reserved for funeral notices of local residents, was a formal, printed death announcement for Slobodan Milosevic. BORN IN SEPTEMBER 1987, AT THE 13TH SESSION OF THE COMMUNIST PARTY OF YUGOSLAVIA; DIED ON 24 SEPTEMBER 2000. THE FUNERAL WILL BE HELD 5 OCTOBER 2000 IN BELGRADE.

The "death announcement" was surrounded by photographs of demonstrators triumphantly celebrating the last days of the Milosevic reign. As I stood reading the notice, two kids with crew cuts, Igor and Steva, were looting one of Marko's abandoned enterprises, a mobile-phone shop.

"If you need a plug for your mobile phone, or a SIM card, come on in," invited Igor, who was nine.

"Where's the owner?" I asked. Steva began jumping up and down. "Gone! Gone! Marko's gone!"

On Ulica Partizana (Partisan Street), Marko's house was locked up, as was his café and his theme park, Bambiland, which he opened at the start of the war in Kosovo. At the Non-Stop Bakery, another business of his, where I had once bought a croissant and listened to people talk about how miserably they lived while the Milosevics lived grandly, the windows were smashed by rocks. There was a sign on the door. CLOSED BECAUSE OF LOOTING.

"The thief is finally being robbed!" cried my friend Elizabetta. The irony of it delighted her. "Now they know, now they know how we felt all these years."

Marko was gone. He had boarded a Yugoslav Airlines flight to Moscow, where his uncle Borislav—Milosevic's brother—was ambassador. The rumor was that he had been refused entry to China. It was not clear whether he had already shifted the multimillion-pound fortune he had made, or what his father in fact had done with the bulk of their money.

The October 5 revolution that toppled Milosevic, several weeks after the election, was a relatively quiet one as East European uprisings go and considering the damage he had done to his country. When the people came out, they came in droves—the marchers from Cacak, the students, the miners carrying clubs and sticks, the Otpor hierarchy who had been beaten and humiliated by the regime. They were all there.

Only one person died, and that was an accident. There could have been more. What we truly believed was that Milosevic, with his family history of suicide and depression, would launch an all-out massacre, killing hundreds of people before going down himself. The day it was supposed to come, the weather shifted in Belgrade. The heat dropped, the winds from the east began. The winter was coming.

In the city, there were barricades set up and workers and peasants had come from the countryside to protest against Milosevic. They were armed and ready to fight against Milosevic's army and his tanks. But it never happened. A group stormed the Federal Parliament and Radio Television Serbia. The resistance groups had also organized to take over Radio B-92, which had been seized during the war in Kosovo.

It happened in a matter of hours. Milosevic did not even impose a state of emergency, failing, comically, to get the signatures needed from his colleagues. The army never attacked. The tanks never rolled into the city.

Earlier, during the buildup to the revolution, Zoran Djindic met Commander Legiya from Frenki's Guys. The two men sat for two hours in Tashmajdan Park. By the end of it, in an act of brilliant diplomacy which would also ensure his own legacy as a peacemaker, Djindic convinced Legiya—who had been ordered by a desperate Milosevic to attack the crowd—not to touch them.

Milosevic was waiting, powerless, in his villa, Mira and Marija alongside him. The fact that he had failed to mobilize the army or the antiterrorist police caused him great despair: in the past, he could always rely on the army to crush the protesting mobs. His power was slipping from his hands, and he could not control it. General Pavkovic had told him there were no drivers for the tanks poised to roll into the city. When he tried to order the air force base at Batajnica, north of Belgrade, to prepare his jet for a flight to Athens, the request was refused.

He had no choice but to concede defeat. He did it on the condition that he would not be extradited to The Hague.

After the revolution, Milosevic stayed holed up in his house at Uzicka 15, pacing the floors. One of his lawyers told me he was refusing to look at a television set and was as restless as a caged animal. The authorities opened an investigation into Milosevic's abuse of power in Serbia.

For several months through the icy winter, crowds of Milosevic hard-liners held vigils at his house. Alongside them was a smaller group calling for Milosevic to save the country by surrendering himself to The Hague.

For months, Milosevic lived every day not knowing when they would come and get him. The only certainty was that they would. Carla del Ponte, the chief Hague prosecutor, had been putting intense pressure on Western governments not to make deals with Kostunica unless they had full cooperation.

As the American-imposed deadline, March 31, 2001, for the Serb authorities to arrest Milosevic or forfeit aid money drew nearer, I stood in the midst of that crowd. The tension was high. Milosevic's bodyguards stood near the gate; a line of police stood on the other side. The crowd swayed and chanted.

Milosevic had been promised by Pavkovic, his chief of staff, that if he conceded defeat, Kostunica would not hand him over to The Hague. As long as he remained in Yugoslavia, he was told, he would remain safe from the war crimes tribunal. But the government did not keep its promise. The first attempt to take him to prison came on March 30, when a SWAT team was beaten back by Milosevic's guards. The second assault came the following day and was led by Legiye, Milosevic's former henchman. The men entered Milosevic's fortress, which by this point had been under siege for thirty-three hours with no electricity and no water.

At gunpoint, the former Yugoslav leader surrendered and was read a list of charges against him: financial misdealings; damaging Serbia's economy and introducing hyperinflation. A statement was presented, signed by Kostunica, Djindic, and Serbian President Milan Milutinovic, indicating that criminal proceedings against Milosevic were not instituted by The Hague and guaranteeing the safety and property of Milosevic and his family.

At 4:30 A.M., the winter sky still dark, Milosevic was led off. His daughter, Marija, could not stand the humiliation. Fueled by a heady cocktail of sedatives and cognac, she followed her father, firing five shots in the air from her handgun, screaming at him not to give up: "Coward! Why not commit suicide? Kill yourself!"

Gallantly, Milosevic apologized for his daughter's behavior. He was taken to Belgrade Central Prison, where he became prisoner number 101980. A few days later, European Union leaders met, and sanctions against Belgrade were eventually lifted. Aid money was allocated to rebuild the city.

The weather grew better as spring took hold of the city. The cafés were full. After a decade of isolation, Belgrade was seemingly free. Europe's last Communist regime had fallen. *Srbija je ustala.* Serbia has arisen.

While Milosevic was growing accustomed to life in cell 1121, news broke that would make his extradition easier: a series of mass graves of Kosovar Albanians was discovered inside Serbia itself, one near the Batajnica air force base near Belgrade. The corpses had been moved north during the bombing campaign.

On June 28, 2001, the anniversary of Kosovo Polje and an Orthodox holiday known as Vidovdan, or St. Vitus Day, Kostunica—who had said in the past that he would refuse to hand over Milosevic—briefly stood back. All week, Milosevic's lawyers assured me that he could not be sent to The Hague, that there was no hard evidence and the constitution protected him.

But in the end, Milosevic was taken to The Hague on the basis of the provision in the Serbian Constitution which stipulates that the Serbian government may take over if the federal government collapses. It was Djindjic, the prime minister, who was given the dirty job of sending Slobodan Milosevic off to The Hague for crimes against humanity in Kosovo. Djindjic would be gunned down in front of his Belgrade office in March 2003, allegedly by the criminal underworld.

The decree authorizing Milosevic's extradition was approved by fourteen votes to one, the sole dissenter being a member of Kostunica's party. The Yugoslav Parliament had taken advantage of a loophole in the constitution that, ironically, Milosevic himself had introduced in 1990.

The move was not entirely popular. Some Serbs saw it as a betrayal, and claimed that it was no coincidence that the donors' conference for the Former Republic of Yugoslavia was coming up at the end of the week. Without Milosevic in The Hague, it was unlikely the government would get more aid.

Within days, the government collapsed under the pressure of his removal. Thousands of people were back in the streets. On the walls of buildings that once said GOTOV JE was scrawled SLOBODA ZA SLOBODANA. Freedom for Slobodan.

I had been waiting in Belgrade for weeks for it to happen, and when it finally did, I reached for my phone. The first person I called was a friend in Sarajevo, a friend from the war, a soldier. This is what I was thinking: Sarajevo—1,200 days of siege; 12,500 civilians dead, among them 1,600 children, most killed by snipers who saw their victims before they shot them. Srebrenica—an estimated 7,000 Muslim men massacred. Estimated death toll from the Bosnian war, 200,000; 24,000 missing.

I wanted to be in Sarajevo that day, not in Belgrade. I wanted be with my friends: the commander with the dog; the young soldier in Mostar; the doctor from Kosevo Hospital. I wanted to sit in a café called the Blue Point that stayed open during the war. Or see a poet friend who was losing his mind during the siege, and still tried to get food for his puppy. Or see the determination of a young girl, a swimming champion, who had lost her breast from shrapnel.

My Mostar friend, when I reached him on the phone, reacted strangely. He had been a good fighter, a sniper. His eyesight was perfect. The last time I had seen him, a few months before, he told me a joke:

"How do you know it's summer?"
    "Because my grandmother came from Srebrenica in her slippers."

Bosnians always had the best sense of humor of all the former

Yugoslavs. During the war, the jokes hid a lot of pain. But when I reached my friend on the phone and told him what was happening in Belgrade, he sounded bored. The lead-up to the RAF jet landing at a Dutch military base with Milosevic on board seemed to draw no emotion.

He said nothing, only breathed. It was rush hour in Sarajevo, he was driving in his father's old Mercedes. I could hear cars honking, traffic, music playing.

"It doesn't matter anymore if they got him," he finally answered. "It won't bring back the dead."

Then, after a while, it did not seem real. Milosevic had not only destroyed a country, but thousands of lives, families, shattered memories. The day they came for him, the day his political career really ended was, strangely, the anniversary of the day it began. Milosevic had launched his political career in 1989, and in 1914, on the same day, Gavrilo Princip, a Sarajevan Serb, assassinated Archduke Franz Ferdinand, putting into motion the events that led to World War I. In 1948, on the same day, Stalin's Cominform expelled Yugoslavia, which meant for may Serbs years of more deprivation and isolation after World War II.

Milosevic was taken by helicopter to Tuzla, a city where thousands of refugees from Srebrenica had gone after the city had fallen in April 1993. He had one final look at his former country, Yugoslavia, and by midnight, he was on a jet bound for the Netherlands.

Aleks, a Serb, and I sat in the car. I kept thinking back to Sarajevo, to Srebrenica, to Gorazde, to Foca, to Kosovo. It was over. We listened to the radio, smoking Serbian cigarettes. The report said Milosevic had asked to change into a suit and pack his slippers.

Aleks said, "I feel kind of sorry for him. They didn't have to humiliate him like that."

The radio said Milosevic had a small bag and got into the car, not protesting, not fighting, not complaining. But he mumbled something about being sold so cheaply.

Only when he boarded the helicopter did he turn around and say to the guard. "Do you know it's Vidovdan?" The guard nodded.

"Goodbye, Serb brothers," Milosevic said. He asked someone where his overcoat was. Then he turned his back on Belgrade, on Yugo-slavia.[4]

Sometime later, Aleks and I were drafting down the Danube in a boat, crossing flat, infinite plains, toward Smedervska, near Palanka, middle Serbia, old Serbia, heart of Serbia. It was high summer.

The village consisted of a few winding lanes, some cattle, a café, some kerchiefed old women. People were friendly, but openly stared. Nearby were deep forests, bowers of wildflowers. Everything was the same as it had been for decades: simple, rural lives.

In 1989, Milosevic had given a speech here, and people remembered it. It seemed they were headed for good things after the long Communist years. Things would change. Money in the bank! More jobs! They still supported him here, had done so all during the wars, all during the betrayal. They kept his portrait on the walls, even after Kostunica won.

Outside the small café, called Pobra, we sat at a small rickety table while the owner, Predrag, brought dishes of red peppers and onions; slices of lamb; sopska, a mixed salad, and bread. There was the sound of the gusla coming from the kitchen: mournful and slow.

Predrag put down the dishes and sat heavily. We ate.

"It happened too quickly," Predrag finally said. "And on Vidov-dan!" The day was significant, he said, because on Vidovdan, 1989, Milosevic had promised everyone a heavenly Serbia.

"And Kostunica sent him away on Vidovdan and promised us the earth," he said, lighting a filterless cigarette. "Something is wrong. I am not an intelligent man, but something is wrong."

His wife called him into the kitchen. The people who replaced Milosevic, he said, were the same. "During Milosevic's time, we had local thieves," he said. "Now we have government thieves." It was not about nationalism; it was about power. Their own power. Destiny. Serbs. History. Milosevic himself had said The Hague was a political circus designed to destroy the nation.

"It is the same," he declared, "as when they killed Karadjordjevic and sent his head back to Istanbul." He was referring to a leader of the Serb uprising against the Turks in 1804 whose nickname was

Black George. He was executed by another Serb leader and his head sent to the sultan as a sign of loyalty.

Aleks said, looking up from his plate, "It's like a circle, Serb history. Everything seems fated. Everything is destiny."

Predrag got up and slapped the table, hard. "That's it exactly!"

His wife came and stood in the door, frowning. "I need you here," she said, looking at the dirty plates.

"Bad luck is following us," Predrag said darkly, and went to join his wife in the kitchen.

Chapter Six

Bosnia Herzegovina casts a spell on all who live there and who were privileged in the past to acquaint themselves with the republic. Sentimentalism plays very little in this—it is through the middle of Bosnia that East meets West; Islam meets Christianity; the Catholic eyes the Orthodox across the Neretva, the lines of the Great Schism; Bosnia divided the great empires of Vienna and Constantinople; Bosnia was perhaps the only true reflection of Yugoslavia. It is both the paradigm of peaceful, communal life in the Balkans and its darkest antithesis.

Misha Glenny, *The Fall of Yugoslavia*

You can forgive but not forget . . . we think that love is greater than hate. . . . but it is a small step to go from hate to love; love to hate. It is a very thin line.

Zeljko Kopanja, editor, *Nezavisne Novine*,
Banja Luka, August 2000

Northern and Eastern Bosnia
August 2000

We crossed the River Sava as the light was fading, arriving in Bosan-ska Gradiska at the hour when the bathers were wading into the murky river. Across the long bridge that links the Bosnian Serbs to their lifeline, Croatia, a faint breeze came from the east, the wide plain that runs through Serbia, through Romania. It was high summer and very hot.

From the border bridge, fishermen cast poles into the gloom of the water. A tugboat moved slowly in the distance. The air was utterly still; there was little sound. The local hotel, which had housed soldiers during the war with Croatia, was reflected perfectly in the water.

At the edge of the water, sitting on a wooden bench, was Milka Belina, ninety-three years old. She was carrying a basket of reddish-green tomatoes. She saw me, a stranger, and approached, holding out the basket in front of her. I have something to tell you, she said, and led me back to the edge of the water, to the bridge wall, to sit.

She was a Serb. She had lived through three wars. Now, in this town, Muslims were returning and they were getting all the money, all the benefits. Who felt anything for the Serbs? It was the Serbs who had tried to hold off the onslaught of the Turks, of the Ottoman Empire from the rest of Europe. Did no one appreciate them?

Her daughter Biljana arrived. She was elegant in her pressed summer dress and pearls, but her smile was lifeless and drained. Her life, she said, was a constant struggle for money. For teaching French two days a week at the university in Banja Luka, she got DEM 400 a month, an amount that barely paid the food bill.

The problem, she said, was that post-Dayton, the map had been redrawn. Her home now lay within the boundaries of Republika Srp-ska, which meant the inhabitants did not benefit from economic aid pouring into the rest of the country.

In the distance was a handsome Serbian church cracked with bullet holes. During the war, a sniper had hid in the belfry, firing rounds across the river. Biljana used to pass and see the shadow of the sniper in the window. Now she thinks she sometimes still sees the shadow, a ghost of the war. Life in the five years since Dayton, she said, became more bearable. "But it's still not good," she said, watching the water.

"I still feel grief for Yugoslavia," she said. "I used to say I'm a Yugoslav. Except Yugoslavia no longer exists."

She gave directions for the road to Banja Luka, wished us luck, and walked home, past the road with the church where the sniper used to hide.

Banja Luka
August 15–18, 2000

During the war, Banja Luka, the second-largest city in Bosnia and the center of the Bosnian Serb military operations, conjured an image of darkness. The ethnic-cleansing campaign had been planned and launched from there. The surrounding towns, leafy, green villages where neighbors had known each other for years and years, like Omarska, Sanski Most, Prijedor, were places where evil things had happened. Now there was blood on these towns and the ghosts of too many people. A 1991 census of the area recorded 536,000 Muslims and Croats in the area. By 1995, there were fewer than 45,000. Where had they gone?

Banja Luka was controlled, more or less, by Radovan Karadzic in Pale. The Bosnian Serb leader had chose Pale—a run-down former Olympic ski resort and weekend retreat of urbane Sarajevans—because he wanted to remain close to Sarajevo in order to destroy it. The Sarajevans, who retained their humor even during the blackest days of the siege, dismissed the Pale residents as *papak*, or cow (literally, hoof) people.

Karadzic wanted the city within his sights. It was a short drive from his headquarters to the snipers' positions above the city. From there, he could see everything. But his obsession with Sarajevo eventually alienated the weightier political and economic leadership in Banja Luka.

In 1995, at the tail end of the war, three members of the Serb Parliament, all from Banja Luka, were expelled after they attacked the Pale gang for their tunnel vision regarding the war. Since then, most of the major opposition parties, including the Serb-backed Socialist Party, had set up headquarters in Banja Luka. The local Krajina radio run by the army blasted Pale daily, and two opposition magazines began publication there days after the Dayton Peace

Accord was signed in Paris on December, 14, 1995.[1]

Slowly, Banja Luka started emerging not just as a military nerve center, but as a rival political base. The modus operandi of each center was entirely different. While Pale was dominated by primitive nationalism, Banja Luka was populated by people with a more Western-leaning mentality, who believed they were unfairly paying the price for Karadzic's determination to take Sarajevo. The more liberal politicians in Banja Luka felt that the siege had done them more harm than good—while the front lines in Sarajevo had barely moved from the start of the war, the city was still shelled. What was the point of it?

The point, of course, was Karadzic and Mladic's plan to drive the population to madness. This was transmitted by the international press, which isolated the Bosnian Serbs by depicting the plight of ordinary people struggling to get a bucket full of water from a well in full view of a sniper. The result was that the Bosnian Serbs were unable to obtain help from Belgrade or the Russians.

"The leadership knew it was ruling a small, poor state but thought it did not need the rest of the world. This was very foolish," said Dragutin Ilic, the head of the Belgrade-backed Socialist Party in 1996.[2] Banja Luka also contributed a large number of soldiers to Karadzic's army, and the industries around the city added to Pale's treasury.

By the time Biljana Plavsic became Bosnian Serb president in 1996, Radovan Karadzic was reviled by all but a few of the 1 million Serbs he ruled. He was fading from public view. When Plavsic moved the headquarters Pale to Banja Luka, it widened the schism between the Serbs there and in Pale. Plavsic had by then become the favorite of Western leaders and her move told them that the Serb leadership was more willing to compromise with the West.

Yet one can be deceived by Banja Luka. While it feels more like Belgrade or a Middle European city with its wide boulevards and pleasant cafés, little was done to stop the massacres there. Evidence from meetings now shows that planning for the deportation of Muslims commenced nearly one year before the summer of 1992, when liaisons were conducted between members of the secret police. All the mosques, many of them centuries old, were destroyed and their stone blocks used to build a parking lot or dumped outside the city.

By the time the war actually started, people were perfectly willing to turn on their neighbors. Others, who now claim they knew nothing, chose to ignore the fact that their Muslim neighbors were rounded up and trucked off to a factory, where they would either be tortured or killed.

Few people tried to stop the mosques from being destroyed. Of the forty-eight in Banja Luka before the war, not one remains, not even the four-hundred-year old Ferhat-Pasha. None were destroyed in battle. All of them were devastated by those who had lived next to their Muslim neighbors. The police brought two truckloads of explosives into the Ferhat-Pasha and blow up the priceless treasures. Some of the local Serbs said the Muslims themselves did it.

Even today, few people object to war criminals who walk the broad boulevards of Banja Luka, go to the movies, or serve on the police force or local committees. It is almost as though a door was slammed shut at the end of the war, and its contents buried. "The secrets," Zeljko Kopanja, at Bosnian Serb journalist, told me, "lie in the Bosnian hills."

There were no actual battles fought in Banja Luka. There were shortages and a lack of electricity, heat, food, and water. The city was drained by its war effort. The people felt used by Pale, resentful that they were tainted internationally because of Karadzic's warped ideology. At one point, during funerals for the dead soldiers, who were buried in tennis courts because the graveyards were full, there were shouts of anti-Karadzic instead of anti-Muslim slogans.[3] But by that point, their fate had been sealed. They had thrown in their lot with Pale. Now they were stuck.

As late as 1995, Muslims and Croats were still disappearing from their homes in Banja Luka. Arkan and his Tigers arrived from Eastern Slavonia in the autumn, shortly before Dayton, to show the few remaining non-Serbs that the war was not finished. Rapes were frequent, but not a single person was held accountable. Some Muslims took to moving from house to house because "they hunt us down like rabbits," one former professor at the University of Banja Luka said in 1995.[4] The policy of fear, which had been used as a weapon, was still in evidence.

Non-Serbs were fired from jobs without severance pay and were left without income, pension, or insurance; some were told to report for forced labor. The ones who were captured and put in camps and then released were often obliged to walk across minefields to Croatia or through front lines into central Bosnia. I saw such an exodus in October 1992. Most of them were too shell-shocked, too traumatized, to speak. They did not actually know why they had been sent away from their homes.

Non-Serbs—the ones who weren't deported—had few legal rights. Six Roman Catholic priests and one nun were murdered; other clerics were imprisoned. "I expect to be killed every day," said Franjo Komarica, the Roman Catholic bishop of Banja Luka, who remained under house arrest and continually appealed to the international community to stop the persecution of non-Serbs. "It's like Nazi Germany with its veneer of legality—where the extremists are always accused of actually doing the killing—and it's just that the police never quite manage to catch them," said one U.N. official in 1995.

The U.N. Security Council Resolution 941 in September 1994 demanded that Bosnian Serbs cease their policy of ethnic cleansing in Banja Luka, Bijelina, and other areas under control of their forces, and to grant immediate access to special representatives of the secretary-general. Those conditions were never met. The U.N. and the international community put no pressure on the Bosnian Serb authorities and Slobodan Milosevic to stop the abuses.

The war crimes officially were filed away, and people were supposed to forget about them. Why then, five years later, did Banja Luka still feel eerie, still feel evil, even if the road leading into its center now is as modern as a road in California? There are gas stations, cafés with names like My Way with the usual roast lamb outside roasting, streets full of people buying newspapers in kiosks or ice cream in cafés, modern hotels with security gates. There were bright neon lights in the distance as we drove up, and a modern restaurant where we sat, with a menu in German. At the next table, a group of burly men eating schnitzel and fried potatoes were arguing football scores.

But I couldn't stop thinking that some of these people were responsible for what had happened, even if they walked among normal citizens now, lived normal lives. The war criminals were being protected by their neighbors. The men at the next table might have been innocent, but they might not have been. At any rate, no one here was talking.

"It's frustrating," a high-ranking American diplomat with a reputation for hunting the criminals told me in the winter of 2001 in Sarajevo. "A lot of terrible people who have never been indicted by the war crimes tribunal, and never will be indicted, are out there walking the streets. Thousands and thousands of them are in the streets. You pass them every day."

Predrag Radic, who served as mayor of Banja Luka during the war, told me this: he had been demonized by the Western press. He was held responsible for not stopping the deportations of thousands of non-Serbs. He said bitterly, "The Serbs are portrayed as rotten apples." He claims he did not have control of the police. Yet while he held office, thousands of Muslims were deported. He did nothing to control the paramilitary—such as Arkan—who came to be the "saviors" of Banja Luka. During his tenure, the Ferhat-Pasha Mosque was destroyed, even though he protests he tried to save it.

Radic said he was not a war criminal. He was blunt: "If The Hague wants to send me an invitation, fine! I'll give them my address." He drank coffee with me and said firmly that as a result of his "intervention" on behalf of the mosque, he suffered grave political repercussions in Pale and eventually fell from grace. He is no longer mayor but is a leading player in his political party.

Radic felt uncomfortable talking about the past. Awkwardly, he explained there had been no ethnic cleansing, or, if there had been, it was organized by the police without his knowledge. There were no mass graves: "I told Clinton's special envoy that if he found one mass grave, I'll take the shovel and dig and he can watch me." There had been no genocide. "This was a civil war in which everyone fought everyone else, but only the Serbs were described as the baddies."

"Why should I take all the responsibility?" he said with great indignition. He talked about the 65,000 Serb refugees who had passed the war years in Banja Luka, and how he had looked after them. "If you want the most blatant example of ethnic cleansing, there is Banija, Kordun, and Slavonia," he said, referring to parts of Croatia where Serbs lived until 1995. He spoke of various Muslim paramilitary groups in Sarajevo and said the Muslims were equally guilty of war crimes, but the world chose not to focus on them. "Let me draw a parallel," he said. "Everything that happened here happened on the other side as well."[5]

He spoke for some time. When I left, he walked me to the car. "You know," he said casually, "there are much darker places in Bosnia than Banja Luka."

I had the feeling I did not want to spend another night in Banja Luka.

Zeljko Kopanja, also a Bosnian Serb living in Banja Luka, believes that the city did not act on its own, and that a society must not be punished for the work of individuals. But he also thinks that the past must not be buried. It is not a popular position for a Bosnian Serb to take. As a result, he lost both his legs in a car bomb attack.

As a journalist and the editor of *Nezavisne Novine*, Kopanja initiated an investigation into Serbian atrocities committed during the war by paramilitary groups. While he did not believe the Serbs were "genocidal people," he felt that certain individuals were, and he set out to expose them. His theory was that the orders came from Belgrade.

He was warned to stop. Some of the warnings came from Belgrade. "People were worried they would find themselves indicted by The Hague," he explains. It was also a matter of pride. It was one thing for the Bosnians or the Croats to write critical articles about the Serbs' role in the war—it was not the place of the Serbs. Kopanja was the first Serb to do it.

He ignored them and continued the investigation. He went so far as to name names of war criminals in Banja Luka. On the morning of his forty-fifth birthday, on October 22, 1999, he woke and decided to walk to his office. But the sky changed color as he was having coffee. As the rain began, he returned home and took his car.

That decision changed his life. Opening the car door set off the bomb. He heard the explosion, saw the flames, but what he really remembers is the slow-motion whiteness in front of his eyes. He thought he saw one of his legs lying next to him, but it was dreamlike. He woke up in the intensive care unit of the hospital with both his legs blown off. The sheet just ended shortly above his knees.

When he got out of the hospital, people came up to him in the street with tears in their eyes and thanked him. He went back to his office and continued working. "I'm not an easily scared person," he said. "If I was, I would not have published what I did. I don't believe I live surrounded by the people who did this to me—in my mind, all traces of the crime lead back to Belgrade and the police force there."

Now he has prostheses donated from Europe, and he is able to walk shakily using crutches, but he is still getting fresh death threats in the mail. We cross the small yard in front of his office and sit down on a bench. The short walk exhausts him, having to swing his body to move his prostheses. It is painful to watch him struggle, but he lights a cigarette and shrugs. There is no self-pity, no anger.

"I don't see myself as a symbol of opposition or democracy," he says. Then he smiles. "We believe love is greater than hate." He told me his wife gave birth to a new baby since his accident.

As for his town, he believed people hid because of the shame they felt. Evil things took place here, and they knew it. "I'm an optimist," he said. "This is not the first war to have happened here. I believe there is a time that will come when people accept that it's their destiny to live together and that they have to trust each other and develop tolerance."

Later, he said that he still believed in some kind of unity between the Serbs, the Muslims, and the Croats. "Of course we cannot go back to the old days, if in fact the old days held any real unity," he said slowly. "Did Tito hold everything together? I guess so."

But he still believed in individuals who had the power to make real change. Then he stared down at the place where his legs had been.

"It would be a disaster if I gave up the fight for which I sacrificed my legs," he said.

Kozarac
August 4–5, 2000

Less than an hour away from Banja Luka, outside the village of Kozarac, I sat in an abandoned field where a house once stood— Zlatko's house—while he parted his hair to show me the Orthodox cross that had been carved into his skull. Five Serbs had held him down and burnt it into his flesh because they said he was half Muslim, half Croat, and needed to be taught religion. Zlatko rubs the cross idly. He stared out at the glade, pointing to a beehive.

"It used to be a lovely life," he said, his voice rising. "You have no idea how lovely it used to be here." The bee sound rose. The sun beat down, overpowering. The scent of roses, dried in the heat, drifted from the dirt. Sometimes, Zlatko ran into Serb neighbors whom he used to know before the war. He always said "Good Morning." Then he said: "What happened?"

"They don't answer me," he said.

The field used to hold Zlatko's house before it was destroyed. He lived there, working as a stonemason, with his mother, his six sisters, his two little brothers, and his own wife and two children, until one summer night, when the Bosnian Serbs occupied the town.

First there was shooting, and all the villagers stayed inside. No one thought of running away. No one believed that war was coming. Then the tanks rolled down the hill, and Kozarac was cleared in one day. Women were herded onto buses for Croatia. The Serbs came for the men.

The first night, some soldiers from the Knin Corps arrived and kicked in Zlatko's door. "Come out, Turks!" they screamed, while Zlatko's mother, clutching his arm, begged him to run away, through the back door. But he could not run. The Serbs were inside, with guns, rifling through the house, smashing dishes. Someone punched him in the mouth, knocked out his teeth.

"That was it," he says. "I was a prisoner." They took his two brothers, one seventeen, one fourteen, away with him. He went in a paddy wagon, the boys in a bus with some other men from the village who were already sitting, waiting, frightened and not knowing what was coming next.

Despite Zlatko's ancestry, he would have identified himself as a Yugoslav. During the war, he was classified as a non-Serb. For that, he spent the next nineteen months in various concentration camps.

But first, they took him to Prijedor, to the police station, where he was questioned for four days, and where he recognized two of the men, Serb policemen, who were interrogating him. They set dogs on him and beat him with a garden hose with an aluminum stub on the end. They beat him with a fire extinguisher. Because he was of fighting age—thirty-seven—they wanted him to say if he knew where the Bosnian defenders were. He had just finished doing his military service for the Yugoslav National Army (JNA) a few years before and he was adamant that he did not know.

"How many Serbs have you killed?" they asked him. And, "Where is Aliya's [Izetbegovic] Army?" They made him run through a line of men, all holding wooden clubs, who rained blows down on his head and back. They starved him and beat him so badly that when they finally released him with other Muslim prisoners, first at Keraterm camp, and later, Omarska—a former iron mine and ore-processing plant that had been turned into an "investigation center" by the Serb civil authorities—his body had turned to purple mush. His uncle had to feed him with a spoon, like a baby bird.

At Omarska, he was given the job of collecting the bodies of those who were beaten to death in a room above the canteen. Sometimes their heads had been split open like watermelons and their brains spilled out over the floor. Sometimes their faces were mashed like potatoes, so that you could not tell if they had flat or big noses or a chin. Zlatko kept heaving, puking up his empty guts, after he carried each body to the fire to be burnt. He knew most of the bodies. Once, he went into a bathroom that was left open. The room was full of bodies turning blue. He fell on his knees and threw up.

Zlatko thinks there were about 5,000 Muslims in Omarska. Usually, they were made to stand all day in the beating sun of the courtyard, 40 degrees Celsius, for ten or twelve hours. Sometimes they were pushed into a room and a small bag of food was tossed in, and it would break when it hit the floor, so that they would fight among themselves for the food.

Water was thrown on the floor so that the men had to lap it up, like dogs. Sometimes a fire was built and men were pushed into the flames as the Serbs laughed. Other times, men would be yanked out of line for no reason at all and made to run the "tunnel" with Serbs on both sides with clubs. They lit tires and made the men jump over them, two or three at a time. When a man stumbled or fell or could not do it, he burned.

But the greatest punishment was to be taken to the White Room, the place from which few came back alive. It was three rooms, with a fire burning out front. When the Serbs killed someone, they took his remains and tossed them into the fire.

You could hear the screams at night, coming from the White Room, and sometimes Zlatko's job was to go in and pick up the body parts after the torture session was over. At night, the Muslims heard the women screaming too, the ones who were there, as they were raped. Zlatko knew the women, he saw them with their downcast eyes during the day, but he could not do anything to help them.

One night, they took him to the White Room. Zlatko had three ribs broken, but he was lucky: a friend jumped through a window because he could not take the torture anymore, and they killed him straightaway. Zlatko prayed to die, but every time he opened his eyes, he was still looking at his torturer.

Later, they took him to the Manjaca Camp. There he saw four men have their heads pulled back and the Serbs slit their throats, just like pigs. The beatings lasted all night, and at dawn, at roll call, most of the men would be dead.

He lost so much weight he did not recognize himself—he was 73 kilos when he entered the camp and 46 when he came out. One loaf of bread was split between twenty-two men. He remembers getting a bite and just chewing it, chewing it, chewing it, trying to keep the white flour taste in his mouth as long as possible.

But to Zlatko's greatest pain was that he could not protect his younger brothers. The seventeen-year-old was beaten so badly that he could not walk. And the younger one, Fuad, was sent to Trnopolje, another camp, which was believed to be even more brutal than Omarska.

Zlatko was eventually sent to Serbia, where he spent more than a year, and eventually released in Zenica in October 1993. He joined the Bosnian Army a few months later, and fought under the end of the war, but he came back in the end to Kozarac because it was the home of his grandparents. He says, "I wanted to prove that they can't expel us." He still sits down with his Serb neighbors. He sometimes sees people from the camp, and people who did things in the camp. He says a part of him is dead, he doesn't feel much anymore. "They can destroy me," he says, "but they can't destroy this country."

Most nights, Zlatko has nightmares about the White Room. "I'm dreaming of Omarska and what happened there. What was done, all of it, in my head. . . . I'm dreaming how they're beating and killing people. . . ." He wakes up screaming, grabbing things. Once, he nearly killed his child who was sleeping near him because he was dreaming of being tortured.

Some days Zlatko says he is all right, but then he might go to town and see one of the men who did it, and he gets scared. "The hair on the back of my neck stands up," he says. "They could do everything they wanted to us in the camp. You could not believe your eyes—no matter what I tell you, it is not enough to describe it. I used to think: What did I do? What did I do?"

Zlatko moves through the field where his family home used to be and pulls up a pot that belonged to his mother. She and most of the family live in Germany. He doubts they will ever return to Bosnia, but for him, for some reason, it's important to stay. He wants the Serbs to know he won't be driven off.

It's so hot this afternoon that sweat pours off him. He describes to me what it felt like to stand in the sun day after day, shirtless, without water, for hours. You felt like you were melting, he said, brains, eyes, hair, everything. Melting like a piece of chocolate in the sun. And that's what we were—nothing more. A piece of nothing.

"I don't know why this happened," he mutters, bending low over a piece of rubble that used to be a kitchen stove. "Why? Some kind of hate?"

Then he told me something. "The policeman who turned me in, a Serb, my neighbor, never liked me," he said. He described how they had a petty argument years before. When he saw the man again in the police station in Prejidor, the policeman had gloated. "Maybe now you shouldn't have done that to me all those years ago."

"So," I said, "this all happened—all this sorrow, all this misery—because some people had stupid grudges?"

Zlatko shrugged. It didn't really matter to him in the end. The fact is, it happened. Nothing will be the same again. He moves toward the place where the kitchen garden was, where his mother grew vegetables. He says, sifting through the dirt with his hands, that nobody knows how many people died in Kozarac. Or even why they died.

"They can't carry this earth away," he says quietly. "The earth stays."

Kozarac was 98 percent Muslim before the war, which made it a prime target for ethnic cleansers. The Serbs would mark the Muslims' houses with a blue X in a circle, so the cleansers could be sure they got it right.

You can't see the marks anymore. But the string of villages in the Banja Luka area is an example of how difficult it is to forge peace, to push reconciliation, or more realistically, to stop renewed ethnic conflict. The area is crisscrossed with the invisible markings of inhabitants who have been moved around, shifted, displaced, and then shifted again.

Kozarac, for example. Its Muslim population is nowhere near what it was before. People creep back, but slowly and carefully, as though they are about to plunge off a high dive into a swimming pool with no water. In a sense, they are.

Article VII of the Dayton Peace Accord declared 1998 as the year to resettle all refugees and displaced persons. But the idea of re-settlement is more complicated than simply rebuilding a house that has been burnt down. Kozarac is an example of how difficult this task is. Eight miles from Kozarac is Prijedor, which lies within Serb boundaries and has an exclusively Serb population. Once, there were Muslims in the town. South of Prijedor on the Sana River is Sanski Most, which has been given to the Bosnian-Croat Federation, but which was occupied by Serbs for most of the war. There, the Muslims who are coming back are frightened, and the Serbs who are forced to leave are angry, or vice versa.

They're coming back from Sweden, from Holland, or Norway and camping in the burnt fields where their houses once stood. "This is Bosnia and it will remain Bosnian," they say defiantly.

But it sounds hollow. People at the Blizanci Grill, which makes cevapcici and soggy french fries, are still too frightened to talk. Down the road, not even a five-minute walk away, is the Serb café, and there, sitting at the front table drinking a beer, is one of the infamous Tadic brothers. Dusko Tadic, who led a round of ethnic cleansing here, is sitting in a jail in Germany for war crimes, the first man convicted in The Hague court, which was established in 1993. His brother, Mladan, who spoke in his brother's defense at The Hague, owns the café, and the walls are lined with photographs of himself in various karate moves, sometimes with his young children.

Mladan has pale, flat, dun-colored eyes. We sit together in the late afternoon, over a beer. He frightens me. He tries to justify the war, justify his brother's brutality. "This war was one where brother killed brother. We are the same people with different religions. People higher up made us take up arms, and only innocents ended up suffering." As for his brother, he wasn't even in Kozarac when the Muslims were taken away! He's a "Serbian Dreyfuss! A victim of grave injustice!"

Then he said: "What happened here was the worst sin and the most shameful act of the Serbian people. We won't be able to wash away the shame from our faces and our hands." But as he says it, it sounds so artificial. I pay for our beers and leave. He watches with flat eyes full of contempt.

He gave me directions to the southern part of town, where the Serbs live. Their houses are neat and whitewashed. At the Mustang Café, there is pig roasting. But the men at the next table are friendly, even if they all look like war criminals. One, Mirko Grahovac, offers a plate of roast pork. He invites me to meet his family. He wants to talk about the war.

Mirko's home is not far away. He built it himself in 1973, and there is a grape arbor with bursting fruit, and a few turkeys wandering around, taking refuge from the heat. Mirko brings some cold drinks, but his wife does not want to come out and sit with us. She shakes my hand but regards me coldly, with suspicion. Marko tells me she thinks everyone hates the Serbs.

Mirko is a truck driver who traveled the roads of Slovenia, Croatia, and Bosnia over and over in the buildup to the war. Because of that, he knew the war was coming. Then slowly, he said, the mood changed in Kozarac. The army moved in and people became separated by politics.

"Even though I could see it coming, I can't believe what happened here," Mirko says, coming with the drinks and kicking one of the turkeys back into the road. "People were forced to flee. Before, everyone got along. We were good before the war. Nobody bothered with anyone's nationality."

His wife and parents fled the village when the army arrived, and he soon followed, "for my own security." Then he had to deliver supplies. "I had the only milk supply on my truck." When he returned, several weeks later, he said all the Muslim buildings were destroyed, all the Muslims were gone.

It was eerie, he said, as he walked through the town to see the place emptied of his former neighbors. "I had Muslim friends and they were sent to the camps," he says. "I heard about the camps, but how could I go rescue them? It would have been dangerous for me."

He doesn't know about leaving now. He admits the town is haunted. But life will eventually return to normal, he says. Resentments, hatreds, fade away.

But how can they?

The Muslims, in the upper, or northern, part of town, are still frightened of the Serbs, still have a kind of passivity that victims carry with them. "If it happened before, it can happen again," said one man who had survived four camps and had moved to Western Europe. He was only visiting for the holidays; he could not imagine himself actually living here again.

Some were building houses on the ruins of their old homes. The builders did not want to talk. At sunset, in the destroyed mosque, the late light filtered through the cracks in the walls made by sledgehammers and guns, bullets and fists. Someone hated this building so much that all their anger, all their vengeance, came out on the stones and mortar.

"Who did this?" I asked a farmer passing with his goats.

He stared at me. "No one. No one knows."

"But you must know! You were here."

He rushed off with his goats.

Then there's another old man. He's called Blagovic, and his house is the one nearest to the mosque. He's on crutches. An injury, he says, from when he was tortured in Trnopolje. His only son, born in 1962, was killed there. "Now my wife and I are alone," he said. "We're not going. Even if the USA is full of Bosnians. I'll stay a citizen of this country, a country that no longer exists." He begins to cry. I stand helplessly, unable to say anything. Then he wanders off, dragging his useless legs between the crutches.

It was getting dark. The crickets sang behind the deserted mosque. The crescent moon in the just-deepening blue sky came up behind the overripe plum trees. From somewhere not far away, the noise of construction drifted in. Then the muezzin—the call to prayer began as the sun sank in the hills.

The same Bosnian hills where all the secrets lie.

Sanski Most
August 12, 2000

> One day, I'll die from my love
> One day, I'll be killed by my hatred.
>
> *Jodgor Obid*

Albasa Kurbegovic is bending low over the headstone of her husband Husein's grave. She's bringing him flowers, a ritual she performs once a week. She kneels by his grave, quietly saying a prayer, and something about love.

It's a big week in Sanski Most. Muslims are reopening the mosque that was destroyed during the war. Albasa, who has a delicate, fine-boned face, is not going. The mosque reminds her of too much. After the old mosque was destroyed, she kept telling her husband that they should pack their bags and leave. But he stalled and stalled and stalled. He trusted people, Albasa says.

It's the second time I met her. The first time was a year after Husein, an important judge in Sanski Most, had been murdered, his body tossed in a mass grave, in the last wave of violence in the autumn of 1995. The paramilitary, invited by the Serb mayor, had staged a final push to cleanse the town of the few remaining Muslims. It was only a few weeks before the war officially ended. Albasa and Husein almost made it through untouched.

They took it for granted that they would survive. Even though Albasa hated what had happened to her town, how it had been overrun by her Serb neighbors, people she had known since high school, and even though she had to retire without a pension, and was forced to barricade herself in her apartment—she did not ever really believe hate could do so much.

As a teacher in Sanski Most, she had been loved by the generation of Serb, Muslim, and Croat children in her classes. When the war started, she saw her Serb students in the street, but now they were hostile. "It must have been what they saw at home that changed them," she says. "They moved around in gangs, they looted, they went into empty apartments, they banged doors, they attacked people in the street."

Once, during the bad days in Sanski Most, she had gone to her old friend, the Serb mayor Nedeljko Rasula, and begged him to give her the pension she deserved. It was humiliating for such a proud woman, but she was desperate.

Rasula gave her coffee and a cigarette, but when she asked him for her payment, he said, "Do you know my father was hung from a tree here in World War II?"

"This is not World War II," Albasa replied. "I'm talking about now. I teach all children, irrespective of faiths. Why can't you be like that?"

Then Rasula said, "You could end up hanging from that tree."

Albasa stared at him, hard. She asked him to give her and Husein a pass to leave the Serb-occupied town. The Serb mayor, her old schoolmate, laughed heartily.

"No, no, there is no reason for you to leave. Everything will be fine. You can't leave. You will get your pension on Saturday."

It never arrived.

When the mosque was razed, she began to have trouble sleeping. Husein told her to calm down: They had gone to school with Mayor Rasula. They knew the police, the soldiers. They had good Serb neighbors. But Albasa argued with him. She said, "They will eventually kill you, and when they execute you, everything I am now telling you will come back to your mind."

And they did kill him, on September 20–21, 1995, two months before the Dayton Peace Accord.

In those days, while Arkan's men roamed the street, life in the town was horrendous. Before the war, there had been a mixed community in Sanski Most; 47 percent Muslim; 43 percent Serb; the rest

Croat. But now the few Muslims who were left—professional people, doctors, lawyers, teachers—were made to dig trenches and chop wood, or clean the streets. Others stayed inside, praying for their lives. People locked their doors and did not venture out. The last of the Serb forces, mainly irregulars, Arkan's men, were going from house to house in a final cleansing operation. In the last days of war, in September 1995, they killed 500 people.

Albasa and her husband stayed in the flat, venturing out onto the balcony for an occasional breath of air, not even going outside to buy a book of matches. It was too late for them to run away, and there were two other Muslim families in the building. Serbs lived in the remaining seven flats, but they were friends, and Albasa believed they would protect them. She was wrong.

Eventually, she believes, it was Rasula who called Arkan's men to come and cleanse the area of the last Muslims. He's the one who would have supplied the names, the addresses.

"That's why I am still here," she says, walking out to her balcony to water some flowers. They took everything from her, she says, but she will not let them take her memories.

The first sign that there would be trouble was when a neighbor, a friend for years, suddenly disappeared. In retrospect, Albasa believes she knew that the Serbs would come for the Kurbegovic family. When Arkan's men came, they tied up Husein in front of her, beating him, even as she was weeping. They took her into another room and cocked their guns at her head. They told her she would die, and she believed they would have killed her, but then one man burst into the room with a wallet full of money.

"Let's go," he barked.

They took Husein with them. Only later, she found out, he was in a hotel, where they beat and interrogated him. Then they put him and the other prisoners on a bus and drove them to the next village and they dug their graves. They tied his hands behind his back. Then they killed him and threw him into a mass grave. His body landed next to some very young people, and some children.

There were sixty-eight other bodies in that grave. When Albasa first went to search for him in that pit the following summer, after it was dug up again, she was looking for him in the jeans he had worn when they had taken him away. She was looking for a face with the mustache she knew so well, for his funny, wobbly capped tooth.

She finally found him through the Red Cross, with the back of his head blown away. A police officer held his head and she saw he had been shot in the neck, at close range. She ran out of the room and vomited.

They buried him on September 25, 1996, in a plot of land that had been his grandparents'. Albasa felt lucky for that; the land had meant a lot to him, to his family. There were people who never found the bodies of their husbands or their sons. "At least I managed to find and bury mine," she says. "That was hard, very hard, but I do know where he is. I go visit and take care of the grave. Even if it's a piece of land, it doesn't matter."

She stayed in her apartment, with the same neighbors who turned her in, with the same door that was kicked down when they came for her husband. There are only two Muslims left in her building now, and from her small balcony, when she goes out to water the geraniums, she sees small children playing with toy guns.

It's strange to think of her staying in that same place, but it's the last place she saw her husband, and his grave is here. She will never leave that. Albasa now sees people in the street whom she knew participated in the death of her husband. This is my home too, she tells herself when she feels their hostility. It is where she went to school, married, helped raise a generation of Sanski Most kids, went to the shops every day, waved at the man who sold newspapers.

Adir Dragonovic, the former Supreme Judge in Sanski Most and a Muslim, went to the mass graves that following summer to sift through the mud. After he was released from Trnopolje Camp, where he had been taken in May 1992, he went to live with his wife and two daughters in Germany. But shortly after Sanski Most was liberated by the Bosnian Army on October, 10, 1995, he came back. He could not stay in Germany living a decent life while the murderers still walked the streets. He knew who they were.

The reason Adir was taken to the camps was because he had fined a Serb policeman for traffic violations. When the man came to take him, he mentioned this, and he referred to it again several times after he had been beaten badly. "So now you'll never give me a parking ticket again!" the man sneered. It was surreal.

Adir knew he was lucky to be alive and, like a lot of survivors, had some guilt about why he lived and others died, but he still wonders about the motives behind the wave of violence that suddenly ripped Yugoslavia apart starting in 1991. Nationalism and politics are often cited, but past hatreds and grievances are also candidates. "Will we ever learn?" he asks me, as we sit in his garden eating Bosnian cake and drinking coffee. He's looking at his two daughters, both exceptional students. Will the next generation learn?

He had a lot of time to think about these things when he was in the camps. He also thought about it when he was exhuming graves, when he uncovered earth and saw the face of someone he knew, like Husein Kurbegovic, his old friend and mentor.

Adir began to get letters recommending that he leave Sanski Most as early as May 1992. They told him to take his family and go, before bad things happened. The writers said they would kill his wife and children if he did not get out. They said they would kill his children before his eyes and roast them on a spit.

He sent his wife and girls away, but he stayed. The mayor, Nedjeljko Rasula, told him these were idle threats. But on his radio show, he was less encouraging—the Serbian propaganda was ugly. On May 25, 1992, having got his parents safely out of the town, Adir was stopped in his car and arrested by Serb police. Then the artillery attack started on the town, from the hills, aiming at the Muslim areas.

Adir listened to the attacks from his 2-by-2-meter cell, which he shared with nine other men, for twenty-four days. He did not know if it was day or night. He was beaten and interrogated. Once a day, the Serbs took him out, and he looked up in the sky and wondered what had happened to Sanski Most. "We had no idea what was going on in the outside world," he says. "At night, we heard mortars and the sound of people screaming in pain from the building next door."

In June, he was transferred to Manjaca, a camp the Serbs called an "investigation center." The beatings, Adir remembers, were incredible. "I did not think I would survive." He was hit with wooden sticks 1.5 meters long and thick electrical cables. He stayed there until December 14, when the camp was disbanded by the Red Cross. Twenty-four of his relatives in Sanski Most had been killed: "Killed for no reason other than the fact that they were Muslim. They were taken from their houses and killed in front of a school in Kljuc." His elderly father was severely beaten and had died in August, while Adir was still in Manjaca. Adir felt he had nothing left. He crossed the border to Croatia, then on to Germany, to find his wife and his daughters.

After the liberation, he made his way back to Sanski Most. "As a victim, and a judge, I felt I had to do something." He began working with Hague investigators, collecting documents and exhuming mass graves outside Sanski Most. They pulled 700 bodies out of various graves. Some of them were dead from the first round of killing, in 1992, but others were from 1995.

In June 1996, Adir organized an exhumation after two survivors brought him to the site. The two had been covered with corpses and managed to stay still until the Serbs left the site. Then they ran away.

The grave is not far from the main road, which links Sanski Most with Banja Luka, 61 kilometers away. It's the road the Serb Army and the civilians took when the Bosnian Army (ABiH) liberated the town on October 10, 1995. Inside were the remains of 65 Muslim civilians, all killed after they had been rounded up and taken to the Hotel Sanus, where Arkan was staying on the night of September 22, 1995. Some came from prison. The Serbs had brought people on a bus, tied their arms behind their backs, and executed them at night.

The excavation team moved away some earth and there, not fully buried, was a body of a young man in jeans and a shirt, hands tied. He still had his papers on him. They dug more and the rest of the corpses emerged. Most were shot in the head at close range. There was a woman in the grave, and children. Some had their documents on them. Then the Serbs dumped them in the pit and bulldozed the earth. But they didn't bother to cover all the bodies—some legs still stuck out, some bits of clothing.

That was when Adir saw the remains of Albasa's husband, and two civilians he knew from a nearby village, Teslic. With his team, Adir brought the bodies to a field in Sanski Most and buried them.

"They were all established, distinguished people whose only crime was that they didn't leave Sanski Most when the Serbs took it," he says, standing at the edge of site of the grave.

Slowly, with witnesses, he reconstructed that night. Local people heard screams of pain, but were too frightened to come out. Now they gave testimonies. It was raining afterward, but it still did not cover up all the thick blood on the road and in the ground. The Serbs had taken the prisoners in twos from the bus, begging for their lives, and executed them.

The area is mined, but Adir kept going back there. He still does. He can't stop thinking about the people being forced to get out of the bus, cross the road, and follow the short trail up the hill to the grave before they were shot. What were they thinking, knowing there was no way out? And some people are still missing. He thinks there are more bodies, buried in the ground, so he keeps searching. He says he is not going to stop until he finds all of them.

Srebrenica
July 11, 2000
Fifth Anniversary of the Massacre

Summer is the most beautiful time in eastern Bosnia. The fruit trees ripen, the valleys and plains take on a golden, tawny color. The rivers are full. But high above Srebrenica, in Stari Grad, the ancient Muslim cemetery is crumbling with neglect. The sinking headstones are wrapped with ivy and weeds, and further up the steep rocky trail, an old man, Sacir Halilovic, is trying to rebuild his house.

Although his family has been on this hill as long as the trees, Sacir, who is eighty-six, is the last in the line of males. The rest are dead from the most recent Bosnian war. His only son, Sejad, a doctor, was killed when a shell split his head open in 1994. Three of his four daughters' husbands and his four brothers were led onto a bus on July 12, 1995, when the Muslim enclave fell to Bosnian Serb forces, and never returned. Until that day, when Sacir hid in the woods for three days before escaping by foot to Tuzla, then Croatia, he had never left his hill.

Now, after five years in exile, the old man has come home with his eighty-year old wife, Mevlida, to die. "I was born in 1914," he says. "I remember the old Kingdom of Yugoslavia. I survived three wars. I fought with Tito as a Partisan. Nothing could keep me from coming back to my house. I belong here."

But out of a prewar population of some 38,000 in the municipality, of which 73 percent were Muslim, Sacir and his wife—from whom Sacir was separated for more than a year while they searched refugee camps for each other—are the only Muslims to return.

According to international monitors, some fifty others came back to villages in the surrounding area. It's a slow return. "If you were Muslim, would you want to come home?" asked one of them.

Oddly enough, Sacir is not frightened. There are American SFOR guards at the bottom of his hill, but if someone wanted to burn him out, it wouldn't be difficult. So he's decided that he isn't leaving his land, not ever again. Not even to go to Potocari, the site of the former U.N. compound, for the fifth anniversary ceremony for the dead in Srebrenica. He just does not want to leave his bill. He says he expects never to come down again.

Srebrenica was a victory for ethnic cleansing. Here are the facts: 43,000 people were driven from their homes, and between 7,000 and 8,000 boys and men murdered. By the summer of 2000, only 3,968 of the bodies had been found, only 76 identified, only 2 survivors returned home.

It has been five years since the fall of Srebrenica, and I drove up from Sarajevo the night before the anniversary and stayed in a hotel near the spring believed to have curative powers. It was difficult to sleep. My door did not lock, and the Serb townspeople that afternoon had made it clear that my friend Benjamin and I were not welcome. A young girl I saw on the street ignored a request for directions. Others jeered at us with our Sarajevo car plates. In the dimly lit hotel, I shared a lavatory with three or four Serbs who did not return my forced morning greeting. The floor was sticky with urine. The bathtub had a trickle of rusty orange water.

We ate breakfast and drove to Potocari, where the relatives of the 7,000 missing were gathered in the empty compound to pray for their dead. We joined a solemn line of people walking to the site.

These people had lived in Srebrenica for generations. Now they are coming in busloads from across Bosnia: from Tuzla, from Prijedor, from Sarajevo, from Vogoska. It was the first time many of them have been back since the massacre took place. They began to pray. From a surrounding hill, a group of Serbs were shouting curses and waving the three-finger salute for Orthodox unity.

The crowd, mainly women, tried to ignore them. Some of the women were crying uncontrollably, their shoulders heaving. Some were throwing themselves on the ground. They all told grim stories: losing all the men in their family; saying goodbye, believing they would meet in Tuzla; or hearing of their fathers' deaths from a witness. After taking testimonies from five or six of them, I sat by the side of the road and digested all that I had heard.

There was little closure. Most had not seen the bodies. Most did not know if their husbands or brothers or fathers or sons were alive or if dead, or where their body parts lay. The secrets were somewhere in the Bosnian hills. Some still believed that their men would one day appear. One woman told me she still prepared a plate for her husband when she sat down to eat, because he might come home, he might be injured somewhere, he might have amnesia or have been taken prisoner . . . While she talked, her friend put an arm around her and looked at me, as if to say, Please don't mind her. She lost something a long time ago.

Amira Dotovic was standing by the side of the road watching the Serbs across the hill shouting. She said she didn't remember much of her father anymore; she was only ten years old the night she and her parents arrived at the U.N. compound with a bag of clothes and food. They were looking for protection, and they fell asleep together outside the compound that night, believing they had arrived in safe hands. Srebrenica, her father told her, was a safe haven. She remembered sleeping, feeling safe. Her father was with her. What could go wrong?

But when Amira woke, her father was not there. He had gone outside, and came back with his face drained of color. "As white as a ghost. He said he had just seen a month-old baby have its head chopped off," she said, in a monotone voice. Then the Serb soldiers came, and while the U.N. soldiers watched, they separated men from women. Everyone was screaming, it was complete chaos. She remembered being taken away from her father; she remembered him being led on to a bus and then she remembered seeing his back.

"That's all," she said. Her face crumbled a little bit. "We never saw him again."

There were 25,000 people in the compound that day; but there were only 3,000 at the prayer ceremony in Potocari. There was a terrible moment when the Hodza, the highest Muslim cleric in Bosnia-Herzegovina, Rais Ceric, called the men to step forward first to pray. A few rows of men silently moved. That was all that was left. The rest was a sea of scarved women.

Hamza Umradic had traveled from a village near Tuzla. She lost 28 members of her family that day. She said, "The Bible and the Torah and the Koran say that hatred is not allowed. I don't hate men as men." She looked away, toward the hill. "But what they did, you have to hate."

In the wet spring of 1993, during the Serbs' "final offensive" at Srebrenica, I waited in Tuzla for the town to fall. On March 11, General Philippe Morillon, the top U.N. officer, had managed to break the siege. He arrived in Srebrenica only to find that the desperate people, many of them homeless in temperatures of −20 degrees Celsius, refused to let him go. During the first months of the Bosnian war, Srebrenica had become a refuge for Muslims from surrounding areas, and the population swelled. There was little food, few supplies, and unrelenting cold and misery.

Morillon, having entered and witnessed the desperation, was virtually held hostage. He climbed out of his vehicle and addressed the crowd, reassuring them that they would be protected. Then he raised a U.N. flag, effectively declaring Srebrenica single-handedly a safe area, and causing major problems back in New York.

When Morillon returned to Sarajevo, he was triumphant. He contacted a few reporters at the Holiday Inn, then brought us back to the Delegates' Club, where he resided. I was stunned when someone produced champagne and Morillon announced that "there was a street in Srebrenica that was once called Marsala Tito Street. Now it is called Phillipe Morillon Street." His vanity, given the circumstances, was astounding.

While the French gloated over their short-lived triumph, things got progressively worse. From Sarajevo, I would climb the hill to a freezing office in the Presidency building and sit with one of the

Bosnian officials who was trying to reach Srebrenica by radio. When he finally got through, the voices on the other end were always frantic, were always full of terror. They begged us to do something, anything. "Does the world know what is happening here?" The line would go crackly, then dead.

By early April, despite a Serb "cease-fire," the onslaught on the enclave had increased; the territory designated as a safe haven had shrunk. On April 10, General Mladic refused to allow Canadian peacekeepers inside for the third straight day. "Over my dead body," he said. People were dying as they waited for medical attention. There was no food. The refugees were crowding in gymnasiums and schools in Tuzla.

There were mortar and howitzer shellings of Srebrenica. On the night of April 13 alone, 56 people—15 of them children—were killed and 106 wounded. Minutes after NATO planes began enforcing a U.N. no-fly zone, the Serbs launched shells against Srebrenica, set to explode in midair to wreak the greatest havoc on people caught in the open. It was clearly not a military strategy aimed solely at the Bosnian forces.

"The Serbs are in control," a U.N. spokesperson told us. "We now expect to be slowed down considerably." Louis Gentile, a Canadian U.N. official who witnessed the attacks, said: "It was very clearly intended to wound as many civilians as possible. Bodies were being piled onto oxcarts or anything that would move. I say 'bodies' because some of the people were still alive, others were not. Some were not really looking like people anymore. There were body parts. There were people whose intestines were falling out, people whose brains were coming out of their eyes. I saw two children who did not seem to have any faces left."

Mladic had told his men to shell "only human flesh. Don't do anything but shell human flesh."

One day, I met a child who was blinded when he went out to play football and got caught in a mortar attack. To stand by his bed while he fumbled around with the sheets, the thick bandages covering his useless eyes, tears running down from the yellowed cloth, was horrible. The shrapnel wounds coated his body like pepper.

Some of his family—the ones who weren't killed—sat by his bed unable to control themselves. His mother just cried and cried. "If only I knew what happened to my eyes," the boy kept saying. "If only I knew what happened to my eyes."

The boy's plight came to the attention of Margaret Thatcher, who railed the European Union about Srebrenica. But Thatcher was one of the few politicians who did anything. On Easter Sunday, a rainy day made more grim by the industrial wasteland of Tuzla, I went to mass in the Catholic church with a colleague. We stood near the doorway while the priest asked people to pray for Srebrenica. The church went silent. Afterward, I walked in the rain to a nearby radio station that had linked up with some ham operators in Srebrenica.

It was in a basement, and the operator and I sat around the radio, huddled against the chill and smoking cigarettes. We had spoken for several days, and each time the man in Srebrenica was growing more desperate. There were times when he would ask simple questions: "What kind of cigarettes are you smoking there in Tuzla?" As if he wanted to know anything from the outside world.

This day, the man's voice would catch, then he would start again. Yugoslav troops—not Bosnian Serb forces, but troops from Serbia—had crossed the Drina and launched their own offensive. The shelling had gotten so bad, he said, that the people were like the walking dead. Did anyone outside there know what was happening to them? "In the name of God," he cried, "do something!"

No one did anything. By the end of April 1995, U.N. officials proclaimed Srebrenica "dead" and imposed tighter sanctions against Serbia and Montenegro in an attempt to halt the Bosnian Serb aggression. A U.N. relief column headed for Srebrenica had tons of aid confiscated by rebel Serbs. Diego Arria, the Venezuelan ambassador to the United Nations and the leader of the powerful U.N. nonaligned bloc, called it "slow-motion genocide."

"No water, no physicians, no electricity," he said. "I repeat, a slow process of genocide."

Arria and the nonaligned countries tried to push through a proposal that Srebrenica be declared a "safe haven"—obliging the U.N. to defend the town—but it was rejected after opposition from Britain, France, and Russia. Instead, it was agreed that it would be a "safe area," meaning that none of the warring parties could operate militarily within the enclave.[6]

Srebrenica limped by for another two years. Both the international will and the soldiers—at the end, 110 lightly armed Dutch peacekeepers—could not ensure the city was safe from attack. When General Mladic demanded that the Muslims disarm, the Bosnian forces, led by a former bodyguard of Slobodan Milosevic's, Naser Oric, were forced to hand over their guns. In exchange, they were assigned a few U.N. soldiers who could not actually protect them. Srebrenica had effectively become a concentration camp.

The Serbs did not keep their part of the deal. They continued to hammer the town, and by July the Bosnian Serb Army had enveloped the 26,000 Bosnian Muslims. The assault began in the early hours of July 6; three days later, they overran the Dutch positions and took soldiers captive. The Bosnian Army begged the retreating Dutch to stay and protect them, and threatened to kill them if they abandoned Srebrenica.

Between July 11 and 12, the Serbs entered Srebrenica. Earlier, Mladic had said he would give Srebrenica "as a present to the Serb nation." Air strikes were ordered, but by then, most of the town was in Serbian hands. Some men, many of them fighters, decided to try to escape by foot, and 20,000 of them set out through the forest. Only one-third were armed. They marched up and down 2,000-meter ascents in the stifling heat.

The Bosnian Serbs hunted them down, trapping them in the woods and either spraying them with bullets as they hid in the foliage, or loading them onto buses or trucks. The injured were left to die from their wounds slowly. Those who surrendered to the Serbs—some wearing stolen U.N. uniforms—were assembled, shot, and buried in mass graves. One group dug a grave and then was buried alive.

Others, many of the elderly men and boys, took cover in the U.N. compound. Meanwhile, Dutch soldiers in the southernmost point of the enclave were being held hostage by Serbs. In the compound, feeling that there was nothing else they could do, the Dutch stood by as the Serbs separated the men and boys from the women and bused them away.

For roughly the next ten days, the Serbs killed and killed and killed. They did not stop until there was barely anyone left.

The men taken from the U.N. compound were crammed into buses or trucks like cattle, then driven down winding, seemingly idyllic country lanes. Fathers were separated from sons, cousins held each others' hands. Some survivors remember sitting in the buses for fourteen hours, not knowing where they would go. Eventually, they were taken to fields outside of Srebrenica, where the lucky ones were blindfolded and lined up in rows and shot quickly. The unlucky ones were herded into rooms of factories or schools and sprayed with machine-gun fire. Very few survived, but the ones who did hid under the dead bodies and were bulldozed into fields, then managed to escape into the woods. "Save yourself, brother," one man, shot in the leg and unable to escape, whispered to a young survivor, who managed to run away from the field.

Denis Begic, who is now twenty-nine, survived. When I meet him for the first time, at a gas station in Sarajevo where he is working, I am reminded of something that the Bosnian poet Mario Susko once told me at the height of the siege of Sarajevo: that it was possible to kill a person psychologically without actually killing them.

Begic is one of the walking dead. A former defender of Srebrenica, he is suffering, according to his uncle Sabit, the former chief of staff of Srebrenica Hospital, from severe posttraumatic stress. It's hard to get him to talk about July 12, because he says he feels guilty that he is alive when so many are dead. He's married to a Srebrenica woman whose husband was executed in a field, and he cannot stop thinking that he lived and so many of his friends died. He talks a bit, then stares with glazed eyes for several minutes. Then talks some more. Then stares.

There are details, however, he cannot push out of his mind. Defending a dying town for three years. Being forced to turn over his gun to the U.N., which declared it a "safe area." What it felt like to walk 40 kilometers from Srebrenica to Tuzla with 120 other soldiers on a freezing mission, transporting ammunition and medical supplies to the besieged town. Watching men die from the cold.

Begic and his brigade were trying to carve out a corridor for civilians to escape, but in the harsh mountain terrain, it was impossible. "Only thirty of us finished the march," he says darkly. "We lost sixty in a minefield. The rest froze to death. I remember begging my friend to get up and keep walking, but he just smiled and said, leave me here to sleep under this tree. We both knew he was dying."

Begic was on the front line near Kladanj when Srebrenica fell. He is one of the few Muslim males remaining who can say they came from Srebrenica. He managed to escape to Tuzla, then Sarajevo. But most of his friends, and 45 of his male relatives, have disappeared forever.

He knows some—who were handed over by the U.N. to the Serbs—were beaten and tortured before being axed to death or shot in the head. He doesn't know where their bones are. Their skeletons are scattered, like thousands of others missing, in the dark earth all over eastern Bosnia.[7]

Sarajevo
July 1, 2001

A few days after Slobodan Milosevic was flown to The Hague, I drove south, through Serbia and Bosnia to Sarajevo. At one point, the car broke down and my Serb friend Aleks and I sat by the side of the road waiting for help. It was the middle of the Serbian heartland: vast swaths of fields, small villages with a single shop that sells maps and Serbian flags. We bought candy for dinner and ate in the car waiting for a mechanic.

When I heard the news of Milosevic's arrest, I wanted to leave Belgrade and go to Sarajevo. I wanted, more than anything, to be in that city when people who were wronged might finally hope there was retribution. What would it feel like, for all those people who suffered under him for so long, to have something like justice?

We arrived in the early hours of the morning, as the sun was rising. We came out of the tunnel and there was Sarajevo, glittering in early-morning summer light. Aleks dropped me at my bed and breakfast near Bjelave and said he was going to the market to buy cevapcici. He had not been to Sarajevo since the war. But he felt uncomfortable having Belgrade license plates. He drove back to Serbia an hour later.

My arrival in Sarajevo came a few weeks before the sixth anniversary of the fall of Srebrenica. The healing process was painfully slow. Bodies were still being pieced together. There was a creeping realization that the West connived to sacrifice Srebrenica in order to draw up a more effective peace plan, and that the U.N. deliberately delayed air strikes until after the massacres were over.

Yasushi Akashi, the former special representative of the U.N. secretary-general, and General Bernard Janvier in particular are singled out and bear responsibility for the lack of NATO air support.[8] Serbs living in Bosnia still deny that any massacre took place. In the autumn of 2002, a report delivered to The Hague claimed that the death toll after the Serbs seized the town was not between 7,000 and 8,000 Muslims as the U.N. maintained, but "only" 2,000, and they were not murdered. The report claims they died fighting and that 800 Serb soldiers also died.

Testimony from one of the participants was dismissed. Sergeant Drazan Erdemovic, a twenty-three-year-old Bosnian Croat fighting with the Bosnian Serbs, wept when he said he killed more than 70 men because he was ordered to, but that he aimed for the Muslims' hearts because it was kinder. For his crimes, Erdemovic would get four years in prison. A man in Sarajevo who murdered his mistress in an act of passion got seven.

The 2002 report also contended that Drazan Erdemovic was "mad." As for General Mladic, he did not commit war crimes against civilians; he "risked his own life to lead them to safety."

All of this is little comfort to people like Advia Sehomerdjic, a Srebrenica widow, who actually did not care that Milosevic was in The Hague. The person Advia wants to see stand up in The Hague will never get there—he's not famous or important enough. He's called Dragan Jovanovic. Her face crumbled as she said his name.

Jovanovic was Advia's Serb neighbor from Srebrenica, the one who burnt down her house, who took away her sons and her husband. He is the reason she cannot go back to live there. He now has a prosperous business rebuilding homes, the ones that he burnt down. UNHCR buses frequently run back and forth between Sarajevo and Srebrenica. When Advia went back once to visit, Dragan saw her, grinned, gave her a three-fingered Serb salute and jeered, "If I'd never burnt down those houses, I wouldn't be in business today!"

In a few weeks' time, it will be the sixth anniversary of the last time Advia saw her sons and husband. She's written one of her sons a letter, and she handed it to me, looking ashamed. "Read it out loud," she said.

> *My dear son:*
> *Your mother is writing you a letter, although I have never received an answer to the letters I have written, because I have always sent them to an unknown address. Serb soldiers took you away from me. Your two brothers and your father, who started their journey through the woods, have not come back to me either. For five years, I have been living alone and waiting for you to come back. Forgive me, I have no more tears to shed, they have already dried up, and I don't know how much longer I have to wait. . . .*

And so, the question I wanted answered was answered. No one here is celebrating about Milosevic. The big fish are getting caught, but the ones who really did it—the "executioners," as people call them—are still living peacefully, walking the streets. They are the men who raped and killed and burned and now sit in cafés in Foca and Srebrenica, confident that The Hague will never find them.

The people who believe the least in justice are some of the 800 women from Srebrenica scattered in the Sarajevo area. I visited them in Ilidza, in Sarajevo, in Hrasnica. Their stories were all horrible: seeing the last of their husbands and sons and brothers. "I just want him to feel what we feel!" said Bajrami, who lost a husband and son, when I asked her about Milosevic.

They started a support group called the Movement of Mothers of the Srebrenica and Zepa Enclaves. Their office had only a fax machine, a united sense of deep sorrow, and the conviction that they would not let Srebrenica be forgotten. "We're searching for truth and justice, to find out how they finished, how they died," said one of the women, Munira Subasic, who lost a husband, a son, and 22 other men in her family.

Every month, they gather on the eleventh day to pray for their men in the mosque. Some of them, like Raifa Mehic, still cannot believe that her husband, who disappeared with 50 other men in her family, will not walk through the door. "He might be a prisoner somewhere," she said. Her sallow face brightened slightly.

At the Potocari prayer ceremony the year before, other mothers had said the same thing. "It is important for survivors to still have hope," one of the mothers said. They've got photographs of their lost ones all over the walls: "Your mother has not forgotten you."

"We want to find our dead, we want to bury our dead, and we do not want people to forget," Munira says. "'Missing' does not mean 'forgotten.' We asked for the bodies in 1995 and we are still asking. We will never stop asking."

Pale
July 2, 2001

The day Milosevic was scheduled to appear before the Hague tribunal for the first time, I drove up the mountain to Pale and watched his appearance in court on a small-screen television in a seedy café. People cursed as I drank my cappuccino. "How can they do this to us?" a blond woman screeched. "After all we've done!" Milosevic came out in his suit and red, blue, and white tie, and everyone cheered. Then, anticlimatically, the television went dead.

The local radio station where Sonya, Radovan Karadzic's daughter, worked, was as quiet as the grave. A lone reporter came out and said that the Serb people had nothing to say about The Hague. Around the corner, Karadzic's house was locked up; he's got a $5 million price tag on his head, and he's thought to be somewhere in Montenegro. A hostile guard told us to go back to Sarajevo.

When I tried to talk to people about Srebrenica, the anniversary of which was approaching, I got blank stares. "Why does no one ever talk about the seventy Serbs who died in Kravica?" said Sasa, a twenty-four-year-old Bosnian Serb. "Do you really think seven thousand men died? It's all propaganda."

Mirza Hajric, a Bosnian government advisor, told me that Bosnians are still a long way off from truth and reconciliation. "Srebrenica is a black hole in Serb politics," he admitted. "People still say it didn't happen. But every Serb knows—they might only admit it over a coffee, and not publicly, but they know. But I still dream of the day when the Serbs will come out and say 'We are sorry.' "

Today in Srebrenica—where before the war the population was 72.5 percent Muslim and 25.5 percent Serb—the houses where the Muslim families lived are now inhabited by Serbs who pushed the Muslims' things aside, or burned them, and hung their own clothes in their closets.

"We went back today to our old house for the first time in five years," said Alma Hasanovic, who was nineteen when I met her at the prayer service in Potocari the year before. Her father disappeared July 11, 1995, and she was leading her weeping mother to prayers to remember him. "There was a Serb family living in our house. We just wanted to get our things. I just wanted my clothes. They wouldn't let us in."

On August 2, 2001, General Radoslav Krstic, the commander of the Drina Wolves unit of the Bosnian Serb Army, was sentenced to forty-six years in prison for the massacre of up to 8,000 men and boys in Srebrenica in July 1995. A soldier who had lost his leg early in the war and fought brutally and ruthlessly throughout, Krstic was the first Bosnian Serb commander to be convicted of genocide by the war crimes tribunal in The Hague.

On September 11, the Mothers of Srebrenica and Zepa Enclave marched to the Sarajevo mosque as they have every month, to pray for their dead. This year, they also prayed for the dead in New York and Washington, that they would not be forgotten, that their bodies would be returned to their loved ones. "We prayed for us," they said, "but it is also for them."

In April 2002, a report on Srebrenica carried out by the Netherlands Institute for War Documentation was released. It chronicled not only the fall of Srebrenica, but the run-up and how the Ministry of Defense and government dealt with the aftermath. The main conclusion was that the Dutch troops were naïve, ill prepared, underarmed, and assigned under a flawed pretext.

As a result, the entire government accepted responsibility for Srebrenica and resigned, including Prime Minister Wim Kok, who was finance minister at the time of the massacre. They did not, how-ever, go so far as to apologize to the families and to the Mothers of Srebrenica, who attended the presentation of the report in The Hague. But in the final days of his ministry, Wim Kok traveled to Srebrenica to express his sorrow and regret.

As for the Bosnian Serbs, they still call for investigations into Muslim atrocities, which undoubtedly occurred in the region. Under Bosnian Army commander Naser Oric, the most notable was a raid on January 7, 1993, in Kravica, in which it is believed 70 civilians perished. But even that horror cannot justify what happened in July 1995.

The Bosnian Serbs still deny the scale of the massacre. They explain the deaths simply as casualties of war.

Somewhere near Brcko
March 1, 2001

We had driven for hours north from Sarajevo, twisting and turning down muddy roads piled with snow until we came to the entrance of a camp in this remote mountain village. There was barbed wire and a fence. There was a long road leading to some sort of compound, and on that road was a group of children walking to school. One of them wore a pink parka with a hood and had pale leggings tucked into her knee-high boots. Her hair was pulled back with a dark blue band. Her face was unspeakably beautiful, angelic. She had a snowball in her hand and froze slightly when we approached.

This was Lajla.

"Stop! That's her!" said Meliha, a woman from the Association of Former Prison Camp Inmates of Bosnia and Herzegovina. She jumped from the car in the snow and reached out to the child. Lajla shyly approached her.

"Ah, Lajla," Meliha said, hugging the child. "Lajla, this is Dzenana. She's come to see your mother."

Lajla nodded. She looked older than eight. I stared at her. Her features were precise and even. Her skin was honey-colored, her hair long and shiny. She was exquisite. How could such a beautiful child have been born from such violence?

Meliha watched me. "I know what you're thinking," she said sadly. Her eyes welled with tears. "I often think the same thing too."

They raped her mother. Over and over and over, so many of them that she does not remember which one could be Lajla's father. After a while, they all looked the same, had the same rank smell—they never seemed to bathe, and they drank, all they did was drink slivovica. After a while, Azra tried not to think about what they were doing. Some nights, it was five, six, seven, or more, one right after the other.

They had taken Azra from her house in Foca and brought her to the building. In Foca, the Serbs had quickly set up sites where Muslim women could be available to soldiers: some women were taken to houses where soldiers on a fifteen-day rotation basis could be satisfied; others went to the Partizan Hall. This is where they brought Azra.

In the hall, there were girls as young as eleven, she remembers. She tried not to look, and to stay calm. But they made her lie in a room full of mattresses that were covered with blood, and very quickly, the men arrived. There were so many of them, she lost count. It went on for weeks, months. She felt dead inside, and when she realized she was pregnant, she wanted to be dead, to kill herself, but they watched her all the time. "We're going to make a good little Serb soldier," some of them shouted as they were raping her.

Azra did not care who the child's father was. This was *her* child; it was up to *her* to protect her. She hoped, and she prayed more than anything, that her lovely little daughter would never have to go through what she did. She kept her daughter. Most of the other women who conceived babies in that place—hundreds were born to Muslim women in Bosnia in those years as a result of rape—gave them away.

I used to go see them. There was a dank orphanage in Sarajevo, on Bjelave Hill. The rape children were kept in a separate room from the other boys and girls. It was a terrible stigma, the place where they had come from. Late in the afternoon, after I finished my work, I would go there and hold them. There weren't a lot of people left working at the orphanage, and the kids were neglected, but it was the babies, who needed to be touched, who probably suffered the most.

We brought some things to take to Azra, who lives on nearly nothing: what the NGOs give her, and a small amount from the Association of Former Prison Camp Inmates, whose budget is not large. We stopped at a kiosk in one of the villages and purchased a bag of oranges, a bag of tomatoes, an assortment of vegetables, a couple bags of pasta, a carton of cigarettes, some yellow cheese, some chocolate, some toothpaste, some shampoo.

The compound where Lajla lived with her mother was a one-story building, cold, and with a shared sink at the end of the hall, a shared bathroom, and a shared kitchen. Their cubicle has a small bed, some dolls, and a curtain behind which blankets are neatly folded. There is a small table with a bit of lace over it—an effort to make the place more cheerful. There is no television. "Lajla loves cartoons," says Azra mournfully. "But I can't afford it."

No one in that compound—all displaced people, all refugees—knew anything about Lajla. They thought Azra came from near Zenica, that the father was a Bosnian soldier who went away and married someone else from his village. Azra said it was not lying. "It's easier that way."

Lajla knew her birthday was August 21, 1993, but that is all she knew of her history. Azra said she would die before she let her daughter find out her mother was raped and deliberately impregnated in order to wipe out her Muslim gene pool. "I do not want Lajla to *ever* find out what happened," Azra said, shaking. "I *will* keep it a secret." She lit another cigarette, the third since we arrived twenty minutes before.

She does not see many people. She is three hours' drive from Sarajevo. Her father was killed in the war, and her sister and mother are also refugees. Her grandmother and uncle were murdered in front of her in her house in Foca, the night the soldiers came to take her away.

Her last memory of a normal life is going to buy her father cigarettes, in June 1992. The Serbian Army had entered the town, and she slipped carefully out of her house. She heard the sound of shooting. When she saw the guard, she politely said good morning, then she realized—to her horror—that the guard was her neighbor. Other women had gathered in her house, for protection. A few days later, the soldiers, tipped off by neighbors, came for the women. They took them away, put them in a truck, screaming insults about their religion, about Alija Izetbegovic. Some of the girls were so young. Azra was afraid, but the young ones—she knew how frightened they were.

Sometimes, she goes to Zenica to see cousins. But she will never go back to Foca, which now lies within the borders of Republica Sprksa and is renamed Srbinje. When she finally got out of the rape camp, she went to Turkey with an aid organization, where Lajla was born. She does not want any link to the past, any chance of Lajla finding out what happened.

Her rapists still live in Foca. They sit in cafés, they drink coffee, they marry and have children. "Can you imagine?" Azra says. They live normal lives now. Many of them work in the police force, the town assembly, the elementary school—the place where returning Bosnians send their children.

The Hague will never find them, she said. But a week before I saw her, three of her tormentors, Dragoljub Kunarac, Radomir Kovac, and Zoran Vukovic, were found guilty of rape, torture, and enslavement in Foca. It was the first time that rape and enslavement were defined as crimes against humanity, and the first trial to focus on sexual crimes. The men were given sentences of twenty-eight, twenty, and twelve years respectively. Azra shrugged and lit another cigarette. She didn't want them behind bars. She wanted them *dead*. "I want them to hang from a tree," she said simply. "That's how much pain they make me feel.

"Besides," she said, "there are fifty other men from Foca who did it, and they're still wandering around. If I saw any of them, do you know what I would do? I would find a tool and kill them.[9]

"I don't want to think about those animals anymore," she said. "I feel ill. When I hear about The Hague, I have to leave the room. There is no medicine that can help me. I just lie in bed and sweat."

There's another reason Azra can't go home, but she doesn't like to talk about it. For a Muslim, the stigma of being raped is so great that most of the women who were held in the camp for months and repeatedly raped have never actually told their husbands or their families about it. Nearly all of them gave away their children.

"They believed they could forget the nightmare if they didn't talk about it," said Meliha quietly to me in the car on the drive up. "But it all comes back to them, the minute they get pregnant again, and when they give birth. You can't escape memory, however bad." Meliha and her association try to trace some of the children, but it is nearly impossible: no records were kept; many of the children were illegally taken out of the country. Others are in orphanages. I remember, when I first came upon the rape babies in Sarajevo, meeting a Frenchman who had come to adopt one, to smuggle her out through the Serbian checkpoints. That child, like Lajla, is now nearly ten years old. She's growing up in France. She will probably never know her origins, how exactly she came into this world.

The figures for how many babies were actually born from rape during that time is unclear. Irfan Ajanovic of the Association of Former Prison Camp Inmates said, "We're never going to find out the exact number. Balkan women find it too shameful."

Azra says, "The war is finished, but the pain is not." She shakes as she lights a match; she shakes when she sits quietly on the small bed in the cubicle where she lives with Lajla; she shakes as she eats pizza at the restaurant we bring her to later in the day. Her head shakes, her wrists shake, her knees shake. When she digs out the packet of pills that she lives on, the pills that keep her alive, her hand shakes so much I have to steady it so I can read the label. Antidepressants, but there are also tranquilizers and sleeping pills. Sometimes, she admits, she takes too many. Lajla has to shake her awake, has to make her get dressed. There are days that are just too difficult to face.

She has terrible nightmares. She dreams of the room where she was kept and can almost hear it again: the screams of the other women. She can smell the blood. She can see their faces exactly. "I see pictures of them." Nights are the worse. She gets panic attacks from the nightmares, and then the sweats. She lies there thinking, Who will take care of my daughter if I die?

As a result, Lajla is actually the mother. At night, she hears her mother crying and goes to her bed to comfort her. She massages her mother's aching temples. She brings her a towel to dry the sweat. She does this, as well as maintaining the highest grades in her class. "She's such a good girl," Azra says, saying that the thing that makes her saddest is that she can't buy her clothes, or a pet, or a real apartment to decorate, or a television. More than anything, Lajla asks over and over for a television. It pains Azra.

"I'd like to think of a better future," she says. "But what's a future if you can't buy your daughter a television?"

We pick up Lajla from school and take her to lunch at a pizza restaurant. "Please, no spaghetti," Lajla says. "All we eat is spaghetti." Azra orders something, but smokes instead of eating. She's painfully thin and her skin is pale from anemia. "It's my stomach," she says. "It's ruined from taking tranquilizers on an empty stomach. I don't feel hungry a lot." She laughs and tells me that cigarettes and coffee are her medicine.

Azra doesn't work, either. For the past ten years, since her capture in the camp, she has moved from refugee camp to refugee camp. She's been here for thirteen months. The neighbors are all right, she says, but she wouldn't call them friends. "It's just Lajla and me," she says.

Lajla eats a pizza and talks and talks. About school, the doll, the television set. She does not look much like her mother, although it is impossible to imagine what her mother—who is now only in her mid-thirties—looked like before she sank into hell.

"I really want a television set," she says, eating the pizza diligently with her knife and fork. "For the cartoons."

"Why cartoons?" I ask her. What does she like about cartoons?

She looks at me solemnly. Then she begins to laugh a little. "Because," Lajla says in a grown-up voice, "it's not the real world."

Chapter Seven

But I wonder if you understand how mighty hatred can be.

—Rebecca West, *Black Lamb and Grey Falcon*

10,615 persons, out of whom 1,601 were children, were killed in Sarajevo. More than 50,000 persons were wounded, a great number of whom remain invalids. The siege of the city lasted from May 2, 1992, to February 26, 1996, or 1,395 days, which is the longest siege in the modern history of mankind.

Suada Kapic, Sarajevo, 1996

One afternoon in March in the early days of war, ice hanging from the shattered buildings, breath coming out like frozen clouds, I saw a dog with a human hand in its mouth. At the time, I didn't know it was a hand. All I saw was a dog driven to madness by hunger, running with a prize in its jaw, a piece of meat dripping blood. It was somewhere near the Presidency building, a location that was never safe during the siege. Shells whistled, hit the ground, burst into stars, and dug their poison into the flesh of whoever was nearby. Afterward, the starving dogs feasted on the flesh while the humans tried to shovel the remains and identify the bodies, too stunned, too exhausted to cry anymore.

It was the first winter of the siege of Sarajevo. Afterward, when I would read the statistics of those killed inside the encircled city, it seemed a cold and remote number. It meant nothing. It had no connection to those people. The dead were, after all, still living and breathing in memory: not just lifeless figures buried in Lion's Cemetery or the converted football field, but faces with life in them, hands, legs, minds.

The dead were more than just the names on the wooden grave markers or lifeless figures lying on the slabs in the morgue at Kosevo Hospital. They were, to me, still there, still floating around the city. Still present. They weren't really dead—the commander who walked me across a front line; Klea's elderly neighbor; Zlata's school friends, who got hit as they played in a courtyard; or the middle-aged woman who was afraid to leave her house but who got a sniper's bullet between the eyes as she stood at her kitchen window.

In Joseph Roth's novel *The Radetsky March*, which tells of the dying days of the Habsburg Empire, the hero, a young soldier, cries out in great emotional pain: "The dead! Father! I can't forget the dead!" In Sarajevo in those days, it was also impossible to forget the dead. They followed us everywhere in the thick yellow fog that hung over the city, and you could feel them everywhere even if you could not see them. They were so close you could almost feel their breath.

The wounded were not just Red Cross statistics on a sheet to be faxed back to Geneva, either, but faces for me, in flesh and blood: the teenage swimming champion who lost a breast when a sliver of mortar sliced through her pectorals and embedded itself in her chest; the young boy who went out because it was a beautiful day and took a bullet in his spine; the girl who was sleigh riding near the Television Center who lay in a coma with her hands curled in birdlike claws.

We speculated about who was actually doing this, pulling the strings, watching the city wither into a dried bone with no life and no breath left. They were the ones with big black marks on their souls, with hollowed-out eyes that saw and felt nothing. Of course, we knew who was doing it—we saw them sometimes when we drove around Sarajevo and into the hills of Pale, the foot soldiers who pulled the triggers and launched the mortars. Sometimes we stopped and talked to them before the worst of the slivovica set in, but we always left feeling weighed down with a sick feeling in the stomach, the presence of evil.

We also saw Karadzic, Koljevic, Plavsic, Momcilo Krajisnik,

president of Parliament, holding court in Pale, the team that was essentially winning the war. We sat with them, uneasy to be sharing a drink or a table with the killers of Sarajevo. But it was also compulsive, in a sick way. As vile as they were, you couldn't help having a grudging respect for their tenacity and the simple fact that they just did not care what the world thought of them. Once, during an offensive on Mount Igman, General Mladic, resplendent in combat gear, with touches of red and gold on his hat, slammed his fist over and over on the hood of my car. "Go home!" he bellowed, red-faced and angry. And as much as I despised what he was doing, I could not help but be strangely fascinated by this man, by the cult that he inspired. He believed in what he was doing.

It is not to say we had no contact with the other side of the war. We bought black-market gasoline and fresh eggs from a farmer in Pale, and stopped at a hotel in Jahorina to eat quickly, too intimidated to enjoy the heat and the hot food. If we passed a night, it was always hard for me to fall asleep without the sound of the shells that I had become used to. The mountain town seemed oddly quiet.

We did not like to linger; Pale seemed tainted with evil, and we did not like to be out of Sarajevo too long, for fear it would either fall without us in it or our route would be blocked. So we drove back in the morning, while the gunners were sleeping off their hangovers, across the battlefield of the airport.

We were guilty, we knew, of perhaps covering one side of the war, but for us there *was* only one side: the side that was getting pounded, that was being strangled slowly, turning blue and purple. The truth wasn't necessarily objective; it was where we were sitting, what we were seeing. Maybe it wasn't fair, but it wasn't fair, either, to kill 10,000 civilians just because they were in the wrong place at the wrong time. "Bad luck!" an old wizened man once called out to me as he was pulling some firewood behind him that he had just chopped down from a tree in the city park. Bad luck! A shell had fallen on the street behind us. There were people running back to see if they knew anyone who had been hit. But the old man and I were speeding away. Bad luck!

Afterward, when it was all over, when the war was finished, we went back, and Sarajevo was a strange place, full of shiny Mercedes and Scandinavian aid workers and Internet cafés that had not existed during the siege, run by returning Bosnians who had missed those 1,300 days, who did not know what it was like to turn on a tap and have nothing happen. Or to stand in the queue for a box from Caritas that contained some feta cheese, spaghetti, and wheat: supplies for a month.

The destruction was still there, however, even if the Austrians and the Germans and the Swedes were sending large sums to reconstruct the city. I could still smell the smoke and the ash. What had not changed was the mentality, and I wondered what was going on in their heads, those men up in Pale, on the mountain, now that it was all over. Did they care about the damage they left behind? Were they haunted by the carnage? What happened to the rapists in Foca, the murderers in Srebrenica, the soldiers I wished I had a gun to kill, the ones who were dug into the trenches above Sarajevo and so gleefully showed me their sniper rifles, and how precisely they could pinpoint a child's knees? Was the man who suddenly moved into the house next door to you the same man who murdered your husband or son? Who were your neighbors?

Whenever I thought of them, the leaders of it all, the ones who wreaked most of the havoc and got away with it—or did they?—I kept thinking of a poem by Langston Hughes I had learned as a child. It kept bouncing into my head and refused to be put to one side. What happens to a dream deferred? *Does it explode?*

I knew what happened to my friends in Bosnia, but I did not know what happened to the losers, the former bullies, the big kids on the playground. What was going through their heads? Were they dreaming black dreamless dreams at night? Had they forgotten? Or were they simply trying to survive, to run far away and not get caught?

February 1997
Pale, Republika Srpska

The day, six weeks ago now, that Nikola Koljevic, Shakespearean scholar, former vice president of the Bosnian Serbs, and architect of the destruction of Sarajevo, put a gun to his head and pulled the trigger was an unremarkable day in the Balkans. Clouds hung low over Pale, where Koljevic lived in "exile," as he liked to call it, since the beginning of the war. There was mud on the streets and snow on the peaks framing the gloomy village. The sky was thick with fog.

Nikola Koljevic was only sixty years old, but he had aged dramatically during the war. On January 17, he went for a walk with his wife, Milica, had lunch, stopped at a shop to pick up some passport-size photos, and then returned alone to his office in the bland and soulless government building. He worked for a while and then excused himself, went to the bedroom above his office where he sometimes stayed, locked the door from the inside, and shot himself. For a reason that was not understood, there were two wounds in his temple.

Koljevic did not die immediately. He fell into a coma and lived for nine days, attached to a life-support machine in a Belgrade hospital. I wonder if he knew what was happening around him, if he knew he had failed on his last quest. Or perhaps he was simply oblivious to his surroundings, to his family hovering near the bed. At any rate, Koljevic eventually died the way that many Sarajevans, miserable at the height of the siege, hoped he would die: slowly, painfully, without dignity.

Exactly what was in Koljevic's mind is not clear. He left a suicide note, but it was not published. Perhaps it was fear that drove him to take his own life. There was talk those days, in Belgrade, in Pale, that Slobodan Milosevic would probably be brought to a war crimes tribunal. Throughout the war, Koljevic, the meticulous, brilliant professor, had kept detailed notes of their discussions. It was likely he would be called as a prosecution witness.

Was it remorse? A wartime ideologue of ethnic cleansing and the man who was nominally in charge of Serb concentration camps, he must have felt some guilt. For his role in the destruction of Sarajevo, he must have gazed down from time to time at his former city and felt a hollow feeling in the pit of his stomach. It was, after all, a literary revenge he had taken on the city. The respected academic who had written eight books on Shakespeare never felt he received the advancement he deserved. He turned to right-wing nationalistic politics and rose in the Bosnian Serb leadership.

When the bombardment of Sarajevo began, he was safe in Pale, and as an architect of the city's destruction, he made sure that the National Library was demolished. When it was hit, scores of texts from all over the former Yugoslavia were consumed by fire, and a blizzard of ashes from the burned books—including his own—covered the city. It hurt, in those days, for people to burn just one book to use as firewood when the nights turned cold and the snow hit the ground. To see the majestic Ottoman-style library on the banks of the Miljacka go up in flames was horrible.

But the library was multiethnic. It was everything Koljevic loathed.

The news of Koljevic's attempted suicide was reported on Pale television and broadcast in Sarajevo. Some people who watched the evening news were shocked; others were overcome with a sense of righteousness and triumph. But Gordana Mikulic, a forty-eight-year-old teacher, dropped her head in her hands and wept. She and her husband were among Koljevic's oldest friends. They had known him before he had been corrupted by power and war and thwarted ambition. She'd last seen him in the spring of 1992, when he and his family and other prominent Bosnian Serbs fled the city for the safety of Pale.

Pale had been the place where wealthy Sarajevans built ski chalets or weekend cottages, where they went to buy fresh produce or breathe the mountain air. No one, least of all the urbane Sarajevans who prided themselves on their sophistication, would have dreamed of living in Pale. The only ones who could thrive there were the *papak*, or cow people, the rural inhabitants who had gigantic chips on their shoulders and who would eventually destroy them.

Shortly after Radovan Karadzic and his gang arrived and set up camp in Pale, with orders drifting down from Belgrade, Koljevic gave the first orders to launch the mortars which would destroy the city. Sarajevo was the multiethnic and cosmopolitan of the cities in the former Yugoslavia; therefore, it had to be crushed.

But Gordana Mikulic did not think of that. She had suffered more than a personal betrayal. As she watched the news from Pale, she had a sharp and sudden image of a young Koljevic, twenty years earlier, not yet tainted with ultra-right-wing nationalism. She could see Nikola standing in front of her, with his good tweeds and his faint British accent, quoting *King Lear*, a book in his hand. Then she had another image, this one more painful. Shortly before the Koljevic family left Sarajevo in 1992, she began hearing rumors that the city was going to be bombed. Terrified, she rang Milica Koljevic to ask whether she should take her young daughter and flee the city as soon as possible.

Milica calmly lied to her friend. Knowing full well what was in store for the city, she advised her good friend to stay put. "Milica reassured me over and over that nothing would happen to Sarajevo," Gordana said. "She said that she and her family were going to Pale for a week, maybe two. She said she would be back, that I was not to worry for myself or for my husband and daughter, who was only seven at the time. We would be safe, she said." Milica did not say she had already sent her own daughter, Bogdana, to Belgrade to ensure her safety the week before. The Koljevics' Pale sojourn stretched from two weeks to two months to four years. They never returned to Sarajevo.

Gordana, the wife of the popular Sarajevo writer Marko Vesovic, believed her. After all, they were good friends, all of them young and talented, moving through the Sarajevo intelligentsia with a confident assurance. Both men taught at the university's Department of English and wrote poetry. Koljevic, who had two boys, had encouraged the younger couple to have a child, telling them that family was the most important thing they could experience. There were long nights spent over bottles of wine, discussing the state of the world, picnics, idyllic bucolic moments like something from a Tolstoy novel.

In the days that followed his death, Gordana mourned him. She remembered mushroom hunting at Nikola's weekend cottage near Olovo in central Bosnia, a town that would later become one of the bloodiest front lines of the war. The women cooked; the children played in the forest. Koljevic had built the cottage himself, out of wood and stone.

Sometime later, when Gorazde was getting attacked and ground down to a fine dust, Gordana saw Nikola on television, calmly explaining the logic behind the onslaught, as if he were explaining the different kinds of mushrooms in the woods. Gordana saw him again and again on television after that, always giving excuses, explanations. Once she sat speechless with anger as he described how it was necessary to attack Srebrenica because the Muslims near Tuzla were launching assaults on Serb civilians.

Gordana stared in horror at her friend on the television, but her heart also sank. "I could not believe," she said quietly, "that this was the same man." She thought of his kindness, his tenderness, of him playing jazz on the piano, of him making jokes. "When I was pregnant," she says, "he called every day to see how I was feeling. *That* is what I think of. Not the war criminal."

Gordana knew another detail from Koljevic's other life, the life that so many people did not see when they looked at the Bosnian Serb vice president. January 16, 1997, was the twentieth anniversary of the death of his eldest son, Djordje. The seventeen-year-old, a mathematics student, was killed in a skiing accident on holiday in Austria. Neither his father nor his mother ever really recovered from the tragedy. According to Gordana, who spent forty-eight hours with the family after the news arrived, Nikola's hair turned immediately from black to snow white. Milica, unable to shoulder the sorrow that her oldest child had died on a faraway hill, had an emotional breakdown. Their youngest child, Srdjan broke out in red hives, which covered his body for two years.

"Let us say that from that day on, the family was never the same again," Gordana said.

More significant than his hair color was Koljevic's inner turmoil. The day his son died, Nikola went through a radical transformation. "I understood what he was doing when he tried to kill himself," says Gordana's husband, Marko Vesovic, who loved his friend but never really recovered from Koljevic's betrayal. "He was closing the circle."

The day Djordje died, a cycle of events began that would continue over the next two decades. Vesovic explains it this way: "After that death, the circle carried Koljevic into the strange world of Orthodox mysticism, of religious fanaticism, which led to his rabid Serb nationalism and his rise to political power. That led to the destruction of Sarajevo, a city where he lived and taught but which he ultimately betrayed." Vesovic paused from his speech only long enough to light another cigarette. He blew the smoke from his nose and stared out into space.

"And that, ultimately led to his own death."

In the last days of the Bosnian war, Koljevic paced the floors of his office in Pale, like his hero King Lear. He believed he was an innocent trapped by fate, by circumstance. After the war, stuck in Pale and later in Belgrade, banned from Sarajevo, and banished from Karadzic's inner circle, he felt himself slipping from power and helpless to stop it. Karadzic regarded him as a traitor.

As early as 1994, he had begun to fade from public view. Prior to the Dayton talks, Koljevic had chosen to back Milosevic rather than Karadzic. He thought it would weigh better in his favor. Karadzic never forgave him. "They threw him away like a used rag," says Marko Vesovic.

It was a cruel disappointment. While Koljevic had been crucial at the Geneva talks, and in dealing with the British diplomats Lord Carrington and David Owen, he was largely ignored and powerless at Dayton. Shortly after the signing, shortly after the war was officially over, he was formally pushed aside. Karadzic stripped him of his role as vice president and assigned him a post as head of the Writers' Union. It was a true Balkan-style punishment: not only had he lost Sarajevo, but now Koljevic was barred from the inner circle in Pale. It was the same cruelty and cunning that Milosevic used to send his former mentor, Ivan Stambolic, into exile.[1] The banishment, the sense of exile, left Koljevic distraught. Those who knew him wondered if he was torturing himself with guilt and remorse, or if he was convinced that this was yet another blow from the hand of God: his rightful punishment.

Koljevic was in fact superstitious and guilt-ridden. Throughout his life, he felt he was being punished for sins he had committed, the betrayals to the people he loved. Alone in his office that January night, staring out onto the vast nothingness of Pale, while Karadzic, nearby, plotted with his new deputy, Koljevic may have heard the voices conspiring against him. God had come at last to administer his final justice.

And just what *was* his crime against God? When I went looking for it a few weeks after he died, literally knocking on doors in Sarajevo with a list in my hand of those who knew him, the reaction was extraordinary. Some people cried. Some held their hands over their mouths, tears in their eyes, and silently shut the door in my face. One man raged at me in perfect English: "You have no right to interfere with the will of God! God alone will judge Nikola!"

I began to have an almost biblical image of the man: as Judas roaming Golgotha after the crucifixion of Christ; a man who had in effect destroyed a huge part of himself to no avail whatsoever. In Sarajevo, no one remembered his poetry or his Shakespearean lectures. Instead, Koljevic was regarded as the prime mover of the destruction of the city. It was he, as the story goes, who signed the order for General Mladic to begin the bombing of the National Library.

The antiaircraft guns started pummeling the fine stone on August 25, 1992. From Pale, high above the city, the rockets looked like firecrackers, but in Sarajevo, what people remembered most from that terrible night was the smell of the paper burning and the ashes from the books drifting like fat, wet snowflakes.

By the time the bombing finished, the building was a hollowed shell of plaster, the bricks and mortar crumbled like the inside of a wedding cake that had been sliced open. For months after, I could still smell the fire inside, and when I would wander through the rubble, I felt anger at whoever could destroy such a beautiful thing. I would still find pieces of books, hunks of burnt bindings that had somehow escaped the fire.

For Koljevic to single out the library was a disturbing but highly telling move: a scholar who loved books, who placed a high premium on intelligence, who believed that words could liberate a human being, had raised his hand and 1 million volumes, many of them rare Ottoman manuscripts, had burned. The library was a symbol of Sarajevo's multiethnic tradition, something Koljevic, slowly growing mad in his Pale isolation, came to hate more than anything on earth.

The day the trams began running again in 1994 during a short-lived NATO-imposed cease-fire—a day I will never forget because of the sounds of the bells ringing after two years of silence in the hollowed-out city—it is said that Koljevic looked down at Sarajevo with even more hatred and venom: the people were meant to crumble, to collapse under the siege, he told someone, not to remain dogged and resistant. It made him frantic, watching the resourcefulness of the Sarajevans who refused to cave in rather than seeing them fall on their knees. The screenwriter Abdulah Sidran, who also knew Karadzic, said that shortly after Nikola left the city, he began to develop a "Sarajevo complex."

Sidran and I met in the Writers' Union, behind a vacant field in Sarajevo that we used to have to run through to reach the Holiday Inn. We ate thick Wiener schnitzel and drank red wine. In the distance, through the windows, were the twin blue shadows of the bombed-out Unis Towers, the tallest buildings in the city. Before the war, people called the buildings by the names of two famous characters from Sarajevo jokes: Momo and Uzeir. The names are of different national origins, and since the buildings were of equal height, they were meant to symbolize brotherhood and unity. The Serbs destroyed them both. The buildings had been equipped with advanced fire-prevention systems, but the people had already emptied the water reservoirs, and so they burned and blackened and remained like two mirrored shells. Constant reminders. Wounded, but still standing.

Sidran stared at the Unis Towers as he described his old acquaintance, Koljevic: a pleasant chap, if slightly disturbed by nationalism, who hid it well enough. "Although," Sidran noted dryly, "one always had the sense it was waiting to burst out."

Then, he explains, Koljevic went to Pale. "He caught the syndrome of those people who hid in the forest. He and Radovan Karadzic thought they would be back in two weeks, having conquered Sarajevo. Imagine—you think you're going to your weekend house for two weeks. That's okay. Then a week goes by, then two weeks, one month, two years, four years, and you're still in the woods. Remember, Koljevic was a city man with sophisticated habits."

Then Sidran raised his forefinger and his thumb to his head and imitated an exploding handgun blowing a temple apart.

"He could not destroy Sarajevo," Sidran said quietly "and that destroyed him."

In late December 1992, I left a frozen Sarajevo with a colleague and in his armored Land Rover began the slow and arduous drive across the airfield—then in the hands of the U.N. but littered with both Bosnian Muslim and Bosnian Serb checkpoints—to Serb-held territory, and eventually Pale. Climbing the city halls above Sarajevo, we stopped at Bosnian Serb positions to look through their gunsights at the city below. It was a sinister but fascinating moment when one of the gunmen, a toothless, drunken *papak*, pointed out our rooms at the Holiday Inn with sniggers. Beneath us, Sarajevo, without electricity, water, or gas, the naked buildings gutted by the relentless bombing, looked as vulnerable and rickety as an empty doll's house.

We needed information, so we had to stop for a while and drink with the *papak*. I swallowed a homemade slivovica in his wooden shack, admired his icons and his pictures of Karadzic tacked to the wall, and thought of a story a British soldier once told me. He had found himself alone with one of the Serb snipers who was proudly demonstrating the ease with which he could pick off civilians at their knees as they ran across the intersections: powerless little stick figures who hit the ground silently and would then no doubt have to undergo amputation at the hospital with limited anesthetic. He, the sniper standing high above them on the hills, would roar with laughter as they skidded on their bellies, the bullet lodged in their knees or their spines.

My friend had a gun with him, a handgun, and for a moment when the Serb turned his back, my friend had to stop himself from releasing a bullet into his brain. "I had one moment to waste him and do humanity a giant favor," he said. "No one would have known."

He hated that man with so much emotion, hated that creature he saw as the lowest form of humanity. And I also hated this old man who was proudly showing me the rooms where we slept, my colleagues and I, where we worked, where we hoped and prayed our plastic windows would not invite this scum to shoot. I did not see him as a man with a family, with an ideology, as someone who was manipulated by men like Koljevic who were far more intelligent and urbane. I saw him as an instrument of evil.

The shack was suddenly stifling, despite the cold temperature outside. The slivovica, the man's breath too near my cheek, the guns and the racks of ammunition, made me feel sick.

Can we go? I asked my friend, who had an extraordinary ability to talk at length to anyone. As we pulled away, the old man and his colleagues gave us the three-fingered Serb brotherhood salute: Only Serbs in Serbia.

In those dark, early days of the war when it seemed as though the end would never come, Koljevic was a man of great power. He was a scholar who spoke perfect English, an official who was wheeled out to give sound bites on CNN, to meet foreigners, to try to explain the logic of bringing a city to its knees. With his literary references, his Western-style manners, his urbane appearance, he was the kinder, gentler face of Radovan Karadzic.

Ejup Ganic, the vice president of the postwar Bosnian-Croat Federation and a leading figure in the Bosnian presidency during the war, told me that Koljevic always reminded him of the kid in the film *American Graffiti,* the small boy "who has to do terrible, terrible things to be initiated into a gang. The one they used to do the dirty work, and he did it to be liked by them." Ganic remembered Koljevic from the days before the war, when he was one of the seven elected Bosnian Serb officials with a new office in the Presidency in Sarajevo. His old office, ironically, later went to Aliya Izetbegovic, the former president of Bosnia.

Ganic and Koljevic used to meet for coffee between sessions and talk. Ganic felt a kinship to the man for his intelligence and his sensitivity. "He was the only Serb I felt I could communicate with. I felt oddly comfortable with him." But, Ganic adds, their coffee-drinking days were a good year and a half before the barricades went up in Sarajevo and the shelling began. "In a year and a half," Ganic noted, "a man can change a lot."

That winter night, we reached Pale by nightfall. Koljevic was holding court in a seedy, broken-down palace, one of the old ski resorts in Jahorina, the Hotel Panorama. He kept us waiting for hours. It was biting cold, and the hotel was unheated. His secretary would come out, grumpily, every hour or so simply to say she had no idea what time he would be finished with his meeting and when he would see us. Various unsavory characters—unshaven, drunk, in combat fatigues—wandered in and out of the lobby. In my hard chair, I wrapped my arms around myself to keep in the warmth and tried hard not to fall asleep.

Near midnight, or what seemed like midnight, someone led us down a long, peeling corridor into a room where Koljevic sat behind a long table. There was a sheaf of papers in front of him. He did not smile, but he rose to greet us. Stooped and balding, a short man, he was rumpled and looked like an owl or a benevolent professor. He was utterly unremarkable; he would have been insignificant in a crowd. But it was a deceiving demeanor: he looked less deadly than he was. Behind his spectacles, his eyes were ice-cold.

We began to drink, and he lectured us, as though we were students in a hall at Sarajevo University. "We are not the monsters you paint us," he said several times. Then came the Serbian history: Turks, Kosovo Polje, World War II, Tito, Cyrus Vance, clashes between Serbs and Muslims on Mount Igman. The Serbs, he said over and over, were misunderstood. Hours passed, my chair seemed to draw in a deep cold. Every time I looked up from my notebook, my small glass was full of plum brandy. Koljevic was smiling, drifting into another world, talking of Shakespeare and King Lear. Of Sarajevo. Of the fact that he had never been made a full professor.

I grew bored as he droned on and on. I scrawled in my notebook. My attention wandered. I came back to attention only when he would point his finger at me and demand an answer.

"You must be hungry," he said. Plates of fatty pork and potatoes swimming in fat appeared, along with bottles of slivovica.

I wish I remembered more of that meeting, which continued so long into the drunken night that I retreated into my mind, to a place where I was warm and getting ready for bed. His voice droned on. The bottle never seemed to empty. Two or three times, my eyes closed and I drifted into a false warm place, the slivovica place. Then they snapped open. Koljevic, the teenage sidekick of Karadzic, was on his feet, sputtering that he had never gotten the recognition he deserved as a brilliant academic. For this I was wide awake.

"They never . . . ," he spat, his face purple with rage. *"They never made me a full professor!"* He slumped back into his chair, exhausted by his admission.

Was he joking? Now I was wide awake. The room was painfully still. Outside, I could hear the faint rumble of guns in the distance. No one spoke. I looked sideways at my colleague, but he was also staring at Koljevic, equally stunned by the sudden realization that the deconstruction of Sarajevo was in the hands of a man who had a terrible, terrible inferiority complex.

We left shortly after that. Perhaps he was embarrassed; perhaps the strong slivovica had loosened his tongue. But he finally called a halt and said we could pass the night on the floor of the room where we were talking and eating. Perhaps he was embarrassed; he suddenly seemed terse and distant.

We didn't sleep on the floor. We stumbled somewhere else, down a snowy path and into an unheated and dilapidated former hotel, and we became the guest of one of his ministers, another extraordinary figure, another ludicrous character out of an Emir Kusturica film. He was dressed oddly: dressing gown over his clothes, perhaps to keep warm, a scarf wrapped around his slender throat. He talked for few hours, this time of poetry.

The minister had a room full of young students churning out news bulletins. It was nearly three in the morning, but he was opening more bottles of slivovica and shouting orders. It was a parallel universe, Pale, a place where no one slept, where everyone appeared to be on twenty-four-hour war duty.

We did get to sleep, eventually. At dawn, the crusty ice cracked and a gray light came splintering through the freezing room where we slept. Sometimes, I think I dreamed that night, but a few years later I came across a Cyrillic version of the poet's verse, inscribed to me in French, and the date. It really did happen after all.

As for Koljevic, he had lied to us that night. He was, in fact, a full professor, had risen high on the academic ladder. In the midst of the bloody and brutal war, he was so bitter that his memory could only focus on the imagined injustices that happened to him.

In fact, others who were in the English department alongside him remember clearly that it was *he*, never them, who made a grand issue of his Serbian roots. One female student, now a lecturer at the university, recalls having to defend her thesis to a group of professors, among them Koljevic. What startled her was his turning to another professor while she was in mid-sentence and saying, "She's very bright, very clever"—pause two beats—"even if she is a Muslim."

It is too easy to say that Koljevic suffered from a Napoleon complex. It was far more complicated. This is a man who fainted—literally lost consciousness—when he heard the news that the Serbs had lost their claim to Sarajevo at Dayton. The place he had invested so much in destroying had destroyed him.

Go back to his roots, to the roots of his insecurities. He was born in Banja Luka in 1936. His father owned a prosperous shop in the days before communism, but once the Communists "liberated" the area, he lost it, and his money. Marko Vesovic talked a lot about Nikola and his brother Svetozar's deep aversion to communism as they were growing up.

"His father talked of nothing else for many years," Vesovic said. "How he had something and how it had been abruptly taken away from him."

Although the young Koljevic was close to both his parents—he is now buried alongside his mother, who drowned in the River Verbas—it was his brother Svetozar, five years older, who influenced him the most. Their relationship was disturbing, and, according to his closest friends, "was the deep pain in his psyche." From childhood until his death, he lived in the shadow of his brother.

Nikola was recognized as a competent scholar but Svetozar, also a literary authority, was regarded as a genius. Five years after he left Sarajevo, students of English still grow enthusiastic over Svetozar's vibrant and moving lectures on James Joyce and his impassioned readings from *Ulysses*. Veskovic says that in modern Serbian literary criticism, "Svetozar was legendary." Both brothers were English scholars who nurtured an affected English humor, but Nikola simply did not have the literary abundance of his brother and was not as good a writer. The younger Koljevic stumbled through life feeling wholly inferior to his elder, more gifted sibling.

On one occasion, a professor from Zagreb, upon hearing Nikola's name, began to shower him with praise. Nikola listened carefully as the professor ended with a high compliment: that his book, *The Triumph of Intelligence*, was standard reading for all Croatian university students. Nikola visibly paled and took a step back. In a small voice, he replied, "I am afraid that you are confusing me with my brother."

The brothers studied at Sarajevo University. Nikola paid his expenses by playing the piano during a horse act in a traveling circus that toured the former Yugoslavia. Both devoured English and American literature with ferocity, learning about turn-of-the-century Manhattan from Edith Wharton and the Midwest from Sinclair Lewis. Both spoke impeccable English. But it was Svetozar who won the first scholarship abroad. When he took off for the United States, he left his fiancée, Milica Medic, in the hands of his loyal and devoted younger brother, Nikola, for safekeeping.

For Nikola, the seduction of his brother's fiancé was a golden opportunity, payback time for all the small insults and degradations that had marred his young life. Whether or not it was sincere, or whether or not he did it out of spite, Nikola and Milica became lovers. By the time Svetozar returned home from America, she was pregnant. They married shortly after the birth of their child, but Svetozar was mortally wounded: the two people he loved the most had betrayed him. He was then forced by his family into marrying Milica's sister.

And so Nikola had his revenge, but it would torture him with guilt. He could not enjoy his new wife, his new baby, without thinking about how it had come to him, how much he had pained his brother. When his son Djordje died nearly twenty years later, he was convinced it was God's will—that he was being paid back for stealing his brother's wife, that his crime was being punished in a biblical way.

"For about two years after that, he drank heavily and steadily," remembers Gordana Mikulic. "His family really suffered." Milica, already a high-strung and emotionally delicate woman, got pregnant again and lost the baby. Nikola saw this too as another punishment, and when she finally gave birth to a little girl about a year after that, he insisted they call her Bogdana, which means "gift from God." He said that the birth of his daughter was a sign from God that he was meant to go on living.

"He quit drinking," says Mikulic. "And about this time, he entered into the world of mysticism."

He told friends that he believed God was punishing him because he had not been a good Serb. Up to that point, he had practically thought of himself, his self-image, as a well-turned out Englishman. Now he found a new identity. "From now on," he told friends, "I am a Serb."

His grasp of mysticism was vague. It sometimes took the form of lengthy philosophical sessions with an Orthodox priest, and strange customs, such as always leaving a plate at the dinner table for the deceased Djordje. He had never celebrated Orthodox Christmas or Easter before, but suddenly, to the astonishment of his friends, he demanded that religious rituals be performed methodically and with great enthusiasm. Gordana Mikulic says she was baffled by the change.

"It was almost as though he was grasping at the tradition for comfort," she says, "to escape the tragedy." What is certain is that it was religion, heavily entwined with nationalism, that sent him down the political road.

Politics was the one area in which Svetozar could not outshine Nikola. The younger brother felt he could at last come into his own, finally receiving the attention and the power and the devotion that he craved and believed he deserved. Svetozar, confused by his brother's willingness to jump into the fire of the Serb Democratic Party, would later say that when his brother became a member of the Bosnian Serb presidency, he did not know whether to wish him success or failure as a politician. To wish him success among so many sharks, Svetozar said, would have been entirely cynical. By 1992, in the run-up to the war, Svetozar claimed that he had lost all "human contact" with his brother.

He recalled heated arguments in which Nikola would rant and rage that the only way forward was to live separately from Muslims. Svetozar would stare in amazement, not quite believing this was the same person with whom he had shared parents, memories, childhood. It was as if he had changed into something else, had adapted the habits and the words of another person. As if he were possessed by the spirit of nationalism that was sweeping through Serbia and Bosnia.

Svetozar would infuriate his brother further by responding to his tirades about separate lives from Muslims with a quote from Nikola Pasic, a renowned Serb politician: "The question is not who you can or cannot get on with, but who you must." Nikola would storm off, his face reddened, his hands clenched in fists. "We don't have to any more!" he shrieked at his brother.

The Parliament buildings in Sarajevo once stood—I say "once," because during the war they became charred skeletons of buildings bombed into submission by the Serbs—next to the university, but the walk from one to the other symbolized a radical transition for Kolje-vic: from professor of Shakespeare to hard-line member of the Serb Democratic Party (SDS). He had, it seemed, finally found his place.

One day, he took his old friend Marko Vesovic to see his new office, moving through the hallways and the rooms with a kind of pride that Vesovic had never seen before.

Later, Vesovic would remember that day, because it was the first time he realized that Koljevic had probably gone into politics because he was "bored with teaching and bored with being compared to his brother." Here, in the Parliament, he had found his own world. His initiation into the SDS was fast: his mentor was the history professor Milorad Ekmecic. Their plan was to create a Greater Serbia where threatened Serbs could live and work together without Muslims and Croats. In a sense, it was a harsh metaphor for Koljevic's own life: he had totally isolated himself and his politics from all the people he had loved before, from family, friends, from Svetozar.

Emil Habul, the deputy editor of the Sarajevo daily paper *Oslobodjenje*, recalls that gradually people began to see Koljevic as a prophetlike character who could predict the future of Bosnia. He gathered around him a loyal band of devotees and lectured them about what must take place in their country. At first, he said that the Yugoslavs could achieve this and separate without bloodshed or war. "People believed him," says Habul. "Because they had to."

The movement gained momentum. One had the sense that soon everyone would be hurled into a deep crevasse. People were frightened. When Radovan Karadzic, a psychiatrist who wrote terrible poetry and was loosely connected with the Sarajevo literary cognoscenti, became their leader, Habul remembers wondering whether or not these characters were actually doing this to gain power and riches. It all seemed crazy, a spiral spinning out of control. "It didn't seem to be a Sarajevo thing at heart," Habul muses. "Remember, the entire strategy was planned in Belgrade."

It was around this time, 1990, that Koljevic began making frequent journeys to Belgrade to meet with Slobodan Milosevic and be indoctrinated into the true meaning of Serb nationalism: a blend of communism and nationalistic symbolism. He remained close to Milosevic, which would ensure that the other Pale political strongmen always resented him as being Milosevic's puppet. But at this stage, the professor of Shakespeare felt that he was being accepted into court.

Later, Milosevic would turn on him and humiliate him. At

Wright-Patterson Air Force Base, where the Dayton Peace Accord was being hammered out in 1995, he deliberately avoided his Pale colleagues, treating them with contempt, as though they were ignorant country bumpkins. That included his old friend Nikola Koljevic, who had spent nearly a decade devoting himself to the Serb leader.

Vesovic watched this, saddened for his friend. He saw what Nikola was becoming, believing him to be the real brains behind the SDS. "I compare him to Rosenberg, Hitler's ideologist. He was a scholar, he was well versed, he could have had influence if he had been stronger," Vesovic says a bit sadly, because he loved his friend. "But by that time, he was already far, far away—lost to us forever."

One of Koljevic's last wishes was written down shortly before he died, and read after his death on Pale Television. It was a request that the body of his son Djordje—who was buried next to his grandfather in Bare Cemetery in Sarajevo—be exhumed and the remains be brought back to Banja Luka, which remained in Serb hands after the Dayton Accord. There, Nikola wrote in his careful hand, the family would be united.

President Aliya Izetbegovic's office received the letter shortly after his death. As an act of good will—although the Bosnian Muslim leader certainly could have borne an enormous grudge against the Serb who had attempted, and succeeded to a large extent, in destroying his city—Izetbegovic ordered his men to exhume the body. After twenty years, Djordje's remains were dug up and driven by a special car north to Banja Luka. Milica and Srdjan, the couple's younger son, and Bogdana remained in Belgrade.

I went back to Pale and Sarajevo shortly after Koljevic's death. It seemed as though time had already swallowed Nikola and he had disappeared into its vastness forever. He had become what he had dreaded in his lifetime: insignificant. His friends were too upset to talk about him.

"I was very, very shaken," Jovan Zametica, the Cambridge-educated policy advisor to the Bosnian Serbs, said. Then he stopped talking. "That is all I am going to tell you."

Another man who had traveled to America together with the young, idealistic Koljevic, the man who loved to read Shakespeare and poetry aloud, slammed the door of his Sarajevo flat in my face. Before he did, his face contorted with rage. He said, "He is a closed subject."

I was saddened by their responses, but I thought I understood their resentment, their unwillingness to discuss him. The Dayton Accord, to the Serbs, was a demeaning blow. By the terms of Dayton, they had lost Sarajevo, the city they had tried so hard to destroy. After all the blood, the rhetoric, the diplomatic wrangling, it would remain, more or less, in Muslim hands, even though some Serbs and Croats stayed there.

The muezzin would continue to cry out a call to the faithful. The mosques would reopen. Young Muslims who had left during the war as nonsecular would return after studying on "scholarships" in Malaysia with a newborn fanatical interest in Islam, something that had not existed before the war. The Serb dreams of unity and brotherhood had failed. And Nikola Koljevic was a tangible symbol of their failure.

Vesovic recalls again that when Koljevic read the final terms of Dayton, he fainted. Literally fell to the floor, the blood rushing from his face. The small, rounded professor who used to quote, "The fault, dear Brutus . . . ," while lecturing the likes of Richard Holbrooke, was horrified by what his people, his Serbs, had conceded. He was the first Bosnian Serb to return to Sarajevo, to a meeting with U.N. and Bosnian officials, and to confront the actual destruction, to confront what he had done.

Toward the end of his life, Koljevic was not considered a player any longer, or an important influence on either Milosevic or even Karadzic. He had no power. His drinking increased, as did his rantings. In the aftermath of the war, he seemed to disappear altogether.

Not many people were surprised by his death. Abdulah Sidrun said: "People here think of him as a monster. But he is not a monster. Monsters cannot be killed."

The night of his death, I had dinner in London with a young Bosnian. I felt sad about Koljevic's wasted life. My friend stared hard at me.

"I hate him," he said. "Because he destroyed my life. My friends are dead. I am a refugee. My family is scattered across Europe. He died the way I always hoped he would. With no dignity."

I was ashamed and embarrassed: for what had happened to my friend across the table and for the fact that I could feel something for the man who had ruined him. Too much had happened to allow room for tolerance, or forgiveness.

As for the people who loved him, they still feel haunted, almost obsessed, by the bizarre turnings of their friend's life. Gordana Mikulic believes that Koljevic killed himself because he had a "seed of morality" left in him and he finally realized how far off course he had strayed. Marko, who truly loved him, missed his friend, but the old one, before he was swallowed alive by politics and nationalism and bitterness and rage.

"He was a man who rose to great heights on his own corpse," he said. "He had already carried out an assassination of his moral and spiritual integrity." Others believed Koljevic killed himself because the war crimes tribunal at The Hague had been making inquiries about him.

Vesovic had burned most of his books—the books that he loved and had read and reread hundreds of times, underlying certain passages that he could come back to—during the siege of Sarajevo so that his family could keep warm. Lots of people did, and for people who loved books, it was painful. As he tossed another book into the fire, he would think of Koljevic's essays. There was one about Macbeth. When he could not sleep some nights, Vesovic found his mind wandering to that essay. Nikola had written, "In an attempt to become more than he is, Macbeth virtually destroys himself."

When Vesovic told me that story in Sarajevo, a few years after the siege had ended, a few weeks after his friend had been laid in the ground, his face had a funny look: a mixture of regret, sadness, anger, disappointment.

He repeated the quote from the essay several times. He wanted me to memorize it, because he said that sentence could serve as an epitaph on Nikola's gravestone.

Sarajevo
March 18, 2001

Biljana Plavsic, the former Bosnian Serb president and a wartime colleague of Nikola Koljevic, was at times known as the Iron Lady of the Balkans, the Serb Empress, or the Queen Mother. In Serbia, however, it is common to reduce names to their diminutive, and my friend Sanja, a Croat, used to call Plavsic Billy. It was a ridiculous name because it was far too girlish, too frivolous, for Plavsic, who was as powerful and self-confident as Margaret Thatcher. In many ways, with her helmet of coiffed hair and well-cut fake Chanel suits, her handbag held in front of her like a shield, she seemed very much a Balkan Thatch.

Her views were sometimes so extreme that Mrs. Slobodan Milosevic once referred to her as "Mengele." Seeing this matronly woman speaking with such hostility was shocking. She was the lone woman in the upper echelons of the Serb Democratic Party, Radovan Karadzic's nationalistic Bosnian Serb party. She was also a rare thing in the Balkans, in particular among the Pale mafia: a powerful, outspoken, larger-than-life woman.

But by January 2001, the Pale gang had disbanded. Plavsic was a seventy-year-old who had surrendered herself to The Hague. Koljevic was four years dead, and immortalized in Richard Holbrooke's memoir *To End a War* as a drunken joke. Krajisnik was also in The Hague, fighting to be released on provisional bail. Mladic was defiantly wandering around Belgrade, but Karadzic was on the run with a $5 million bounty on his head. His former villa in Pale was boarded up and guarded, and it was said he slept each night in a different location, growing more and more desperate, sometimes dressing in the robes of an Orthodox priest.

It was Plavsic, or Mrs. Plavsic, as she had always been known, who interested me the most. A few weeks after she turned herself in to The Hague, I went back to Bosnia. March is a miserable time to be in Sarajevo, when the grayness from the mountains envelops the city and the damp cold never leaves your bones. Just landing in the Sarajevo Aerodrom and catching the faint smell of winter sent me back to my mental state in those days. One year, I remember, I spent the whole month of March suffering a low-grade depression, watching the snow melt and drip, and following a street kid, whom I met at the orphanage, as he went about his daily life.

At night, my friend Ariane and I sat wrapped in blankets drinking whiskey in her room. I hated the smoky taste, but I liked getting drunk. It killed the boredom as it numbed the brain cells, and it killed the monotony of living inside a siege. The next day I would have a hangover and devour aspirin, hoping the cold would numb my head. By evening, we would file our stories and start again.

The boy I used to follow, Nusrat, looked more like a monkey than a child. He was adept at theft and survival. To hide from snipers on the Bridge of Brotherhood and Unity, he would get inside a stone urn, wrapping his thin arms around his legs like a human beetle. He robbed from the humanitarian aid convoys by climbing into the trucks and throwing the boxes that were meant to last a month down on the ground to his accomplice, another orphan. Despite his fledging business, I still gave him money and food, which he took dutifully without thanking me.

Nusrat did not trust me, and I did not trust him. Although I pitied him, I was not even sure I liked him, or felt warmth toward him, the way I did toward other children. While he was tragic, he was not lovable: from behind his hooded, dark eyes, he regarded the world as a place where stealing and looting was necessary for living, and where he would stomp on the next kid who was smaller and getting in his way.

In his whole life, he had never been held or told that anyone loved him. Normally, that would have been grounds for me to shower him with love and attention, with hope of getting him out of this place and away from the war, but in my depressed and barely functioning state, it was enough for me to buy him bread and provide him with some money to find a place to sleep at night. I had already given out all I could: I felt, for a while, I had nothing left inside of me to give away.

I was thinking about Nusrat when I took a taxi in March 2001. This time, I did not check into the Holiday Inn, fearing the ghosts of the past and afraid to see the same faces I had known, now older. I did not want to tell them what had happened to me in those years, where I had been, how my life had changed. I felt cold and numb; I did not want war nostalgia.

I checked into a new hotel, near the old market which got mortared so many times that the mortar holes had been filled with a red waxy substance and were now called Sarajevo roses. I spread my papers out on a lumpy bed with a flammable synthetic bedspread. My visit to Sarajevo was so different this time. Before I used to follow Nusrat to his favorite haunt, the flooded, broken-down Europa Hotel. Now it had been renovated into some modern monstrosity. Even the old orphanage where he sometimes slept had been cleaned up. Once, going to visit the orphanage, some of the older kids maneuvered me into an abandoned room and locked me up for hours. They finally let me out when I promised them cartons of cigarettes. Now, I was following not Nusrat but Plavsic, or rather, the ghost of Biljana Plavsic, the former president of the Republika Srpska. In the morning, I woke up and walked through her old neighborhoods. I visited her childhood friends, going past markets that were now open and not selling powdered eggs which had been stored since World War II, but flowers from Holland and chic Italian leather boots. I went to Plavsic's old classrooms and apartment buildings while she sat alone in a cell, meeting occasionally with her lawyers, sometimes bursting into tears, protesting that she was innocent.

Since Plavsic conceded defeat in the 1998 Bosnian elections to a hard-line nationalist, Nikola Poplasen, she had chosen to live openly in Banja Luka. She knew she was being pursued by the International Criminal Tribunal for the Former Yugoslavia (ICTY), but she believed she was innocent. There was always an air of arrogance around Biljana, and she convinced herself she was not in the same league as Karadzic and his cronies. But following Momcilo Krajisnik's arrest—he was taken screaming and kicking from his home in May 2000—she became increasingly anxious. She noticed intruders on her property, shadowy figures whom she thought were soldiers. When she called the police, she was told it was SFOR (NATO-led security forces) who were looking for someone else and had gotten the wrong address.

"Don't worry," they told her. "It's not for you."

But Plavsic did worry. She knew it was a lie. She convinced herself they were checking her home for a swoop operation, to take her the same way they had taken Krajisnik. The protection she always assumed the West would give her was beginning to peter out.

"Biljana began to panic, she freaked out," said Mirza Hajric, a member of the Bosnian government. "She suddenly realized she had no protection."

At that point, Plavsic may have lost her power and her position within the SDS, but she still did have pride. She did not want to go to The Hague, but she knew it was inevitable. When the fear and paranoia became too much, she turned herself in. On January 9, 2001, she arrived at The Hague, the only woman sitting in the detention center waiting to go to trial for war crimes.

Madeleine Albright—whom Plavsic would later face in The Hague in December 2002—called her decision "courageous," but Plavsic actually had no choice. A Hague official later told me that "it was the only dignified thing she could do. What else could she have done? Wait for them to drag her away?"

She was offered a safe house by the Dutch government, but she turned it down, preferring to be "with my boys"—the other Bosnian Serbs. In prison, she was given an extra room where she could sit, study, prepare her defense.

But unlike Milosevic, who would later adopt a defiant stance in court, bullying the prosecutors, the witnesses, and the judge, Plavsic seemed very vulnerable. Her former lawyer, Krstan Simic, told me that Plavsic, a religious woman who prayed throughout her ordeal, was baffled as to why she was in prison. She protested her innocence.

"What have I done?" she asked Simic frequently. "Explain to me clearly: What have I done?"

On October 2, 2002, Plavsic reversed her verdict and declared in front of the International Penal Court of The Hague that she was guilty, in particular on charges of crimes against humanity in Bosnia. The court decided to raise the other seven charges weighing against her, in particular, that of genocide.

"I recognize that I am guilty," Plavsic told the court.

It had taken her more than a year and perhaps a great deal of soul-searching to come to that conclusion.

At the height of her power, in the old days when the Bosnian Serbs were winning, and later when the West would pluck her from the gang running the Republika Srpska and choose to deal with her alone, Plavsic would stride into the Parliamentary Assembly meetings in Pale like a warrior. Her gold-tinted hair shone. Her well-cut suits molded to her strong figure. She looked strong, and she was: she liked to fight. Once, in 1994, she told a Serbian newspaper, "I don't have faith in political negotiations. One good battle would settle the war."

But by the time she reached The Hague, the Iron Lady was tired of the old battles. Nikola Koljevic was in his grave. Karadzic was hidden somewhere in Montenegro. She had had enough.

Going through old newspaper cuttings of Plavsic in her finest hours, storming the battlefields and kissing murderers like Arkan on the cheek, it would have been easy to hate her, as easy as it was to hate Koljevic or Karadzic. Her nationalism, at the height of the war, seemed even to exceed theirs; she believed Muslims were "genetically deformed." She did nothing to help fellow women who were suffering dreadful consequences as a result of the war. She was so extreme that Milosevic suggested she seek psychiatric help. She, in turn, loathed Milosevic for his "willingness" to cooperate with the West: she refused to shake hands with him in 1993 because he endorsed the Vance-Owen peace plan, which she saw as pro-Muslim.

That same year, a year of horrendous suffering for Bosnian Muslims in cities such as Gorazde, Srebrenica, Foca, and Maglaj, she toured the wasted countryside in Bosnian Serbia. After seeing hospitals, troops, and cities held by their forces, she remarked blithely, "I'd like to see eastern Bosnia completely cleansed of Muslims." Later, she tried to backtrack. "When I say clean, I don't mean ethnic cleansing. The international community has imposed this term on us, for a completely natural thing."

The year before, in Bijeljina in 1992, she had planted a kiss on the cheek of Arkan, who had just razed the place. "I always kiss the heroes," she gushed. "When I saw what he'd done, I told myself, this is a real Serb hero. He is a real Serb. We need men like him."

There was another Biljana Plavsic, though. Lonely, childless, driven to succeed in the male-dominated world of Bosnian Serb politics. Proud, unloved, highly ambitious: trying to forge her way in an oppressive and sexist world. Sometimes she became less of a monster and more of a three-dimensional creature. Sometimes, I even saw her as extraordinary: standing up to Karadzic and Krajisnik with strong, if illogical, arguments, rooting herself firmly in her high heels and waving her finger at them, lecturing them as if they were ill-behaved children in a classroom. Even if I hated what she stood for, one had to have a grudging respect for her.

After Plavsic left Bosnia, people had different visions of her, largely centered around her sexuality. It was rampant sexism, because no one ever made comments about Koljevic's or Karadzic's private life, no matter how much they disliked them. Yet people felt free to tell me, unsolicited, that she was cold, remote, driven. Depending on whom I spoke to, she was either flirtatious, sexually voracious, sexually frigid, or a lesbian. I disregarded all of these accounts: in the end, I concluded she was an emotionally detached woman who gave little time to her private life. The war had engulfed her completely. Who really knew what went on in her head at night, after the rabid parliamentary sessions, after staring for hours at maps of Bosnia?

Her relationship with Sarajevo, where she had been raised, was equally complicated. Unlike Nikola Koljevic, she did not have a vendetta against Sarajevo or its people. Like Koljevic, she *was* a true Sarajevan, even if she was born in Tuzla in July 1930. She had loved Sarajevo, thrived on the intellectual ambiance of the university. But Plavsic, even more so than Koljevic, grew to hate the Muslims with a ferocity that shocked even her Pale colleagues.

Dr. Ejup Ganic, the former Bosnian vice president, was the man Biljana once called "Genetically deformed." During the war, I had sat with Ganic for hours—largely because his office in the Bosnian Presidency had some heating and his English, honed in Chicago, was impeccable. After the war, he had left office and had gone back to his former profession, teaching engineering and writing textbooks.

That March afternoon, I found Ganic in an old building near the university. Night was falling. It was verging on early spring, but it was cold, the frost hanging on the windows. The days were still short. We drank lukewarm coffee as the sky darkened in intensity. I could hear the bells from the tram stop outside.

Ganic had often been sent to deal with the Pale bunch during the war, but as he spoke of Plavsic, he grew visibly uncomfortable. He had known her, as he knew Koljevic, from before the war, from Sarajevo University, and his relationship with her, like that with Koljevic, was cordial. They met in 1990 when both served on a seven-man shared Bosnian presidency. The two—one Serb, one Muslim, both scientists with a taste for empirical order—liked each other. They met for endless coffees, discussed politics and families. Ganic even remembers sending Plavsic flowers for a holiday, before the war broke out. "I liked her," he said simply. "She was intelligent. I could talk to her freely."

When war finally did erupt, Ganic was horrified to find that his old friend, the only woman working in Karadzic's inner circle, was doing nothing to halt the crimes that were being perpetuated against other women. He felt she bore some responsibility.

"As a woman, she had the chance to stop some of the more horrifying crimes that happened to other women during the war: rape, mass torture," Ganic says, his voice rising. "And yet, she stood by and did nothing."

Night after night, Plavsic sat, first in the Serb-held suburb of Grbavica where she lived, later in her Pale retreat watching Bosnian television, and witnessed exactly what was happening. She saw children running from snipers; she saw the deportation of Muslims from central and eastern Bosnia; she saw aid convoys being turned back from Gorazde and Srebrenica under orders from General Mladic. She knew about the rapes, about the babies being born, about the gymnasium in Foca where women were held and gang-raped.

"I knew she was watching it all in Pole," Ganic insists. "Because she used to call me frequently and complain about something I said. She knew what was going on. The biggest crime in this war was the war against women," he says angrily. "And what was her role?"

For sixteen years, Biljana Plavsic had taught at Sarajevo University, eventually rising to become Dean of the Faculty of Natural Sciences and Mathematics. She had entered those cavernous, chilly classrooms and instructed future biologists. She would often visit front lines from which Sarajevo was shelled. She could see the concrete shoe-box buildings of the university where she drank coffee; gossiped with friends; developed ideas; invented, after many years of research, a new type of microscope; and struggled, like Koljevic, to be part of the gang. How could she have stood there and watched the city bleed without feeling something? She once remarked that "Sarajevo has come *too much* to the world's attention." She explained that she had believed the city would fall within days and "how it spread to this line of fire, I honestly don't know."

"It's strange to have a woman behaving like that," says Ganic, genuinely baffled. He puts it down to the same syndrome that Koljevic suffered from: the small kid in *American Graffiti*. "The kid who will do anything to be accepted, to be part of the bigger boys, the gang."

At the height of her power, Plavsic was, certainly, accepted into Karadzic's gang. In 1996, after she was elected Bosnian Serb president, the West embraced her. With great conviction, she tried to expose corruption within her own circle. It was admirable, but it was also a cunning move, calculated to bring her closer in line with the Western diplomats. In terms of her relationship with her Pale colleagues, it was suicide. For this treachery, they cut her dead.

When the ICTY charge sheet finally arrived, the charges summed up her private war years: crimes against humanity, genocide, persecution, extermination, deportation, willful killing, inhuman acts, violation of the Geneva Convention of 1949. It said Plavsic was guilty of the violation of the laws and customs of war. Her charge sheet read that she was guilty of "complicity in the planning, preparation or execution in the destruction of Bosnian Muslims or Bosnian Croat communities, including:

1. The mass killing in mid-June 1992 of 47 Bosnian men from Rajlovac Camp in Novi Grad.
2. The execution in mid-July 1992 of 150 Bosnian Muslim and/or Bosnian Croat males at Omarska Camp in Prijedor.
3. The execution in late July 1992 of 150 Bosnian Muslim or Bosnian Croat males at Keraterm Camp in Prijedor.
4. The mass execution in August 1992 of Bosnian Muslim or Bosnian Croat males in Trnopolje Camp in Prijedor.
5. The repeated beatings, torture, and killing of 36 Bosnian Muslim males in July 1992 in Foca.

6. The killing in August 1992 of 20 Bosnian males from Kalinovik.
7. The inhumane treatment and/or torture of Bosnian Muslims, Bosnia Croats, and other non-Serbs—including beatings, torture, sexual violence, and death threats on a daily basis.
8. Involvement in the planning, preparation, and execution of the forced transfer and deportation of tens of thousands of Muslims, Bosnian Croats, and other non-Serbs.

I read the charges, faxed from The Hague, sitting on my Sarajevo hotel bed. That day, the air was tinged by exhaust fumes. My bitter Nescafé got colder as I held the charge sheet between my fingers and tried to replay all the crimes Plavsic had, in effect, committed.

Omarska, Keraterm, Trnopolje. I saw Zlatko, the Omarska survivor, sitting in a field near Prijedor telling me about the night he was taken away. The barbed wire; the cries from the White Room. Zlatko screaming over his shoulder for his mother to run away as he was dragged to the interrogation center. Then, horribly, nineteen months in camps. Where was Plavsic while Zlatko was getting beaten with rubber hoses in Omarska and made to crawl simply to get a cup of water?

Omarksa is now closed. But inside the three courtrooms of The Hague, the past is still very much alive. Foca, Prijedor, Vukovar, Racak. Towns that probably were pretty little villages once and now are synonymous with evil. Where did it come from, this evil? What had driven these people to do this to each other?

Reading the charge sheet, I drifted between past and present, holding it in my hands. In real time, there was early-morning Sarajevo traffic. In the past, there was no traffic because there were no cars. Snipers aimed at cars. There was no fuel. By the first year of the siege, the number of vehicles fell from 105,000 to 5,000, and of the two hundred city transportation routes, there remained only one. If you had a car, it was probably a VW Golf which had been made in Sarajevo before the war, and you drove *fast*. There were signs posted the first few months of the siege: DRIVE CAREFULLY, DON'T GET KILLED IN VAIN.

Biljana Plavsic was not charged in connection with snipers, but she should have been. All of the Pale gang should have been convicted of murdering the city. Of building fear, which in fact became their strongest weapon because it caused people to run away.

Now, in real time, postwar, there was a traffic light outside my window on the corner. There were packets of sugar on my table in an Alessi-style bowl. The freshly renovated tram was running. A bell was ringing, designating a stop. During the war, people listened for the tram bell like Pavlov's dogs. If it rang, it meant the trams, built in Prague many years ago, were running. It meant the war was over. When I hear that bell again, my friend Klea had said, I'm going to scream with happiness.

For me, Plavsic was most guilty of stealing years of people's lives. But she didn't think so. When she read the charge sheet, she cried, believing that somehow she was different from the others.

"After she received her invitation to The Hague, she cried for days," says Suzanna Andjelic, a journalist in Sarajevo. "She believed The Hague would treat her the same way it treated Mladic, Karadzic, or Krajisnic."

Ironically, after all those years of fighting to be treated the same as her boys, she now wanted to be treated carefully, like a woman.

Biljana Plavsic was a strange child. Growing up in the Marijin Dvor neighborhood of Sarajevo, she was taller than the other children, more remote. She was blond and solid, with ramrod good posture, and her dresses and school uniform were always clean. The daughter of a wealthy scientist–turned–museum director, she lived in the world of books and studies, so much so that the other children were a little afraid of this big, silent girl.

Biljana seemed older than the other kids, those who played games on the streets in front of their grand Austro-Hungarian–style apartment blocks not far from the Miljacka River. Many years later, when the war raged here, there was a street in Marijin Dvor, not far from Biljana's house, called Trscanska. On this street, more civilians were hit by snipers than anywhere else in the city. There were large cement blocks put in place so that people could walk or run behind them without being seen.

But that's fast-forwarding. For now, Biljana Plavsic is still a little girl. The rabid nationalism that would later emerge is buried very deep. All she cares about now is studying. It's almost as though she doesn't concern herself with the world outside. When everyone got a bit older, and it was customary to follow young couples walking home hand in hand, throwing a few stones to tease them, no one ever threw stones at Biljana. That is because none of the other kids can remember seeing her walk home with a boy, even though she was growing into a beautiful teenager with pale, silky hair and a clear, unfurrowed brow.

In a faded photograph taken of the Marijin Dvor gang in the summer of 1938, a group of friends stand slightly agog, staring into a forgotten photographer's lens. The country was still called the Kingdom of Yugoslavia, the name given to it in 1918. Tito had not yet taken control.

In the photo, Biljana, eight years old, stands slightly apart from the other children. She is elegant; there is no raffish expression on her face, no sign of mischief. She has a straw boater on her head and white knee socks. She towers over the rest and looks stronger.

"She was like a horse," says Drasko Vognovic, a childhood friend who was six years younger, but is also in the picture as a skinny boy. "As strong as a horse. She was *big*." He tries hard to explain, with his hands, that he does not mean just physically big. It was an air; it was her presence. Biljana always seemed slightly disapproving, he said.

Everyone remembers the Plavsics as nice people, good neighbors. Her father, Svetislav, originally from Brcko in northern Bosnia, was a biologist who later became director of the Botanical Gardens at the National Museum in Sarajevo. Her mother was a schoolteacher. They had money, but when communism came, they lost it all, and Biljana never forgave the Communists.

Later, when referring to Slobodan Milosevic, she would call him, with disdain, a *Communist*. Her brother, Zdravko, was a good athlete, a star basketball player who later went on to play for Partizan Belgrade. He was considered *raja*, a buddy, a mate, one of the gang.

At sixteen, Biljana was an attractive, pale blonde with blond eyelashes that fluttered when she spoke. The war years had not deprived her; she had filled out to be a lovely young woman. Still, she walked to school and home alone, without a boyfriend to carry her books.

She was serious, studious, removed. "Oh, she was cold, cold,

cold," recalls Ibrahim Busatlija, a professor of geography at Sarajevo University who knew her from the beginning of the 1950s, when he recalled a beautiful young woman in her early twenties.

In those days, he remembers the two of them, just starting out at Sarajevo University as teachers, going swimming with another male colleague. One of the men teasingly put his hand on her knee.

"Then we both put our hands on her knee, joking with her," he says. "And she acted as if we didn't exist. She just kept on talking." What surprised Busatlija the most—and I was wary of his story, thinking perhaps that he might have been a rejected lover and therefore wanted to speak ill of her—was not that Biljana objected to their touch, but that she had seemed oblivious to it. "She was in another world when it came to that," he said. "No interest in a man at all."

Another of her colleagues in the Department of Environmental Science, Sulejman Redzic, remembers her as "an unusual woman . . . and I say that in a positive way," he stresses. "She was attractive, intelligent, elegant, and rich." He said that even at the beginning of her career she knew what she wanted and her focus was like a laser: for instance, she was one of the first people in the early 1970s to insist on advanced technology in her laboratories.

Redzic had no indication of any nationalism in those days—in fact, like most of her university colleagues, he assumed she was a Croat because she had gotten her Ph.D. at Zagreb University and preferred Croatian textbooks in her courses.

Redzic, who calls Plavsic "my mentor," was shocked when he saw what she had become, because she did not seem capable of such actions. When he first learned that Plavsic had joined the SDS and gone to Pale during the war, he believed, as did many of her former friends, that she had been manipulated by her SDS colleagues.

"She collaborated with brutal people," he shrugs. "She might have been disoriented. I don't think she had the education to be a policy-maker. She was an academic."

Academics should know better, he added. But in fact, the core of the Pale mafia—Karadzic, Koljevic—were brilliant intellectuals. And Biljana Plavsic, Redzic knew, was far too tough to be pushed around, which left him with a disturbing conclusion.

"How could someone so highly intelligent be manipulated?" he asked himself out loud. When he saw Biljana on television during the war, he called his wife to watch. He was heartsick: the woman on the television bore no resemblance to the professor he idolized, who had taught him so much. "She had changed her personality," he said. "Most of us in the faculty felt the same way." He said she even looked physically different, but it was just the animosity on her face.

The Sarajevan journalist Suzanna Andjelic, who followed Plavsic closely, always felt that she compensated for her absence of private life by channeling it into her politics and her nationalism. So is the common theory in Sarajevo, where her lack of children is constantly pointed out.

Plavsic *did* marry, a lawyer, Mirko Banjac, in the 1970s, but the marriage did not last long. When she divorced, she confided to a friend that now was the time for her to rise. But Ahmed Buric, a journalist who met her often in the early 1990s, believed she grew bored with academia. She needed more challenges. Buric takes the same line as Suzanna Andjelic: "Because she had virtually no private life, she focused on politics and nationalism," he says.

Plavsic entered politics at the academic level. When she could not get an electronic microscope that she needed for her research, she campaigned heavily at the university board and was elected vice-dean in charge of finance. She got her microscope—paying for it out of the university budget.

"One of her characteristics was that when she wanted something, she got it no matter what the consequences," said one of her former students.

By the time she left the university to join the Bosnian presidency in 1990 as a member of the SDS after eighteen years of teaching, she had gone as far as she could. "My party," she said happily, talking of the SDS to a friend almost as if she was talking about a lover. "The party I have been waiting for." It seemed as though this outsider, this girl who was never asked to play, had found her place.

By April 1992, the Bosnian war had begun. Plavsic joined Karadzic in Pale and, between 1992 and 1995, was one of three vice presidents of Republika Srpska. Her role was, at times, crucial. *Newsweek* referred to her as "a weak but active participant in the political decisions behind ethnic cleansing." She traveled extensively throughout the war in her VW station wagon (unlike Karadzic and Krajisnik, both of whom drove Mercedes), watching the military maneuvers and often goading Mladic into pressing his men further. Her insensitivity and fever for war was astounding.

"There are twelve million Serbs in the former Yugoslavia," she remarked once. "And if we lose six million on the battlefield, there would still be half left." That remark led former Russian envoy to Bosnia Vitaly Churkin to conclude that Plavsic was "infected with war insanity."

"She was merciless at that point," recalls her former colleague Ibrahim Busatlija, adding somewhat cruelly, "She had an emotional defect . . . an odd frigid virgin." Suzanna Andjelic adds that "on a couple of occasions, she showed herself as uncompromising, worse than Karadzic or Krajisnik."

As one of the few women in the SDS, she would often complain to her friends that being a woman set her apart. It annoyed her. Swanee Hunt, the former American ambassador to Austria, often met with Plavsic after Dayton in various secret locations to discuss diplomatic tactics. Plavsic did not want the others to know she was seeing Hunt, and one location she suggested was in a cemetery, where Plavsic lit candles for her dead mother. As she held a burning candle, she confided to Hunt that her position as the sole woman in the midst of a macho, political world was not easy. "At that moment, I saw her as a woman, not as a politician," Hunt later said.

After Dayton, after she was elected Bosnian Serb president, Plavsic began to make unpopular changes within her own party with all the sensitivity of a charging bull. To the horror of most Bosnian Serbs, she launched an investigations into car and cigarette smuggling, among other things, and the "K Mafia"—Karadzic, Krajisnik, and Dragan Kijac, the interior minister. It was a time when the Serbs were already feeling downtrodden. Now they felt betrayed by their own.

"During the war," she stated. "I was aware that many things were being done in an illegal way." A Bosnian government official, Mirza Hajric, remembers that time and remembers reevaluating Plavsic for what she did. "Even though she did horrible things during the war," he says, "because she was leading that investigation, I thought that deep down, she *was* a decent person."

As president, Plavsic was bolstered by Madeleine Albright, Prime Minister Tony Blair, and Foreign Secretary Robin Cook. Her style—

straightforward, intelligent—was more acceptable to Western leaders than Karadzic's. "They felt she could be trusted more than Karadzic to implement the Dayton Accord," says Hajric. "Even if she had championed the siege of Sarajevo and urged on Mladic and Karadzic." The former Fulbright scholar who had studied in America charmed the West in a way that Karadzic, now persona non grata, could not.

"She really enjoyed that rule," Ejup Ganic says. "She was like the Queen Mother."

But while the West embraced her, her colleagues were drifting away. Her final vengeance on the SDS was to move the capital from Pale to Banja Luka, creating an immediate split among the leaders: the West backed Banja Luka and Plavsic; the Eastern-bloc countries remained loyal to Pale. In return, Krajisnik, then interior minister, fired anyone who gave information to her and dismantled the police loyal to Plavsic. "Plavsic is the queen of Banja Luka propped up by NATO," he once remarked bitterly.

Among her own Bosnian Serb people, made angry by what they saw as unfair treatment after Dayton, Plavsic began to lose power and popularity. Like Nikola Koljevic, her descent was rapid, and she grew paranoid and depressed. On one occasion, flying from London to Belgrade, she was detained by police. She later said she believed she would be kidnapped, and on Milosevic's orders, taken to a psychiatric hospital, declared mentally ill, and stripped of her powers. Milosevic had not forgiven her for slighting him in 1993.

The West did eventually abandon Plavsic, as her friends always predicted. By the time she lost power in 1998, she knew, as one Sarajevan friend put it, "she had no one to protect her." As early as 1996, the year she became president of Republika Srpska, she realized The Hague would come after her. During the four years she served as vice president of the RS (1992–96), she was a member of the Supreme High Command, which gave direct orders to the military police, and she was part of a united team of leaders that included Karadzic, Krajisnik, Koljevic, and Mladic.

During the trial of Dusko Tadic, one of the Bosnian Serbs convicted by The Hague in 1998, the prosecution showed footage of Plavsic congratulating and kissing Arkan after the massacre of Muslims in eastern Bosnia. The legendary kiss had come back to haunt her, but she still convinced herself that because she had enjoyed American support, The Hague would not touch her. "Madeleine Albright is my friend," she once told a journalist.

She was wrong. Eventually, her "invitation" arrived. For Orthodox Christmas 1999, she traveled to Belgrade to see her family. Her friends say she spent the holiday distraught—frightened, anxious, and crying. She jumped when the telephone rang. She did not want to go on the run like Karadzic. She did not want to be dragged off in the middle of the night like Krajisnik. And she did not want to die like Koljevic.

"Being an indicted war criminal is pretty lousy," a Western diplomat told me shortly after Plasvic decided to surrender. "Radovan Karadzic spends his life running from place to place. Physically and emotionally, it's no way to live. You either go underground, or you turn yourself in." Plavsic chose the later. By giving up, she had a greater chance at ensuring a "provisional release" so that she could await her trial in Yugoslavia and not in jail.

But she deliberated handing over her freedom with great sadness. On New Year's Eve 2000, as the world braced itself for the millennium celebrations, Plavsic was alone. She made a call to her old friend and former assistant at Sarajevo University, Cerima Mujacic, a Muslim who had known her for thirty-five years. During the war, Mujacic was one of the few people that Plavsic actually helped. She was trapped in a Serb-held Sarajevan neighborhood, and Plavsic frequently came to her aid. For this, Mujacic remains fiercely loyal.

As the two women chatted, Mujacic suddenly was struck by a wave of sadness for the older woman. It became clear she was just calling to have human contact. "She asked me to find some books for her," Mujacic said. "But her voice was so sad." When she put down the phone, Mujacic felt depressed. She suddenly knew she would never see her former boss again.

Many years after the photograph of the Marijin Dvor gang was taken, when Biljana became a Bosnian Serb deputy and a nationalist and, more important, one of the gang that sat in the hills above Sarajevo trying to destroy it, her old friend Drasko pulled out the photo and tried to remember everything about her.

Drasko is a Serb, like her—"I'm Orthodox, not a Serb," he says hotly—but he stayed in Sarajevo and lived through the siege like everyone else. He wanted to gain some insight, some clues about why that tall blond woman would want to destroy her own people. What had happened to Biljana that made her hate the place so much that she would want to see it leveled?

Shortly before the war began, he was listening to the radio in his kitchen and he heard a familiar voice: Biljana. By then, she had become a well-known politician, but everyone still thought of her as the girl who didn't have a boyfriend walking her home from school. Her mother and her brother continued to live nearby. "People don't change much from the time they are kids," he said. "So I thought she was the same."

What Drasko heard on the radio made him feel sick. The way Biljana talked about Muslims was so fierce. He doesn't remember anyone from his neighborhood—which was largely Serb when they were growing up, but mixed with Jews, Croats, Muslims, Gypsies— *ever* talking like that. It was ugly, Drasko decided, and turned it off. What had happened to her? he asked himself. Was it because nobody wanted to play with her when she was little?

Later, Drasko knew something horrible was going to happen in the city because at the very beginning of the war, Plavsic left for Pale, but she *did* come back to Sarajevo. But she came in a UN armored vehicle to pick up her elderly mother. She drove up to her old house and waited outside for her mother to emerge. A soldier who was assigned to guard her that day later told me that when the crowd found out who was in the vehicle, they encircled it and would have pulled her to pieces had they gotten inside.

They were angry that she was escaping while the rest of the city was descending into hell. The Serbs had stopped shelling while Plavsic entered the city; they had made a deal that they would do so until she emerged.

Meanwhile, a convoy of 2,500 women and children were getting ready to evacuate the city. But the convoy was essentially held hostage by the Serbs until Plavsic had left safely. Ironically, it was her old enemies—Ganic and the Bosnian government—who rescued her from the furious crowd and got her safely back to Pale.

"What I remember from that day was that a convoy of women

and children were leaving the city," recalls Benjamin Isovic, now a singer and musician, who witnessed the scene. "They were held hostage while she drove in and collected her family. Once she got out, the convoy and the city got pummeled. But she didn't seem to care. She was willing to sacrifice women and children."

Drasko, her childhood friend, remembers that convoy incident too. By all accounts, he should have hated her. Still, he felt a strange sadness, a pulling at his heart, when he heard that Biljana had turned herself in, red-eyed and swollen-faced, to The Hague. He again pulled out the picture of all of them as kids, before World War II even began. When he was still a skinny kid. When none of them knew anything about life. He stared at it, hard, looking for some kind of answer.

Her plea of guilt stunned those who knew her, particularly those to whom she had protested her innocence.[2] Plavsic could not have done it believing it would give her a shorter sentence, or a minor punishment. Basically, she was acknowledging the fact that she could spend the rest of her life behind bars. Perhaps, as one Hague official put it, "she had a genuine sense of remorse, and a wish to remove the stain of collective guilt from the Serb people."

Her statement read as follows:

By accepting responsibility and expressing her remorse fully and unconditionally, Mrs. Plavsic hopes to offer some consolation to the innocent victims—Muslim, Croat and Serb—of the war in Bosnia and Herzegovina. Mrs. Plavsic invites others, especially leaders, on any side of the conflict, to examine themselves and their own conduct.

The acknowledgment of guilt by Mrs. Plavsic is individual and personal. Legal responsibility can only be borne by persons individually, based upon individual acts and conduct. Mrs. Plavsic's acknowledgment of guilt reflects this principle and affirms that the legal responsibility of an individual, even if he or she is a leader, cannot be attributed to a group of people. Her acceptance of this responsibility will, she hopes, enable her people to move past the

carnage of the past decade, to reconcile with their neighbours, and,
ultimately, to restore their dignity as a respected people.

I spoke with a friend in Banja Luka about Plavsic's motives. My
friend had met her, and said that Plavsic was a deeply religious
woman. She had had time to think about what had happened during
those dark years, and perhaps the only way to forgiveness was admission. "I think she's finished with the war," my friend said. "She genuinely wants to see reconciliation."

In February 2003, at the age of seventy-two, Plevsic was sentenced to eleven years in prison for crimes against humanity. She is
the highest-ranking official involved in the Balkan conflict to be sentenced to date.

High Summer
Sarajevo
July 2001

I didn't like what I saw in postwar Bosnia. In a nostalgic and certainly
selfish way, I preferred the siege. Certainly, there was not then the
same kind of greed that I saw now. For a while, I did not go back
because the oddity of a real flight from Switzerland or Germany with
bankers and lawyers and businessmen wheeling their expensive suitcases behind them was too strong a contrast for me. Everywhere I
looked, I saw ghosts of the way that things had been a decade before.

Instead, I went to other places: Chechnya, where packs of wild
dogs were eating the flesh of the dead and where a houseful of blind
old people sat waiting during a bombardment for someone to rescue
them; Sierra Leone, where nine-year olds high on drugs carried AK-
47s that were nearly bigger than they were and learned how to
amputate hands and feet; East Timor, where the dead were stuffed
down wells; Liberia; Zimbabwe; Rwanda; Israel; Kosovo; Afghan-
istan; Iraq.

I settled in the Ivory Coast to write this book. But very soon after
I arrived, I was lying in my bed reading a report on Srebrenica when
I thought I heard gunfire. It was 4 A.M. and I could not sleep. I

thought I was dreaming—the sound was exactly like the old days in Sarajevo. I heard a grenade burst, very near my walled garden. A few hours later, I found out why: a coup led by rebellious soldiers had been launched, and was spreading into an ethnic civil war that reminded me, too much, of the early days in Yugoslavia. Soon, I was buying candles and bottled water and sleeping with my shoes and my passport near my bed. I now understood what it meant to have war come to your home, not to fly in to report it.

Nothing, of course, felt like Bosnia. The journalist Martha Gellhorn once said, speaking of the Spanish Civil War, that it was only possible to love one war. The rest becomes duty. I did try, but I did not feel the same thing in Rwanda as when I sat cross-legged on the floor, freezing cold with my friends Klea and Zoran and my baby godson Deni at their wartime home, a shack on Bjelave Hill, seeing the night sky turn red from tracer shells or bullets.

After Srebrenica, which should have been saved, after nearly 200,000 dead and 24,000 missing, the rest seemed so pointless. The diplomatic nation building that followed the war did not interest me. The World Bank and the IMF did not interest me. We used to dream of Sarajevo after the war, but that after-the-war time is now, and the city seemed dead and soulless.

By October 2002, Bosnia was the poorest country in Europe after Moldova. It had become a crossroads for smugglers and traffickers, for migrants and sex workers getting into Europe. Gangster culture prevailed. Mafiosi cruised in luxurious cars with tinted windows while half the workforce was jobless. Nationalistic politics prevailed at the October general and presidential elections. Paddy Ashdown—the former British Liberal Democratic leader, who effectively runs Bosnia as the international community's High Representative in Bosnia—said that he saw corruption and criminality as the bane of postwar Bosnia.

My friends didn't have enough money to buy a beer at the Internet Café, which had a Mexican theme and served expensive salads. The only people who seemed to be able to spend money were the internationals who flooded the place, and the mafia. Since 1995, Bosnia had absorbed $5 billion dollars in donor aid without much outward sign of spending. A recent report said another $500 million in budgetary funds are documented to have disappeared. Organized crime succeeded where politics had failed.

I spoke about it to my friends, who would agree, but then again, most of them had long left Bosnia and vowed they would never go back. Klea, whose entire family had emigrated in 1993 and 1994, wrote to me from Canada, where she was living with Zoran and Deni:

> *Hi Janine,*
>
> *It is so good to hear from you. Again, I'm sorry I didn't mention that Deni did get the money and he is unstoppable on the scooter!*
>
> *I don't know what to tell you about your bad experience in Sarajevo. I think that people that had the heart and soul of the city are somewhere in the world, scattered still with the same heart and soul. All of us made that city what it is and the city made us what we are today. But it lost its people and it lost its charm. Now you will meet people that wanted Sarajevo to be what it is today, so I guess they can have it!*
>
> *The rest of us will e-mail each other, gather round when we're not busy, and some will hope that they will meet again somewhere, if ever. A part of Sarajevo is in us forever and it is painful but the reality is never pleasant. What we had is gone. Each day that we let go to the future is brighter. It is hard and takes a long time, but one day the journey will be completed and we will have just our memories—the ones that we want to keep.*
>
> *Zoran is off to work. We work opposite shifts, which sucks. Deni is playing with some friends in the street and I am finishing some work for tomorrow. My mom is back in New York and I miss her already. Hopefully, we will go to New York next summer. I have to see Sandra's baby.*
>
> *That's all for now.*
>
> *Kisses and hugs,*
>
> *Klea, Zoran, and Deni*

A few days later, after that last trip, I went for a drink with a friend in a local café near Karadzic's old apartment. We stayed out late. We talked of the changes in the city and what had been left behind, what had disappeared with all the people who had emigrated. Another friend, Zoran, had told me over a lavish meal in Zagreb a few months before that very little had, in fact, changed from wartime Bosnia to the new federation: "The same old bullies are running the place, just with different faces."

Very late, my Bosnian friend drove me home. This time, I had stayed in the Holiday Inn, for nostalgia. But the place was empty of guests and the hallways were gloomier than during the siege. They had not changed the depressing dark furniture or the curtains, either, although the minibar was working.

My friend dropped me at the parking lot near the church in Marijin Dvor. It was next to what had been a field where snipers often got direct hits. Now there was a fast-food restaurant dropped in the middle of it. He said he would drive me to the airport the next day, and kissed me goodnight.

But I could not sleep. I woke in the morning to my telephone, a radio station in Cape Town that had read one of my stories in *The Times* and wanted a live interview. The reporter, live on the air, began to interview me as though the war was still happening. I suddenly realized he had no idea it had ever ended. As he asked questions about snipers and humanitarian aid convoys, and children being killed every day, I decided that to most of the world this was just another city that had been—or still was, according to this South African journalist—a war. Yugoslavia, or what it was, meant something to only a very small group. It was my obsession, but it was not most people's.

The breakfast was a buffet with a vast display of imported cheeses and meats. There was orange juice and croissants and *pain au chocolat*. There was toast and honey and marmalade, and there was also my friend from the old days, the waiter who used to organize the after-hour football games in the large dining room where we ate en masse, like students in a canteen, during the war.

He wasn't skinny anymore; neither was he young. He smiled crookedly.

"The breakfast is good," I said. We laughed awkwardly. We did not have to say anything more. We both remembered the old breakfasts. When I left, I turned back to look at him in his clean white shirt. I remembered that during the war the waiters always managed to keep their shirts clean, somehow.

Zoran arrived, hungover and red-eyed. We drove down Snipers' Alley. We turned left, down a new, freshly paved turnoff, the place where a bunch of Bosnian soldiers used to sit, and then passed the Serbian checkpoint where they used to demand passports. Someone had washed off the WELCOME TO HELL graffiti that greeted you when you first entered the town.

The Aerodrom was new. It had trolleys to carry luggage and a row of taxis outside. Where were the muddy tracks, the shelter where the Scandinavian soldiers who wore shorts in the summer stamped your passports with Maybe Airlines, Sarajevo? Where were the sandbags? My friend led me up a Philippe Starck–style escalator to a café.

We had coffee. Why did the modern Aerodrom make me feel tearful? Because the fate of Bosnia had been decided on an American air base and it killed its spirit. My friend had said the night before, "Dayton stopped the war, but it also killed our country."

My sandwich arrived—the same thick, hard Bosnian bread, but less stale than what we ate during the war—and I thought of the sandwich that Gordana Knezevic, the former editor of *Oslobodjenje*, had made for me in her office the day I saw the dog with the hand in its mouth. Humanitarian-aid cheese on stale bread. "Sorry," she had apologized. "After the war, I'll make you a better one."

Now, my friend, sitting in the airport, was saying, "Say *Dovidjenje Bosna*. Goodbye Bosnia."

He was right, of course. The war was over, but it would be generations before that stink of evil passed. What could save this place? Bosnia was now being run not by the Ottoman Empire or the Habsburgs, but by the international community.

Milosevic is in The Hague, the first head of state to be tried by an international court, and Karadzic will eventually be hunted down. But is it too late? During those dark years, no one came to save Bosnia. Neither God, nor the Orthodox saints, nor the angels, nor all the candles the old ladies lit in the cemeteries—certainly not the U.N. or the Western leaders—had tried to save it until it was too late.

In return, a whole generation will spend their lives trying to process the horror of what they saw. The stench of the place, the slow smell of death, will erode everything. Thousands of peacekeeping soldiers can't cover it up, and all the World Bank money and the Danish and Austrian economic aid can't fix it.

Zlatko had said to me, in that field in Kozarac, when he showed me the Orthodox cross carved into his skull: "Evil things happened here."

At the airport, a mechanical voice called my flight. I left half the sandwich on my plate. Zoran and I made plans to meet in Dubrovnik that summer, knowing it would probably not happen. At the passport control, I turned back to see him one last time, waving, urging me to move forward. Smiling. I pushed my passport through the window.

On the plane, I sat next to an American engineer from the Midwest. He was living in Sarajevo for six months and spoke of the wonder of his apartment in the Old Town with ISDN e-mail, water filters, a new washing machine. He knew places in Sarajevo I did not know existed, new restaurants that specialized in Dalmatian fish. There was an excellent wine list.

I did not know many restaurants in Sarajevo, aside from Jez, which was opened during the siege by a former Bosnian fighter. The food was not bad—usually black-market or humanitarian-aid cheese mixed with huge cuts of meat that came from Croatia or Pale—and there was a mournful young girl playing the piano and singing on most nights. I remember her short, red hair.

The engineer did not sense my emotions. He had not lived here during the war, when everyone was silent when a plane took off because they wondered if the plane would leave the ground without a rocket piercing its side, so he continued to talk. I felt something stinging behind my eyes; I was remembering so much.

We passed the airstrip where so many people had died trying to cross the road to get outside of the besieged city, and then the entrance to the Aerodrom, where I had hauled my heavy bags so many times from the U.N. plane into an armored personnel carrier to drive down Snipers' Alley. We passed Igman—and I remembered the summer when every morning Ariane and I checked to see if the white flag on the mountain was still flying. The rumor was, if it was gone, the defenders could no longer hold the city. I traced the window with one finger. I drew an outline of the mountain. I remembered the soldiers who died there and got buried in that mountain.

The seat belt light was still on. The stewardess—pretty, Bosnian, but speaking German—smiled from her seat. Was she thinking the same thing I was? What had happened to this country? Who lit the fuse? How far had people gotten this time from past wars, past hatreds, past desires, past petty grievances? Would someone send someone to a concentration camp again in eight or ten years? Would they remember that their grandmother had been insulted by an ethnic slur during World War II? Would they inherit the sense of humiliation and bitterness and the quest for retribution passed on from generation to generation?

Yugoslavia, or rather the former Yugoslavia, is complicated, but it is also transparent. People are smart. Everyone knows that unless they learn from the past they will continue to repeat the same mistakes, over and over. The same web of violence, terror, and destruction. I just don't know if they will get past it. In Mostar, the summer before, I had met a Croat fighter who was convinced the war was not over, that it would return in twenty years.

We passed over the green summer fields of Nedzarici, once a Serb-held suburb, and I had the sharpest, the most painful memories of the war. A nursing home full of old people too frail to be evacuated, and whom everyone had forgotten anyway. The staff had run away because of the danger of the place's location. A December day so cold that people were dying in their sleep and there was no one to remove their bodies, so small in their death. How could anybody be so small? I covered their heads with blankets so they could have some dignity in their last moments before death. I was with reporter friends: Kurt, who is dead now, killed in Sierra Leone, and Peter from the *Washington Post*. We moved silently, from room to room, unable to take in all that we were seeing.

Then, at the end of the hall, near a broken door, there was a room with beds full of dead people, dead old people. I began to count. One, two . . . I got, I think, up to thirteen. I was standing near an empty bed piled with old clothes.

Then a hand was raised up from the pile and grabbed mine, and I saw, to my shock, that it was someone still alive, but barely. It was not a pile of clothes, but a woman, with violet eyes. Not knowing if she was Croat, Serb, or Muslim, only muttering with the last energy in her body, *"Zima, zima."* (Winter. Winter.)

Holding my hand, the skin frail like paper. Watching my face. Her life fading.

"I will go and get help," I pleaded. "I will come back. Please stay alive until I come back."

Faint smile. She knew, I knew, no one would come to help.

She covered herself. She rolled over. She crossed that curtain that separates the living and the dead. She became again a pile of clothes.

Beginning After Everything

After I buried my mother
(under fire, I sprinted from the graveyard)
After the soldiers came with my brother
wrapped in a tarp
(I gave them back his gun)
After the fire in the eyes of my children
as they ran to the cellar
(the rats ran ahead of them)
After I wiped the old woman's face with a dishcloth
(terrified to reveal a face I knew)
After the ravenous dog
feasting on blood
(just another corpse in snipers' alley)
after everything
I wanted to write poems like newspaper reports,
so heartless, so cold,
that I could forget them
in the same moment someone might ask me,
"Why do you write poems like newspaper reports?"

Goran Simic, from *The Sorrow of Sarajevo*

Notes

CHAPTER I

1. The figures were provided by the Organization for Security and Co-operation in Europe (OSCE) and the United Nations High Commissioner for Refugees (UNHCR) at the time of the war, May 1999.
2. Doug Rekenthaler Jr., "Kosovo Humanitarian Distaste Forces Hundreds of Thousands from Their Homes," DisasterRelief.org, March 31, 1999. On April 2, Sadako Ogata, the U.N. High Commissioner for Refugees, said that 230,000 had fled since March 24, roughly 23,000 a day.

CHAPTER 2

1. Human Rights Watch believes the date that the Serbs began taking the women of Dragacin was probably April 18, 1999, although Zoya thinks it was several days later.
2. In 1999, British Foreign Secretary Robin Cook, along with NATO representatives, warned that rape camps, similar to those used by the Bosnian Serbs during the war there, were operating inside Kosovo. This was never confirmed, but the State Department, in May 1999, issued this report: "Ethnic Albanian women are reportedly being raped in increasing numbers. Refugee accounts indicate systematic and mass rapes in Djakovica and Pec. We believe that many crimes of gender violence have not been reported due to the cultural stigma attached to these offenses in Kosovar society."

   That same year, Joanne Mariner from Human Rights Watch said she believed there was no Serb policy of raping women systematically. Instead, "without making light of the subject," she asserted that "here, there are random methods of terrorizing civilians by police, paramilitary and Serb neighbors." Mariner said that the reasons for rape were twofold: one, for "attraction, the other is the humiliation attached to it, both for their women and their men. It is completely taboo in their society."

However, this does not eliminate the trauma inflicted on a society, especially one as closed and traditional as that of the Kosovar Albanians. When told of this specific incident, Mariner said, "That shows the ethnic animus of it. You have to think of the deeper implications of these rapes. It can ruin marriages, prevent marriages. It can make them all feel like damaged goods. Even in a culture not nearly as judgmental as this, you feel vulnerable and powerless . . . and that, of course, is part of the motivation. To humiliate and make them feel powerless. That they don't have power in their soul."

As of September 2001, there are no formal charges of rape on the charge sheet brought against Slobodan Milosevic. However, the chief prosecutor of the Hague International Criminal Tribunal for the Former Yugoslavia, Carla del Ponte, has been quick to point out that this does not mean that crimes have not been committed: it simply means that there is a lack of evidence, because the victims are reluctant to come forward and tell their stories.

Despite this, del Ponte has urged victims to come forward, and The Hague has continued to investigate. According to Florence Hartman, del Ponte's spokesperson, "It's terrible to say, but it's depending on them. If we don't have testimonies, we don't have a case."

CHAPTER 3

1. Based on the author's interviews with Kosovar Albanian refugees between March and July 1999 and in December 2000. According to the U.S. Department of State: "What began in February 1998 as a Serb government campaign against the separatist Kosovar Liberation Army (KLA) has evolved into a comprehensive premeditated and systematic program to ethnically cleanse the Serbian province of Kosovo of its roughly 1.7 million ethnic Albanian residents (also referred to as Kosovar Albanians). Because Serbian authorities have denied access to international monitors, documentation efforts have been too fragmented to estimate definitely the number of missing and dead."

2. From the U.S. Department of State's report on ethnic cleansing, "Erasing History": "The regime of Slobodan Milosevic is conducting a campaign of forced migration on a scale not seen in Europe since the Second World War. More than 90 percent of all ethnic Albanians have been expelled from their homes in Kosovo. . . . refugees report that Serbian authorities have confiscated passports and other identity papers, systematically destroyed voters registration and other aspects of Kosovo's civil registry, and even removed license plates from departing vehicles as part of a policy to prevent returns to Kosovo."

3. LeBor, *Milosevic*, p. 291.

4. Ibid., p. 334.

5. Ibid., p. 4.

6. The figure of 600,000 people killed at Jasenovac during World War II is an official Yugoslav estimate. Franjo Tudjman put the figure at between 30,000 and 40,000. Some Serbs claim that 1 million people died at Jasenovac. A Croatian historian, Ivo

Banac, puts it at 120,000.

7. LeBor, *Milosevic*, p. 3.

8. The ICTY was trying to establish the extent of Croatia's involvement in planning the war in western Bosnia. According to *Scotland on Sunday*, June 18, 2000: "The discovery of secret tape recordings and thousands of confidential documents chronicling the regime of the late president Franjo Tudjman were handed by the country's new leaders to the United Nations War Crimes Tribunal. It is a sensational move that could implicate senior military and political figures in war crimes and other serious criminal acts. The material details contain nine years of corruption, cover-ups and the subversion of an entire country."

According to the SOS, Tudjman enjoyed warm relations with Slobodan Milosevic, and in 1999 "discussed setting up a trade deal worth 250 million British pounds sterling—thereby giving the Serbs an international lifeline around sanctions, and letting the HDZ (Tudjman's hard-line nationalist party) to fill its coffers with the profits. . . . at home, the tapes show that Tudjman engineered deals to steal hundreds of millions of pounds of state property for the benefit of cronies in his HDZ organization . . . but it is the revelations of war crimes that have excited the outside world. The UN War Crimes Tribunal was shunned by Tudjman—and last year threatened trade sanctions as a result. Now it has been invited to investigate war crimes in Croatia and Bosnia. More than 3,500 documents have already been sent to . . . The Hague. . . . in the Bosnian village of Ahmici, . . . evidence has emerged to support his claim that the massacre was the work of paramilitary units who took their orders from the politicians. One tape revealed that Tudjman ordered his own investigation into Ahmici. When given the names of five of the killers by his secret police, he arranged for them to be given new identities and jobs."

As of September 2002, sixteen Croats have passed through the doors of The Hague. Seven Croats are in custody; one is on provisional release; one was acquitted; three were found not guilty and released; three were transferred to serve sentence. For the Lasva Valley crimes—which include Ahmici—six Croats were sentenced, three are on appeal. Another is waiting trial. Some others have been acquitted.

9. LeBor, *Milosevic*, p. 251.

10. From "US and NATO Objectives and Interests in Kosovo," U.S. State Department, March 26, 1999.

11. From "The Eighty Days War"—written by *The Times* of London reporters, including Janine di Giovanni, edited by Bronwen Maddox, 1999; reprinted by the Brownstone Policy Institute.

12. One year later, in September 2000, President Djukanovic would boycott Yugoslav elections. While making contingency plans to prevent violence, he could not endorse voting. Only 24.8 percent of Montenegrins defied their government by voting. Even without Montenegro's support, Vojislav Kostunica had enough votes to win and topple Slobodan Milosevic thus setting in motion a chain of events which ultimately led to the fall of Milosevic after a decade of war and nationalism.

13. Quoted in a briefing given by Fred Eckhardt, spokesman for the U.N. secretary-

general, April 6, 1999.

14. Arkan (Zjelko Raznatovic) was later assassinated in Belgrade, in January 2000. His murderers were never found, but it was widely believed in Belgrade that the Milosevic family, fearing what Arkan would say in The Hague war crimes tribunal, were behind it.

15. Malcolm, *Kosovo*, HarperPerennial, New York, 1999, p. 335.

16. Quoted in John Reed, *The War in Eastern Europe*, p. 00.

17. Some revisionist historians say that the Chetniks—who during World War I had contributed to the defense of the Serbs against the Austro-Hungarian Empire and to the Allies' victory on the Macedonian front—also fought courageously in World War II against both the Nazis and the Partizans in the struggle against totalitarianism in the Balkans. See Misha Glenny, *The Balkans*, for more on the Chetnik movement and history.

CHAPTER 4

1. It is also the poem which partially inspired Dame Rebecca West's epic Yugoslavian journey, recounted in *Black Lamb and Gray Falcon*, published in 1941.

2. Local elections in Kosovo took place in October 2000, followed by general elections in October 2001. Ibrahim Rugova and his LDK party won, but not enough to run the government entirely. Therefore, he is president, but the government is shared among Thaci, Rugova, and Ramush Haradinaj and his Alliance for the Future of Kosovo (AAK). Actually, the U.N. controls foreign policy, economics, and the judiciary. "All the Kosovars really do," explained an Albanian journalist, "is take care of the traffic on the street."

CHAPTER 5

1. Interview with Adam LeBor, Belgrade, November 2001. From LeBor's book *Milosevic*, p. 330.

2. For more on the collective Serb mentality and history, see Tim Judah's excellent analysis *The Serbs: History, Myth, and the Destruction of Yugoslavia*.

3. Goran Svilanovic is foreign minister in the Kostunica government.

4. As of April 2003, Slobodan Milosevic was on trial at The Hague for crimes against humanity and genocide in Kosovo, Bosnia, and Croatia. The prosecution for his offenses in Kosovo, which began on February 12, 2001, concluded on September 11 after 95 trial days, 124 witnesses, and over 300 prosecution exhibits. The prosecution for crimes in Bosnia and Croatia was due to commence in late September and to finish in May 2003, at which point Milosevic would be given the chance to defend himself. It is estimated that the trial will go on until the end of 2004.

CHAPTER 6

1. Chris Hedges, "Top Leader of the Bosnian Serbs Now Under Attack from Within," *New York Times*, January 4, 1996. Permission to reprint kindly granted by the *New York Times*.
2. Ibid.
3. Ibid.
4. "A Cry for Human Rights in 'Cleansed' Banja Luka," *Christian Century*, September 27, 1995.
5. On that point, I agreed with Radic. The Croats were undeniably guilty of atrocities which they have not addressed and for which they have not been punished; they have certainly not been demonized the way the Serbs have been.
6. LeBor, *Milosevic*, pp. 234–35.
7. In April 2002, following the publication of a massive report which detailed the fall of Srebrenica, *Srebrenica: a "Safe" Area* (Amsterdam: Netherlands Institute for War Documentation [NIOD], 2002), the entire Dutch government resigned. The report demonstrated the vagueness of the term "safe area." "The proclamation of the zone as a safe area created an illusion of security for the population."
8. Ariane Quentier, a French reporter who interviewed Akashi shortly after the fall of Srebrenica, was astounded by his lack of compassion and his inutility. She wrote me of meeting with him: "I met with him [Akashi] after the fall of Srebrenica, and when the same was going to happen to Zepa. When I asked what the UN/UNPROFOR was going to do now that the Serbs were about to enter Zepa—and this bearing in mind the Srebrenica experience—Akashi replied, 'We are going to write a strong protest letter to the Serbs.' It became the headline of the newspapers! It was so incredible to dare say such a thing less than 10 days after the fall of Srebrenica, and still he did it! It says a lot about the complete inability of the UN to act decisively and effectively—but with a letter—while people are massacring each other. . . ."
9. In March 2001, Radovan Stankovic was also arrested on crimes against humanity and rape and enslavement. He refused to enter a plea. The court agreed to enter a plea of "not guilty" and appointed a lawyer. Stankovic was part of the Bosnian Serb forces which overran Foca in 1992. He says he was simply doing his job as a member of a militia. By spring 2001, three Bosnian Serbs had been convicted in the Foca case and two were still at large.

CHAPTER 7

1. The former mentor of Milosevic and Serbian Communist Party leader, Ivan Stambolic, was crucified by his protégé at the Communist Party's Eight Session in 1987. Following his betrayal by Milosevic, Stambolic was politically sidelined and remained quiet more or less for thirteen years. In the run-up to the September 24, 2000, Yugoslav presidential election, it is believed that American officials encouraged Stambolic—a popular figure—to run for office. He would not take a lot of votes, but he could have split the Socialist vote. On August 25, 2000, Stambolic went for a jog and, while resting on a park bench, was seen bundled into a white van by eyewitnesses. It is now widely believed that he was kidnapped and killed by Mira

Markovic.

2. For The Hague, Plavsic's reversal of her plea was a major development, because the one count in which she admitted guilt—namely Count 3, persecutions on political, racial, and religious grounds—as a crime against humanity, is an "umbrella" count which covers numerous massacres, detentions in camp, deportation, forced labor, plunder, and destruction of property over large parts of Bosnia-Herzegovina. "Apart from genocide, it is the only other crime in our jurisdiction that has an element of discriminatory intent," said a Hague spokesperson.

Bibliography

BOOKS

Adric, Ivo. *Bosnian Chronicle*. London: Harvill Press, 1992.

———. *The Bridge over the Drina*. London: Harvill Press, 1994.

Almond, Mark. *Europe's Backyard: The War in the Balkans*. London: Heinemann, 1994.

Arsenijevic, Vladimir. *In the Hold*. London: Harvill Press, 1994.

Boulat, Alexandra. *Éclats de Guerre*. Paris: Les Syrtes Images, 2002.

Cohen, Roger. *Hearts Grown Brutal: Sagas of Sarajevo*. New York: Random House, 1998.

Dalrymple, William. *From the Holy Mountain: A Journey in the Shadow of Byzantium*. London: HarperCollins, 1997.

di Giovanni, Janine. *The Quick and the Dead: Under Siege in Sarajevo*. London: Phoenix House, 1994.

Drakulic, Slavenka. *Balkan Express: Fragments from the Other Side of War*. London: Random House, 1993.

———. *How We Survived Communism and Even Laughed*. London: Vintage, 1988.

Filipovic, Zlata. *Zlata's Diary*. New York and London: Viking, 1994.

Glenny, Misha. *The Balkans 1804–1999: Nationalism, War, and the Great Powers*. London: Granta Books, 1999.

———. *The Fall of Yugoslavia: The Third Balkan War*. London and New York: Penguin, 1992.

———. *The Rebirth of History: Eastern Europe in the Age of Democracy*. London and New York: Penguin, 1990.

Gutman, Roy. *Crimes of War: What the Public Should Know*. New York and London: Norton, 1999.

———. *A Witness to Genocide*. London: Element Books, 1993.

Hall, Brian. *The Impossible Country: A Journey Through the Last Days of Yugoslavia*. London: Secker & Warburg, 1994.

Herodotus. *The Histories*. London: Everyman, 1910.

Holbrooke, Richard. *To End a War*. New York: Modern Library, 1998.

Hollingworth, Larry. *Merry Christmas, Mr Larry*. London: Heinemann, 1996.

BIBLIOGRAPHY

Honig, Jan Willen, and Norbert Both. *Srebrenica: Record of a War Crime*. London: Penguin, 1996.

Hukanovic, Rezak. *The Tenth Circle of Hell*. New York: HarperCollins, 1993.

Judah, Tim. *Kosovo: War and Revenge*. New Haven and London: Yale University Press, 2000.

———. *The Serbs: History, Myth, and the Destruction of Yugoslavia*. New Haven and London: Yale University Press, 1997.

Kaplan, Robert D. *Balkan Ghosts*. New York: Vintage Books, 1994.

Knight, Gary. *Evidence: The Case Against Milosevic*. The Evidence Project. Millbrook, N.Y.: de. MO, 2002.

LeBor, Adam. *Milosevic: A Biography*. London: Bloomsbury, 2002.

Maass, Peter. *Love Thy Neighbor: A Story of War*. New York: Knopf, 1996.

MacLean, Fitzroy. *Eastern Approaches*. London: Pan Books, 1956.

———. *Yugoslavia*. London: Thames & Hudson, 1969.

Malcolm, Noel. *Bosnia: A Short History*. London: Macmillan, 1994.

———. *Kosovo: A Short History*. London: Macmillan, 1998.

March, Michael. *Description of a Struggle*. London: Picador, 1994.

McAllester, Matthew. *Beyond the Mountains of the Damned: The War Inside Kosovo*. New York: New York University Press, 2002.

Merrill, Christopher. *Only the Nails Remain: Scenes from the Balkan Wars*. Lanham, Md.: Rowman & Littlefield, 1999.

Naythons, Matthew. *Sarajevo: a Portrait of the Siege*. New York: Warner, 1994.

Norwich, John Julius. *A Short History of Byzantium*. London: Penguin, 1997.

Owen, David. *Balkan Odyssey*. London: Victor Gollancz, 1995.

Pavic, Milorad. *Dictionary of the Khazars*. London: Hamish Hamilton, 1989.

Reed, John. *The War in Eastern Europe: Travels Through the Balkans in 1915*. New York: Scribners, 1916.

Rohde, David. *Endgame: The Betrayal and Fall of Srebrenica, Europe's Worst Massacre Since World War II*. New York: Farrar, Straus & Giroux, 1997.

Roth, Joseph. *The Emperor's Tomb*. London: Hogarth Press, 1984.

———. *The Radetzky March*. London: Penguin, 1995.

Runciman, Steven. *Byzantium: Style and Civilisation*. London: Penguin, 1975.

Silber, Laura, and Allan Little. *The Death of Yugoslavia*. London: Penguin, 1995.

Shawcross, William. *Deliver Us from Evil: Warlords and Peacekeepers in a World of Endless Conflict*. London: Bloomsbury, 2000.

The Stationery Office, London. *War 1914: Punishing the Serbs*. London: Crown Publishers, 1915.

Sudetic, Chuck. *Blood and Vengeance*. New York: Norton, 1998.

Susko, Mario. *Verus Exsul*. Stamford, Conn.: Yuganta Press, 1998.

Tanner, Marcus. *Croatia: A Nation Forged in War*. New Haven and London: Yale University Press, 1997.

Thompson, Mark, editor with Article 19, International Centre Against Censorship. *Forging War: The Media in Serbia, Croatia, and Bosnia-Hercegovina*. London: Bath Press, 1994.

Vulliamy, Ed. *Seasons in Hell*. London and New York: Simon & Schuster, 1994.

Ware, Timothy. *The Orthodox Church*. London: Penguin, 1993.

West, Rebecca. *Black Lamb and Grey Falcon.* Vols. I and II. London: Macmillan, 1944.

West, Richard. *Tito and the Rise and Fall of Yugoslavia.* London: Sinclair Stevenson, 1994.

Zimmerman, Warren. *Origins of a Catastrophe: Yugoslavia and Its Destroyers—America's Last Ambassador Tells What Happened and Why.* New York: Random House, 1996.

DOCUMENTARIES

A Cry from the Grave. Storyville, BBC 2. Nicholas Fraser, editor. November 27, 1999.

The Death of Yugoslavia. BBC 2. Norma Percy, Angus McQueen, and Paul Mitchell, producers. Brook Lapping Associates for the BBC. London, 1995. Six episodes.

Lessons from History. BBC 2 Correspondent. Fiona Murch, editor. Farrah Durrani and John Thynne, producers. Reported by Janine di Giovanni. October 7, 2000.

REPORTS

Human Rights Watch. *The Fall of Srebrenica.* October 1995.

———. *World Report 2002.*

International Crisis Group, November 2, 2000. *War Criminals in Bosnia's Republika Srpska: Who Are the People in Your Neighbourhood?*

Kusovac, Zoran. *"Crime and Culpability in Milosevic's Serbia." Jane's Intelligence Review,* February 1, 2000.

Netherlands Institute for War Documentation. *Srebrenica: A "Safe" Area.* Amsterdam: NIOD, 2002.

Index

To come

A NOTE ABOUT THE AUTHOR

Janine di Giovanni is a senior foreign correspondent for *The Times* of London and a contributing editor to *Vanity Fair*. She is the recipient of a 1999 National Magazine Award for her reporting from the Balkans, two Amnesty International awards for war reporting from Sierra Leone and Kosovo, and Britain's Foreign Correspondent of the Year award for being one of the few reporters to witness the fall of Grozny, Chechnya. She has been the focus of an award-winning documentary about women war correspondents, *No Man's Land*. She is a graduate of the Iowa Writers' Workshop where she received an M.F.A. in fiction and lives in London and West Africa.

A NOTE ON THE TYPE

This book was set in Janson, a typeface long thought to have been made by the Dutchman Anton Janson, who was a practicing typefounder in Leipzig during the years 1668–1687. However, it has been conclusively demonstrated that these types are actually the work of Nicholas Kis (1650–1702), a Hungarian, who most probably learned his trade from the master Dutch typefounder Dirk Voskens. The type is an excellent example of the influential and sturdy Dutch types that prevailed in England up to the time William Caslon (1692–1766) developed his own incomparable designs from them.

Composed by Stratford Publishing Services
Printed and bound by TK